UNFORGIVABLE SINS

Protecting our Children from Predators

Scott Hall

Manor Hou

**Library and Archives Canada
Cataloguing in Publication**

Hall, Scott, 1946-
    Unforgivable sins : protecting our children from predators /
Scott Hall.

ISBN 978-1-897453-06-3

    1. Child sexual abuse--Prevention. 2. Children and
strangers.
I. Title.

HV6570.H354 2008   362.76'7
C2008-905963-8

Printed and bound in Canada
2nd Edition, June 15, 2009
336 pages.
All rights reserved.

Cover design: Michael B. Davie and Donovan Davie
First Published October 15, 2008
Manor House Publishing Inc.
www.manor-house.biz
(905) 648-2193

Scott Hall, Copyright 2008, F.J. Scott Hall Law Corp.
Suite 300 – 848 Courtney Street, Victoria, BC V8W 1C4
Tel: (250) 384-6600/1-800-435-6625
Fax: (250) 388-9406   www.unforgivablesins.com.

We gratefully acknowledge the financial support of the
Government of Canada through the Book Publishing Industry
Development Program (BPIDP), Dept. of Canadian Heritage, for
our publishing activities.

Manor House Publishing Inc.
www.manor-house.biz
905-648-2193

For Patrick, who made me promise to tell his story; for
the children who have been and were sexually abused and
were never able to tell their stories; for Rylan and Sasha
and all the children who, I hope, will never have a story to
tell, this book is written.

I hope I have kept the faith.

Unforgivable Sins offers unforgettable advice in dealing with the sexual abuse of children...

"This book is for the children past who were sexually abused and for the children of the certain future where sexual abuse has been banished from society... It is my belief, based on having heard the stories of over one thousand victims of sexual abuse; approximately one in every five children in North America has been sexually abused... Fortunately, through a combination of education and awareness programs at home and at school, children are now being taught to be more assertive the second they are touched improperly... If this book is about nothing else, it is about the vital importance of teaching children about abuse at an early age. Knowledge prevents sexual abuse. The best people to deliver this knowledge are mothers. The best time to deliver this knowledge is today."
– Scott Hall

IF YOU FIND YOURSELF DEALING
WITH OVERWHELMING EMOTIONAL ISSUES
WHILE READING UNFORGIVABLE SINS, DO NOT
HESITATE TO PHONE THE NATIONAL SUICIDE
PREVENTION LIFELINE NUMBER: 1-800-273-TALK
(8255). The National Suicide Prevention Lifeline is a
national, federally funded network of local crisis centers
providing suicide prevention and intervention services
through a toll-free telephone number: 1-800-273-TALK
(8255). For more information, visit
http://www.suicidepreventionlifeline.org.

FOR MORE INFORMATION, VISIT
WWW.UNFORGIVABLESINS.COM

WARNING! People who have been victims of a sexual abuser may find the information in this book will cause them to become extremely emotional. Such people should take care when they read the words that follow and be sure to do so in a safe environment where there are friends, family or professional caregivers who will support them.

TABLE OF CONTENTS

"I know things no one should know. I know things
everyone should know."
– Scott Hall

INTRODUCTION

I was working as a lawyer under contract to the British Columbia Government in Canada in 1982. One of my jobs was to liaise with social workers who had identified children at risk in the community and, where necessary, bring the circumstances of those children's home lives to the attention of the Court. The Judge was presented with information about how the parents or other caregivers were looking after the children and then decided whether the children should stay in a potentially dangerous situation, be kept on special watch, or removed from the homes of their parents or guardians. Usually, the perceived dangers were neglect or other physical or mental abuse.

For some reason, in 1982 the children started complaining of sexual abuse. Since I worked in concert with over 50 social workers, all of whom were monitoring children who were potentially at risk, there was a significant pool of information about sexual abuse that I drew on. One after the other, the social workers I questioned said that sexual abuse was being reported by children as young as three or four, and was suspected in children much younger than that. This had never happened before. What was going on in my sleepy hometown of Victoria? Was there now a huge new wave of sexual abusers, and if so, why had they chosen this time to become pedophiles?

The sexual abuse was generally being done to both boys and girls by parents or close relatives in the children's home. For the most, part the actual abuse was being perpetrated by men, but it was suspected that women in the household, generally mothers or foster mothers of the children, were aware of the abuse but remained silent and did not report the molestations and rapes.

I had many conversations with child protection workers as to what they thought was happening. On the face of it, there seemed only two alternatives: either this was a new and perhaps localized phenomenon, or it was conduct which had been going on for years and had been unreported by children. It may have been that the child care workers had not identified it because they were not accustomed to looking for sexual abuse of children for whom they were ultimately responsible.

Looking back from this vantage point over twenty five years later, it seems astonishing that it took so long for me to conclude that there was nothing new about the sexual abuse. It was the reporting and the acknowledgement of it which was the departure from the past.

There are many who say that there was a movement in those days, which continues today, to be overly cautious in approaching such sensitive issues as women's and, in particular, children's rights and allegations of sexual abuse to women and children. There are many men and women who believe that the women's movement, in particular, has swung the pendulum too far and that innocent people are and have been persecuted on flimsy evidence and have had their lives ruined by a prank or a spiteful accusation. Those people should have their voices heard.

But in 1982, before the social changes of the two next-ensuing decades, the major questions on the minds of people who cared for children in a professional capacity was: "How do we get to the bottom of this? And how do we get it to stop?"

I started out using the tools I had as a lawyer to do what I could to help the children. That was my job.

Because it took so long to understand this was an underreported phenomenon, many valuable years were lost. Professionals in behavioral sciences, with training and background quite different from those of a lawyer or a Judge, found it difficult to explain why sexual abuse within a family was now being reported where for centuries there had been silence.

I cannot pretend to know the root causes of the proliferation of stories about the sexual abuse of children in the early 1980's, but I can venture a few observations.

First, children were being encouraged by school teachers to be more forthcoming than they would have been a decade earlier. And people in authority were beginning to LISTEN to children as they had never done before. Children had rights and their caregivers knew that and conveyed a new importance to the opinions of children.

Even before governments were telling children to "Just Say No", teachers who had flourished in the 60's were also more sexually aware than their counterparts who were 10 or more years older. Whatever else the 1960's had accomplished, they removed most of society's blinders to its sexual mores. Contemporary child care workers flourishing in the 1980's had earlier been exposed to a society where all things sexual were not swept under the rug, as they had been in the 1950s and before. If sexual abuse was not discussed openly, at least sexual abusers were acknowledged as a sad part of the human family. In the 1950s, societal attitudes to the sexual abuse of children were more of the "Don't Ask, Don't Tell" variety.

A further and equally important rent in the blanket of silence that stifled the truth about childhood sexual abuse came through the media. Pre-school children were learning that they were individuals who had rights, however miniscule those rights might appear in their small world. Television shows such as Sesame Street and Mister Rogers created child self-esteem, perhaps for the first time ever.

Almost every child knows what is appropriate touching and what is not. The older the child the greater the knowledge she has. Most two or three year old kids can tell when they are being touched in an inappropriate manner. In the early 1980's, though, the question was who would listen to the children? Before the 1980's, if the child could have formulated it, the question about disclosing her sexual abuse was "What happened to me may NOT have been wrong. And who will believe me?" In those days few people, including parents, believed a child's story of sexual abuse, or if they did believe it, they often did little about it.

Shame on those parents.

We will never again disbelieve the children.

Beginning in the 1980's, then, children who were in pain, children who believed they could trust child care workers, told of their sexual abuse. And people who were their caregivers, their social workers, for example, began to listen to the children and to agree with the children that something very wrong had happened to the children.

One of the first trials I prosecuted for the government agency in charge of caring for children was in 1984. A boy, age 3, and a girl, age 5, were thought to have been sexually abused by their father, who was sole caregiver after their mother had died. This case became a battle royal. The social worker for the children had become concerned because both of the children had developed red marks around their genitals. The five year old girl told the social worker that the red marks on her vagina were caused by her father's beard and the marks were made when he was putting his tongue into her vagina. The boy was too young to discuss the red marks around his genitals, but the social worker and Doctors believed the father was sucking on the little boy's penis. The social worker had to give the little girl's evidence because a girl of five was not thought capable of telling the truth in Court. The Judge never got to see the girl or the boy.

The father called the family doctor as a witness. The doctor gave evidence that the red marks could have been caused by pinworm and that he had treated the children accordingly.

The Judge was in a quandary because, at that time, evidence given by children was not admissible and evidence given by a third party, about what the child had said, in this case the social worker, was also not admissible. So the Judge KNEW what the little girl had said, but could not base his decision on that information. At the end of an emotionally charged three week trial with dueling experts, including a respected psychiatrist who testified that he believed sexual abuse had happened as the girl alleged, the Judge found that there was insufficient evidence that the father had sexually abused his children and returned them to his care.

I appealed this decision.

The trial Judge was upheld on appeal.

This case was a watershed. Later, the law was changed. Children are now able to give evidence in Court with provisions being made to safeguard them.

I often wonder what became of the two children who were returned to their father, and fear the worst.

It was not a good case to lose.

Sometimes it takes a flagrant case of injustice to result in the law being changed for the better. This was a small beginning in changing the system, and I have been bringing cases to Court for victims of sexual abuse ever since.

The evidence given in Court by a person who has been sexually abused is often, but not always, disputed by the person charged with the offence. Whether in a criminal trial (where the outcome for the guilty person may be jail) or a civil trial (where the outcome may be that the guilty person is required to pay money damages), the likelihood is that when the sexual abuse took place there were only two people present. In most cases, the perpetrator is an older person in a position of authority, say a stepfather, a Priest, or a teacher, and the victim is a child of 4-14 years of age. The power imbalance between the victim and the perpetrator carries on through life to the point where, at age thirty, the former child is likely disposed to think that he or she did something wrong to bring on the sexual abuse or acted in a way to encourage the sexual abuse.

Very often the victims think, even when they are 70 or 80 years old, that no one will believe them because that is the thought they have carried with them since they were raped or otherwise abused, and at the age of 80 most victims who have not had counseling are still ashamed of the abuse that was done to them because they believe, against all logic, that they had encouraged or deserved the sexual assaults done to them.

It is my belief, based on having heard the stories of over 1,000 victims of sexual abuse, that approximately one in every five children in North America has been sexually abused. This abuse can take the form of an uncle fondling the penis of a nephew at a family gathering or a stepfather raping his stepdaughter for a number of years.

In neither case would the child have been likely to disclose the sexual abuse to an elder. In most cases the child had been made to feel part of the act, so the sexual abuse becomes a secret kept by the child and the abuser. Indeed, in some cases the child derives some pleasure from the attention of the elder or the physical touching, which makes the issue of fault or guilt or complicity all the more confusing for the victim – not only in youth but for decades to come.

In many cases, where the abuser is a trusted friend of the family or a member of the family, the abuse continues every time the abuser sees the child and arranges for the two to be alone together. The abuser and the abused enter into an unlikely contract with one another, where all terms are dictated by the pedophile and the child blindly obeys.

Fortunately, through a combination of education and awareness programs at home and at school, children are now being taught to be more assertive the second they are touched improperly. They are being told to report improper touching and the better armed they are with information about what is "good" touching and what is "bad" touching, the safer they will be.

If this book is about nothing else, it is about the vital importance of teaching children about abuse at an early age. Knowledge prevents sexual abuse. The best people to deliver this knowledge are mothers.

The best time to deliver this knowledge is today.

The Courts have gradually come to recognize something that was largely unknown two decades ago: sexual abuse can have devastating psychological effects on a child in later years. Often the syndrome is referred to as "Post Traumatic Stress Disorder". In fact, children become psychologically confused by intimate acts done to them when they are young and they carry the memories of these acts with them for life. Twenty years ago, this statement would likely not have been believed by some professionals. Now, however, we know that damage done to a little boy or little girl by fondling or penetrating them can cause psychological scarring leading to failed relationships, failed jobs, alcoholism, drug abuse, severe depression and sometimes suicide.

Anyone who sexually abuses a child should be prepared to spend a lengthy period of time in jail and to lose significant amounts of his wealth in paying compensation to the child he abuses. The damage the abuser does is almost as painful and long-lasting as if the abuser kept repeating the abuse day after day. In the minds of most abused people when they remember the abuse they are right back in the moment of that abuse. They become children again. A thirty year old trucker or a sixty year old grandmother can instantly become six years old again, and recall the pain of the abuse, the room where the abuse took place and the smells of the abuse. These are memories which cannot be washed away by the passage of time. They are, however, memories which the victim can be taught to cope with through therapy and other forms of counseling.

It has taken some time for the system to catch up with the reality of sexual abuse. There seems to be news every day now of some new sexual horror somewhere in the world. Since about the year 2000, there have been a number of reports concerning Priests of the Roman Catholic Church who have abused boys and girls in places as far-flung as France, Ireland, Boston, Philadelphia, Los Angeles, Dallas, Australia, Tahiti … I could go on.

The profile of childhood sexual abuse has been elevated by these clergy-related cases, but so far the lessons learned have not helped many children.

In many cases the stories of abuse by Priests are similar. The offending Priest has a history of several instances of sexually abusing children, the conduct of the Priest is known to church officials and church officials, rather than removing the Priest from contact with children, send him to another parish where he continues to sexually abuse children. So widespread has this problem become in the Roman Catholic Church that Pope John Paul II directed his Bishops to report all instances of sexual abuse by Priests in their dioceses directly to the Vatican. In particular, to then-Cardinal Ratzinger, later Pope Benedict. Pope Benedict has undertaken to remove homosexual Priests, although not pedophiles, from his Church.

The public first became aware of the sexual abuse of children by Priests in Canada in the mid-1980's, when boys who attended Mount Cashel Orphanage in Newfoundland complained that they had been sexually abused by their teachers and caregivers, members of the Christian Brothers of Ireland in Canada. Although the Christian Brothers finally admitted to the sexual misconduct and voluntarily liquidated their assets to provide compensation to approximately 100 boys who had been sexually abused, the tragedy was compounded by a cover-up by the Church which allowed the abuse go on for a decade after the police first became suspicious of the clergy at the orphanage.

A second and far more widespread story of sexual abuse in Canada became known in the early 1990's when Aboriginal children who had been required by the Government of Canada to attend Residential Schools far away from their homes began to tell of their experiences in those schools. Many of the children, boys and girls alike, had been sexually abused by teachers and other staff at the schools. Run by the Roman Catholic, Anglican and United Churches under contract with the Government of Canada, the schools were a fertile ground for abuse of all kinds. These cases of sexual, physical and emotional abuse have slowly made their way through the Courts in Canada. It is estimated that as many as twelve thousand native children were sexually abused while attending Residential Schools. We will never know the true number, in part because many children have died by their own hand, taking their secrets with them.

The fact that widespread sexual abuse of these Aboriginal children was taking place as recently as 25 years ago and was happening because of the policies of a Government as forward thinking as that of Canada, should make us all pause.

Over the years, I have met with and recorded the stories of people who were sexually abused at Institutions run by churches or by family members or teachers or others. I have been the lawyer for a number of men who were sexually abused by the Christian Brothers of Ireland in Canada and for others, including those who were sexually abused at the Aboriginal Residential schools.

My research has led me to conclude that I may have spoken on an in depth basis with more people who were sexually abused as children than anyone else in the world has ever done.

Children have been sexually abused in ways which only a pedophile could imagine.

Judges around the world, hearing many horrible stories of rape and other horrific sexual abuse, have now, at last, begun to find children to be telling the truth. In Court, the standard for believing the evidence of a victim of sexual abuse is a high one. The abuse generally happened long ago and the only other person present when the abuse took place is either very old or dead. The Court takes care to be satisfied as to the truth of evidence given by an adult about things he alleges happened to him when he was a child.

This is a unique area of law, dealing with psychological damage inflicted long ago. The system has not yet caught up with the needs of the victims. The victims need to hear that they are believed. The Courts and lawyers for the pedophiles finely sift the evidence of the victims for implausibilities and inconsistencies. The pedophiles and the Courts attempt to safeguard the pedophiles' money or liberty, but in most cases the victim just wants someone to say: "I believe you. Now let's see what we can do to help you along."

It is important for people who have been sexually abused and people who wish to better understand this major issue in society to be aware of what the term "sexual abuse" means. In some cases, the cases I believe most of us think about when we hear of sexual abuse, the assault consists of an older person fondling a boy or girl's breasts or genitals either over or under their clothing.

That fondling may progress in some cases to the abuser penetrating the anus of the child with his penis, finger or tongue or an object. The abuser may require the child to perform similar acts on him or her. The abuser may rape the child in the anus or the vagina with his penis. During all this time, the child is powerless to stop the abuse. The abuse often takes place a number of times each week over a period of years.

People who have been sexually abused as children often suffer not only from depression, but from an inability to have an intimate relationship with members of either sex, a fear of people in authority, sexual difficulties, low self-esteem, and substance abuse which numbs the painful memories of the abuse and renders the survivors of sexual abuse among society's disadvantaged people. As a consequence, these victims often lead very fragile lives and do poorly in social settings including socializing with others and excelling at their work. They are a large part of the emotional walking wounded of our society.

Generally, the more painful and frequent the sexual abuse was, the greater the impact is on the life of the person abused. Even today, most victims of sexual abuse are unwilling or even unable to tell anyone of the abuse, so great is their shame and feeling of guilt. But the key to healing, I believe, is sharing the story of the abuse with these who will listen, understand, and, where appropriate, continue to love the victim of abuse and encourage them to continue talking about the abuse.

Most people who have been sexually abused choose not to deal with the impact of that abuse on their lives. Most lock it away or learn to cope, much as they would if they had lost an arm or a leg when they were younger. They get on with their lives, even though they have been deeply affected. The difficulty, however, is that the wound is psychological, not physical. It continues to cause pain in dreams, or in flashbacks triggered by sights or situations whether in day-to-day life, on television, or elsewhere.

There is no control over when these feelings will come about. That is the reason I began this book with a warning that people who were sexually assaulted years ago should be in a safe environment with caring people around them while they read what I have written.

I know these words have power for people who have suffered privately and in silence for many years, afraid of releasing their secret to the world. I have endeavored to choose and build my words here in such a way as to encourage people to consider how they might deal with their demons.

There is help. As doctors deal more and more with victims of sexual abuse, they learn more and more how to help people manage the emotions engendered by the abuse and the triggers which cause the memories.

I have been lucky enough to see people who could barely discuss their abuse and who were in the depths of despair, shake off the shroud of depression and acknowledge that the sexual abuse was not their fault. Once people hold this thought in their minds and, more especially, in their hearts, they are half way home to healing the pain and learning how to manage their feelings of depression and low self-esteem.

There are more and more doctors, counselors and therapists who can help people manage their feelings, take those feelings out into the light of day and gradually diminish the effects of the sexual abuse. I always say that the memories of sexual abuse hate the light of day.

I believe the more people talk about their sexual abuse – their "dirty little secret" – the less power that dirty little secret has over them, until finally it has almost none at all.

Because it is no longer a secret and it is no longer dirty. It loses its control over the emotions.

The victim is no longer a victim but a Survivor.

Another tool that may help people heal from the wounds inflicted by sexual abuse is confronting the abuser. Like speaking of their sexual abuse, or obtaining counseling, this may not be an appropriate avenue for everyone who has been sexually abused, but it has provided many people with an opportunity to tell their story and to be believed.

In some instances even the abuser herself will acknowledge the abuse and want to deal with her past behavior as much as her victim does, perhaps more.

I encourage everyone who has been sexually abused to find a counselor, psychologist or psychiatrist to work with toward healing. Not all counselors are the same. Pick one you get along with, one who has experience dealing with sexual abuse victims. Healing will happen. People who have carried a solitary and heavy burden for five or fifty years can lighten that burden and lead a happier life.

For the people who experience this healing, it is almost a miracle. I have seen this "miracle" happen often. A new approach to the treatment of people who were sexually abused is needed for survivors and doctors and lawyers and Judges.

We can all go there together.

Because we must all go there together if we wish to stop sexual abuse from ruining lives.

You can begin to heal today if you were sexually abused. You must take the first steps yourself when you are ready to begin healing. It will not be easy. Nothing worthwhile ever is. This book will show that you are not alone as you may often have thought you were.

People have suffered what you have suffered and have managed to cast off the hold this horrible abuse had over them and go on to lead fuller and better lives.

You can do this too.

It is often difficult to predict the future with certainty, but in the area of sexual abuse I feel confident that the future will see fewer and fewer children abused.

The reasons are many. Children, their parents, their teachers and Doctors are more aware of these acts and the effects of these acts than at any time in our history. Lines of communication between children and their caregivers are becoming more open all the time. Awareness of the existence and danger of sexual abuse has never been higher. The media, for once, is doing a good job exposing this evil.

People in general have a heightened awareness of sexual abuse and now know that it has serious repercussions. People who would be abusers are aware of this heightened vigilance, aware that they will go to jail if they are apprehended, and aware that they may lose their life savings when they ruin a child's life.

It may be that people fifty years from now will look back and see this decade as being a watershed when the sexual abuse of children finally began to come to an end.

I cannot think of a more worthwhile goal for our society or a better legacy for our children.

This book is for the children past who were sexually abused and for the children of the certain future where sexual abuse has been banished from society.

The key is knowledge. I hope that you will find some of that knowledge in these pages and that you will succeed in banishing the devils who beset you today.

No two stories are the same. If you were a victim of sexual abuse, your story is unique to you. You may not find a story in this book that is even close to the sexual abuse that was done to you or even close to the impact that the sexual abuse has had on your life. But you will find stories that others have told me about what happened to them and how they have managed to survive.

Everyone has his truth and his way of coming to terms with that truth. Your way is the right way for you.

Sexual abuse has always been with us. The toll that it has taken on children and the larger society they inhabit cannot be measured.

We can and should put a stop to the majority of it.

The only impediment to wiping out the sexual abuse of our children is education. The more education we all have, the less likely it is that sexual predators will succeed in dehumanizing our little ones.

Under age 6, about half of the children who are sexually abused today are assaulted by a family member and only FOUR per cent are sexually assaulted by a stranger, according to police records from 2003 and Statistics Canada.

In this book, I cast a number of stones at a number of people and inveigh against them for sexual behavior that is always wrong, always damaging to children and often cruel for the sake of the perverse gratification of the abusers.

While I am truly shocked and astonished by the conduct of the pedophiles I write about in this book, I realize that with a jog here and a turn there in our life, each of us may have become one of them.

I wonder, because so little is understood of the subject, whether there is not a "switch" within all of us either turned on or not turned on that leads us to go from playing doctor to pedophilia, as if that were the most natural transition in the world.

There is, as well, an apparent difference between those whom I call "hardwired" pedophiles and those I refer to as "situational" pedophiles.

The hardwired pedophiles are born with a desire to have sexual contact with children (and often adults, as well) where the situational pedophiles use children for sex when there is no other sexual outlet for them or when a turn of events presents itself and the pedophile, usually a man, but not always, acts on an unanticipated sexual stimulation and has sex with a child.

When he finally confronted the issue of why he had had a sexual liaison with Monica Lewinsky, American President Bill Clinton said that he had done so for the worst of reasons: because he could.

Almost all pedophiles "can" because of the inherent power they have over their child victims.

One of the most important messages in this book is to encourage mothers to give power to their children so that they will know for certain, and so that they will be likely to convey that power and that certainty to a pedophile that touches them:

"No. You can't touch me."

I call on psychologists and psychiatrists to take the information they find in these pages and put it to good use.

The vignettes I relate in this book are all stories that have been told to me by people I believe. I have changed the names and some situations not affecting the importance of certain episodes in order to protect people from further harm.

The language in this book is, of necessity, extremely stark and descriptive. It is not a book for the squeamish. If you are shocked by sexual language which would ordinarily be regarded as clinical, please have someone you trust read this book and provide you with a synopsis of it.

The last thing I would wish to do is to have this work appeal to anyone's perverse or prurient interest. There are many graphic descriptions of the sexual abuse of children in these pages. I believe that it is necessary to describe the sexual abuse the way it happened, the way it was described to me.

Much as people are more inclined to accept the truth of the Holocaust when they see pictures taken at concentration camps, the horror recounted in some of these personal stories will go a long way to educate, to inform, and to help prevent the future sexual abuse of children.

You will find that I often switch back and forth between the gender of the children who are sexually assaulted in order to remind me, and to remind you, that girls and boys are equally targeted by pedophiles. For many years the accepted wisdom has been that if children were sexually abused, they were most likely girl children.

This is not now, and never was true. Boys and girls are almost equally the victims of sexual assault in our society. For reasons I will examine later, however, boys are far less likely than girls to be forthcoming about the details of the sexual abuse done to them by adults.

Finally, I am trained as a lawyer, not as a caregiver. Many of the positions I posit here, or conclusions I have arrived at, fly in the face of beliefs that have been held by both society and the caregiving professions for years.

Conclusions I arrive at, or theories I put forward, have been developed by me after more than twenty years of close work with numerous victims of sexual abuse.

What I say here, what this book ultimately stands for, may be flawed. There will doubtless be criticism of things I suggest. If that criticism is based on gaps in my knowledge of therapy modalities or human dynamics, if these flaws are brought about by my misperception of a proven reality, I am solely responsible for the flaws – as I am for everything else in this book.

While I may offend legislators, Judges, lawyers, doctors, stepfathers, teachers and the clergy, I hope that I will do no harm to the people to whom this book is dedicated – all the children who, through no fault of their own, never had a chance to have a carefree childhood or a carefree life.

Given that I offend so many groups in society, it is inevitable that people will say "Who does this guy think he is? Why should anyone listen to him?"

I have written this book because I had to. Over the years, I have been honored by the faith that people have had in me when they chose to tell me their most personal and horrifying stories. I have built a store of knowledge from these brave people that no one else has. This store of knowledge, if shared by me, may help one other person, perhaps you or a member of your family.

If I can save one child from sexual abuse, it is my duty to try. If I did not write down here what I have learned, I would be breaking faith with those who have trusted me with their stories and their lives.

I learned a long time ago that if I speak from my heart to people who were sexually abused as children, then nothing I say will give offence to the people who have carried their terrible secret for years. It is enough for them to know that I care and that I wish to help them.

It is in that spirit that this book is written.

Chapter 1

EVERYONE INTO THE POOL!

Sexual assault is a unique crime. Very few of us contemplate committing arson, few of us plan to rob banks, and murder is far from the minds of most people in our society. However, some form of sexual intercourse is generally not far from our minds.

Each of us is a sexual being with sexual feelings. Even my second wife. A child in the womb masturbates. A person self-described as being "asexual" has erotic dreams, sometimes wet dreams where orgasm is reached. Men and women in their eighties and nineties often find the spirit and the flesh both willing and act on their sexual urges.

Teenage boys will think of sex upon seeing a shooting star, a basketball or a wall made of cinder blocks. This is because teenage boys (I was one once myself, and speak with authority) rarely think of anything but sex.

Indeed, researchers at the Kinsey Institute for Research in Sex, Gender and Reproduction at Indiana University say most men are always thinking of sex. These researchers published data in 2006 which showed that 54% of men think about sex once or several times a day. Only 19% of women think about sex once or several times a day.

Priests and nuns and teachers and Judges think about sex. Nurses, doctors, social workers, airline pilots, deep sea divers and women mushing their sled dogs through the Iditarod Race in Alaska think of sex. Those nights on the Iditarod can be long, cold and lonely... and look! A shooting star!

Queen Elizabeth of England thinks of sex, as did the Queen Mother and, most especially, the Queen's late sister, Princess Margaret. The late Freddie Mercury of Queen thought of almost nothing but and died from a surfeit of unhealthy sex. Bill Clinton and George W. Bush think of sex, but one probably not as often as the other. Hillary Clinton and Condoleezza Rice think of sex, but probably not for the same reasons. Jesus was the Son of God. There is nothing in the Bible to suggest he thought of, or ever had sex. However, the human part of him thought of sex, and the God part did not. Probably.

Chairman Mao Tse Tung thought lots about sex and often had sex to keep him young, although not necessarily with Mrs. Tung; Gandhi had young girls brought to his bed naked so he could prove his faith was strong by NOT having sex with them, and Fidel Castro allegedly became the father of his country in more than words alone. John F. Kennedy had more sex than Richard Nixon, but Richard Nixon may have thought of sex, say, as often as Kennedy had sex. He MAY have…

Even as I write this sentence, it sounds from the ululations that I hear coming through this hotel's wall, that the woman in the next room is having some kind of sexual relations with some person or thing and is calling on God either to witness what is going on, or to prolong or end it. I will not use the house phone to ask.

There is, I believe, no bad sex as long as it is sexual contact between two or more adult people, none of whom is hurt by it, each of whom consents to the sex that is taking place in bed, in a tree, on the roof of a car or, for our Canadian friends, in a canoe.

The sexual liberation which began in the late 1950's with the Beats and coffee houses and poetry and the stirrings of societal and personal freedom has progressed through the decades to a point where, as the song said before its time, "Anything Goes." That ditty by Cole Porter was probably his paean to homosexuality in the 1930s, but he did not reckon with what was about to happen. Cole Porter could not have foreseen the day when heterosexual anal intercourse was the plot in an episode of Sex And The City which aired on prime time television in 2002. Cole Porter could not have foreseen Hugh Hefner and his seminal Playboy Philosophy published in the 1960's. The essential message of Hefner can be boiled down to the phrase: "If it feels good, and the woman is both of age and willing, do it." Now a postergeezer for Viagra or Folditin or one of the erection drugs, Hefner seems determined to die with a smile on his face and an erection of such magnificence that there will be difficulty closing the lid to his coffin. Well done, Hef. A life with but a single purpose, carried on with tenacity.

Two generations post-Playboy Philosophy, teenagers are having oral sex and anal sex with a frequency which would have shocked their grandparents or perhaps Hefner himself. (Let's face it, ONCE would have shocked most of their grandparents.)

Anal and oral intercourse between teenage boys and girls is often seen as a foolproof way of having sexual intercourse and avoiding pregnancy. I do not condone this. I just record the facts. Teenagers have intimate relations with one another far earlier and more frequently than they did just a decade ago. Because of the ever-earlier sexualization of children, we may soon learn of pre-teens having oral and other forms of intimate genital contact with one another.

And the parents of these children are not far behind. A large and detailed survey in 2005 found that most adults in

North America have sexual relations three times each week. Of course, in the Post-Clintonian world, where the definition of "sexual relations" can be a bit of a puzzler, these three occasions encompass a lot of different behavior that consenting adults are supposedly getting up to.

Two things are clear, however. These comings together feel good for at least one of the participants and the sexual activity is likely not driven by a desire to procreate.

Group sex, bondage, Mazola sex, mile high sex, public place sex, fast sex, tantric sex, the Oriental favorite Seven Orifice Sex, English Garden Gnome Sex, McDonalds Drive-Thru sex, many of these forms of recreational sexual conduct have come into our own homes and gardens since the 1960's, and most are relatively recent developments in industrialized society.

Even with the advent of HIV/AIDS in the early 1980's, the trend to more and more unusual sexual contact has been persistent and shows no signs of diminishing any time soon. Sex, apparently, has a greater hold over us than the fear of death.

Like it or not – and most of us appear to like it – sex in all its pleasure inducing guises is here to stay. There are few restrictions on sexual contact and where there is an imagination at work, tools for the job and a free Saturday evening, things will likely get kinkier before the inevitable backlash sets in and one or two generations from now everyone is back in the missionary position and then only once a year.

In the meantime it is well to remember what Woody Allen answered when asked if sex was dirty: "It is if you do it right."

It is extremely unlikely that a Judge will arise in the morning, rob a bank, and then go to court to judge a case about a man who robbed a bank. A Judge WILL awake in the morning, have sex with her husband, then go to Court and judge a case about a man who had sex with his stepdaughter. Judges have little personal knowledge about robbing banks, but they have personal knowledge about sexual intercourse. Judges, of course, must be impartial and dissociate themselves from personal knowledge of any offence they are asked to sit in judgment on. But the crime of sexual assault is one which has many layers and resonates in the psyche of all who learn the details of the assault. At some point in a trial any Judge will compare his or her own sexual experience to that which he or she is asked to sit in judgment on. The Judge will compare the facts alleged to his or her own personal sexual experience and, in effect, measure the distance between that Judge's own past sexual conduct and the conduct the sexual abuser is alleged to have engaged in. To my knowledge there has been no course offered to Judges hearing sexual abuse cases to give them a point of departure other than a self-referential one in attempting to determine the distance from the societal norm that a perpetrator is alleged to have strayed.

The tension in a courtroom when a sexual assault trial is taking place is palpable for this reason and for many others.

Because we are all sexual beings we must all work hard to come to the understanding that pedophiles pervert our universal sexuality by preferring to have sexual contact with children rather than with adults. Some pedophiles will have sexual relations with adults as well as children, but the fact that they sometimes or always prefer children is what makes them dangerous.

Chapter 2

NOMENCLATURE

Nomenclature is one of the aspects of the sexual abuse problem which is most easily rectified. Unless and until children and adults begin using the proper names to describe parts of the body and their functions, we will continue to talk at each other when we should be talking with each other.

Gertrude Stein famously coined the phrase "A rose is a rose is a rose…" In the movie Citizen Kane, the character played by Orson Welles is supposed to have named the vagina of his mistress "Rosebud." The meaning of the word Rosebud was a mystery in Citizen Kane, but we in the real world should not be so confused about penises and vaginas and their quirky synonyms because confusion about terminology hinders us from getting at the truth and obfuscation of the truth harms children.

The word "penis" is far from perfect. It sounds nasty, emphasizes the urinary function and is difficult for younger children to say. Until a universally accepted synonym can be agreed on, we are all stuck with having to say penis when we mean penis.

Equally discomforting is the verbiage which springs up in place of the word "vagina". I hold no brief for the word vagina itself. Like penis, it is a foreign name, unpleasant to the ear and tough for kids to say. In addition, I'll bet real money that over fifty per cent of all people, including those who possess a vagina, would have difficulty separating the vagina from the vulva from the labia from the pudenda from the pubis. Because doctors, lawyers and Judges have settled on this word as part of their day-to-day parlance, mothers should tell their daughters that their vagina is their vagina, and continue to refer to the child's vagina whenever it is appropriate to do so. In less time than we might think, children become accustomed to employing the word in their vocabulary and that is a step which will help prevent them from being sexually abused.

Similar words must be taught to our children at an early age, not for shock value or for any other reason than to assist the children in communicating with would-be attackers and with their caregivers. Very early on, say by the age of three, all children should be able to correctly identify these body parts by name:

Breast
Vagina
Penis
Anus

Beginning when the child is two years of age and imparting more information as the child progresses in age and comprehension, each mother who teaches the meaning of these words to her children, however difficult she may find the task, will go a great distance to rape-proofing her child.

At the same time, as the child grows and comprehends more, he should be told that these parts of his body are NOT to be touched by anyone other than his mother and, when appropriate, his father.

The child should be taught that if any person other than her mother or father touches her breast, her vagina, or her anus, she is to loudly yell "NO!" and move quickly away from that person, continuing to yell "NO!" at the top of her lungs.

This conduct by children may result in the odd misunderstanding and the occasional false alarm. However, it is far better for your child to know she has the power to say no, the power to protect her own body and the freedom to use that power, than to worry about occasional hurt feelings when a family member or a sitter touches a child in an innocent manner.

You, as a mother, cannot always be beside your child. You must therefore inculcate a sense of power and self-preservation into your child so that she can do the job of protecting herself when you cannot be there.

Again, it is far better to have the occasional misunderstanding between your child and her caregiver who acts without malice than to suffer through the torture of knowing your son or daughter has been raped and that you failed as a mother to do all that you could to prevent the abuse from happening.

Rape-proofing your child puts a great deal of responsibility on you as a mother. Being a good mother requires that you be responsible. You are responsible for your child being here in the first place. You are equally responsible for giving your child his best possible defense against rape.

As the mother of the child, you are the only person who can do this in a natural manner.

If you have not yet begun to rape-proof your children, begin today. It is never too early and it is never too late.

Unless you wait another day.

Then it may be too late.

You will already have thought "Well, I can't have my little boy or girl, two or three years of age, going around using words like that!" Yes you can. Despite our apparent preoccupation with sex, there is a societal aversion toward many things overtly sexual, and words used by children having a sexual connotation fall into this category. These are supposed to be "dirty" words, words not to be used by well-bred, proper children.

That concept is false.

Ignorance of the words used to describe parts of our body plays right into the hands of pedophiles. When a child uses the appropriate word to describe a body part, the person who will be most shocked is the pedophile.

If your neighbor is disgusted that your child knows that her vagina is called her vagina, or his penis is called his penis, your neighbor's child has something to learn.

Imprecise nomenclature aids those who rape children.

We hear almost daily in the media of children who were "molested" or "sexually assaulted" or "sexually abused".

This fuzzification of the sexual acts committed against children does a disservice to them and everyone fighting on their behalf.

The phrase "sexual abuse" encompasses every act from fondling to anal rape. So, too, does the phrase "sexual molestation" or simply the word "molestation" or "abuse," depending upon the context.

It is incumbent on the media to report the facts as they exist and not to engage in self-censorship by employing euphemisms which cloud the issue of sexual abuse. When a victim of crime is shot to death, the media reports the fact in those words, leaving out the details of the scene of the murder. The same must be done with victims of sexual assault, so that parents, children and pedophiles will know the true subject matter of the story being reported.

Much as we find it distasteful, children must know at an early age that no one is allowed to play with their vagina or their penis. Again, it is far better that their young ears and minds be subjected to these words and their meanings than that their little bodies be subjected to the acts themselves.

By indulging in fuzzification of the sexual assaults on children, the media is buying into the concept that the acts are shameful to the child when, in fact, the acts are shameful to the perpetrator. It is not the fault of the child that he was anally raped by his Priest. The child is not to blame. The child did no wrong. The child is not named in the media account. Why, then, should the media give a free pass to the Priest in question by alleging that he "abused" or "molested" a young boy? If the Priest anally raped the boy, we should all know this.

Legal nomenclature ranges far and wide in the fuzzification of sexual assault. In olden times – forty years ago – there were offences at law such as "criminal conversation", which was a legal term for sexual intercourse.

Another phrase which clutters up the courts even today is "indecency". "Sister Cecilia is alleged to have committed "gross indecency" on a young male."

We might all be forgiven if we muttered to ourselves "What the hell....?" What did she DO to the little kid, anyway? Did she invent something new or is it something my wife and I do together after midnight?

Very often, because the law is masterful at fuzzifying sexual unpleasantries, Courts declaim that a young girl was "touched for a sexual purpose" by the accused. Between "criminal conversation", "gross indecency" and "touching for a sexual purpose", who knows what's going on?

A prime example of how legal terms contribute to the problem – albeit in an attempt to protect the victim and a delicate public – is the catchall phrase "sexual exploitation". A lot of people in Canada are charged with this crime. Again, it is extremely unhelpful because no one, not lawyers, not Judges, knows what sexual exploitation is until they see the actual particulars of the offence.

If, by "sexual exploitation", people mean to say that a child was masturbated by a man, then that is what the charge should read. When the man is sentenced to jail for masturbating the child, parents and potential pedophiles will all know that this is the sentence imposed for this act.

The term "sexual exploitation", invented by well-meaning legislators, does more to help pedophiles than to help victims. Whatever harm is occasioned by the publication of the transgression of the pedophile is harm only to the tender sensibilities of the public. And the public should know what these creeps are up to.

I was going to introduce you all to the word "frottage" and the concept that it attempts to encompass. However, I believe I have made my point about imprecise language, and invite you to google "frottage." Some words we will have to keep on using. We need some kind of word to explain what frottage is, and if we didn't already have "frottage" we would have to invent a word to replace it – and we are probably not up to that task.

In olden days, they had the good sense to call sodomy, sodomy and buggery, buggery, but in some jurisdictions in North America "sodomy" is the word used when the act complained of is oral-genital intercourse. The legislators, I suppose, confronted by oral-genital sex, believed that, whatever else it was, oral-genital sex was a "gross indecency", and having no other category in which to put oral sex, they stuck it in the "sodomy" category.

This is fatuous and unhelpful and demonstrates how far people go to avoid speaking the truth about things sexual.

We should all adopt language by which we understand that oral-genital sex is neither a "blowjob" nor "fellatio" nor "cunnilingus", but oral-genital sex. Who did what to who can be sorted out later.

Vaginal rape should be referred to as vaginal rape by a penis (unless otherwise stated), anal rape is anal rape by a penis, and "touching for a sexual purpose" is "fondling of the breast" or "fondling of the genitals" or "masturbation". (Masturbation is, after all, prolonged fondling of the genitals.)

We should try to eliminate the Latin names for sexual acts – fellatio, cunnilingus, analingus – if for no other reason than that no one who speaks Latin has had sexual intercourse for hundreds of years (well, hardly anyone. See the Chapters on the Catholic Church).

Again, if we are to go as far as possible to eliminate sexual assaults on children, we need every possible tool we can get in our tool kit. To leave out such a valuable tool as clarity of speech is to say we can win this fight with the tools at hand.

We cannot.

Knowledge is power. Children are not offended by knowledge disseminated in the interests of saving them.

Anyone else in society who is offended by the spoken truth in their Court reports or on their news should simply take a pill or turn the page.

Chapter 3

WHO ARE THE PEDOPHILES?

Given the high sexual content in all our lives, it is little wonder that the weakest among us will be sexually victimized. This is sexual Darwinism: the imposition of the will of the most aggressive on those least capable of defending themselves.

This book looks for ways to stop our children from becoming the sexual outlet for pedophiles and for ways to help those who have been victimized by pedophiles.

It is a fairly straightforward thing to establish the groupings of people who are likely to sexually abuse our kids. In order they are, more or less:

Stepfathers
Trusted family friends, neighbors or relatives
Authority figures/ Foster Parents
"Helpful" strangers and "friends" from the Internet
Common rapists

We will leave aside the common rapists. These are rapists without portfolio who may stalk your children, then seize them and sexually assault them. These criminals fall outside the mainstream of abusers in that they employ kidnapping, violence and threats rather than attempting to befriend the children or lull them into a belief that everything, including the fondling that is going on, is perfectly normal, perfectly reasonable and based on the "relationship" between the adult and the child.

These swine can be defeated by rape-proofing your children along the lines I set out here. Your children should be taught not to put themselves into dangerous situations. Most street rapists and kidnappers look for a moment of inattention on the part of your child. If they choose a child who has been rape-proofed as a victim, they should drop her like a hot rock when she starts to scream "No!"

And, of course, a rape-proofed child never gets into a car with a stranger or even stops to talk with a stranger, not without putting up an actual, physical fight and screaming "NO!" at the top of her lungs until the stranger goes away.

In this book I will concentrate on those who are likely a greater danger to your children: the people you already know.

And here is the first rule: Trust no one.

I am speaking here to all mothers of all children.

Trust no one with your precious babies. Everyone you believe you can trust is potentially a person who will rape your child.

Your father, your brother, your husband or your son WILL sexually abuse your son or your daughter, given the wrong circumstances.

I understand this is an alarming statement, one you've likely never before encountered, one that's controversial because it is so extreme. However, I rely here on a variation of Barry Goldwater's 1964 Presidential campaign theme: "Extremism in defense of children is no vice."

Or, to rework a quotation from Abraham Lincoln, "No man can be trusted with all children all of the time."

If we are to stop sexual abuse, we must assume for the safety of the children that some man in or near your family who has contact with your children will fondle them or rape them. This is not to suggest that all mothers become frantic in an attempt to ferret out who the potential sexual abuser might be. I simply ask that you be vigilant.

Do not ever leave your children of tender years alone with a male friend or relative, or a woman who will have men in her house while you are away.

Until you are certain that your son or daughter has been rape-proofed, and even afterward, be vigilant about the people they spend their time with when you are away from them.

It is inevitable that many will say this philosophy is too hard on men. It may be. But men are tough. We have broad shoulders. We can take it. Children cannot, however, take sexual abuse, and the statistics show that 95% of sexual abuse of children is done by men. So, as men, we all have to admit that while this may be an extreme position, it is not unwarranted. Our track record speaks for itself.

For men who find this position disturbing, I have one thing to say: pick your best male friend, the one you both know and like, the one you most respect. You have to be out of town for two weeks. You need someone to look after your 15 year old daughter while you are gone. Your best friend offers to look after her for you. What do you do?

Damn straight. You find someone else to look after her.

If the choice is one between bruising a few men and saving ONE child from being raped, let the men be bruised.

We'll get over it.

Chapter 4

THE CATHOLIC CHURCH: PART ONE

The Roman Catholic Church is two thousand years old, give or take a hundred years. It is the oldest continuously existing human entity on earth. Older by far than the British Monarchy or any other present day dynasty in any land, the Catholic Church must have been doing something right to have been growing from strength to strength over two millennia.

The Church has a presence in nearly every country in the world and commands the allegiance of over a billion earth dwellers.

If it can be said that if any organization is in a position to take the long view of things, that organization would be the Catholic Church, which believes with some justification that in another two thousand years it will still be here.

By comparison, the United States of America is about 230 years old and Canada a mere 140 years old.

The Catholic Church has seen earthly empires come and go, governments rise and fall, and has ebbed and flowed with the likes of Genghis Khan, Christopher Columbus, Neil Armstrong, Torquemada, Adolph Hitler, the Roman Empire, and Keith Richards. There is not much the Church hasn't seen. There is not much new under the sun to this organization. Wars, famines, space exploration, nuclear explosions, assassinations, holocausts, newly discovered galaxies, U.F.O.s; the Church has seen them all and continues to survive and to thrive. It has had its ups and downs, times when Popes were held captive, times when many of its parishioners left the fold to start new churches, times when it was outlawed in many countries, when worship went underground. But the Catholic Church always bounces back.

Indeed, today's time traveler advancing through the Centuries to, say, the year 5,000, if he were allowed to take with him one thing only, would be well advised to take a crucifix to identify himself as a friend to the future.

The way things are going only Catholics and cockroaches are destined to be around for any substantial length of time. (And reruns of *I Love Lucy*....)

The Catholic Church has not always been a benign and beneficial entity in helping to order men's affairs. Indeed, there have been times when Popes led troops into battle, encouraged warfare against non-believers, financed and organized crusades against Arab infidels, and urged the Great Nations of Europe to explore the four corners of the world in the hopes of winning more souls for Christ and, occasionally, relieving local peasants of their treasuries of gold and jewels, and then their lives.

Given that the Catholic Church, such a far-reaching entity, was always controlled by the best and the brightest who worked their way up through the Catholic hierarchy until they came to rest in Rome and began to set Church policy, it is only natural that plans would have been made against the day when some of those who had been troubled by the actions of the Church would seek redress.

After all, you can't make boatloads of communion wine without crushing a lot of grapes, nor can you capture souls or booty for two thousand years without making the odd enemy.

The Church claims that a billion souls adhere to its teachings. That leaves at least five billion humans (who may or may not have souls, depending on which cleric you believe) who could have a grievance with the Vatican from time to time.

Any organization worth its salt that has existed for two thousand years (and I can think of one right off the top of my head) will likely have made plans to deal with petitioners who come to World Headquarters seeking reparations for some offence, real or imagined, committed yesterday or two thousand years ago.

In other words, whatever else it has, you can bet your boot that the Catholic Church has a great bunch of lawyers.

Your other boot can be bet as follows: a two thousand year old organization will not likely be stampeded into making any hasty decisions when it fully expects to thrive for another two thousand years. Time is on its side. And whatever travail may appear to be afflicting the Church from decade to decade or century to century, well, this too shall pass, by the Grace of God.

It always has.

In the 1980's came the first alarums concerning sexual abuse perpetrated on little children by officials in the Catholic Church.

Some former children were speaking in public about Priests and nuns who had raped them.

The Catholic Church, from the local priest on up through the Archbishop to the Cardinal, denied that any such abuse had happened and often advised the accusers that if they persisted in making such devil-inspired statements, they would certainly go to hell.

A lot of former children took this advice to heart and Shut Right Up, often at the urging of their family.

Others, less fearful of going to hell, or having already been taken there by a Priest or nun, refused to be quiet.

How brave these people were.

To go against the religion of their parents, to risk their souls being dropped into the eternal fires of hell, to risk all on telling the truth. I am astonished by the courage of these victims who came forward before anyone else had done so, to defy the religious doctrine they had had hammered into them and to throw away their own and their family's chance for an Afterlife in order to get the truth out.

Most knew they would never be believed. Most had been told by the pedophiles who had sexually assaulted them to never tell anyone what had happened to them because no one would ever believe them. Many had told their parents that a Priest or a nun "Touched me" only to have their parents accuse them of lying and to have their parents castigate them for speaking ill of a Priest or nun.

Some of the children who had tried to tell were strapped or beaten by their own parents. Some were made by their parents to go to the Priest or nun, who abused them, tell what they had said to their parents, and ask for the forgiveness of the Priest or nun. That forgiveness was often not forthcoming, but the words "I told you no one would believe you," were sometimes what they heard.

How brave they were, then, after that, to come forward again, to try again to get the truth out.

How like the Church to accuse them all of lying and to stand by that story for decades.

Well, you don't get to be a two thousand year old superpower by rolling over for every kid who comes in with some cock and bull story about his private parts being attacked by a Priest, do you?

The Roman Catholic Church has provided a lightning rod for stories of sexual abuse during the last twenty years, but members of that Church are not alone in their debasing of children.

Chapter 5

MALE TEACHERS – WOMEN TEACHERS – WOMEN RAPISTS?

In May 1968 I was invited to travel from Toronto to Halifax for an all expenses paid interview at Dalhousie Law School to see if I was smart enough to qualify for a law scholarship.

I wasn't.

I had the idea that I could get a scholarship at both Dalhousie and the University of New Brunswick Law Schools, take the money from one and buy a sports car to travel back and forth between the two. The plan might have worked… but I got good and drunk on Moosehead beer at the Hotel Nova Scotia the night before I was to appear before the Law Faculty Selection Committee.

During this preparation for my interview I met another inebriated scholarship candidate in the pub. He was similarly at loose ends and briefing a case of local beer. He had taken his Bachelor's degree in education and was now thinking about going into law. I asked why. He said, "the women." I was momentarily puzzled. "There are decent looking women in law?" I asked, unable to think of one.

In those bygone days there were very few women in law, and most of them not foldout material.

It turned out that my New Best Friend was teaching high school and so, at the age of 21 was coming into daily contact with 17 year old women students whom he found distracting at best and beyond temptation at worst. After a few beers he told me he had had an affair with one of the students he had taught in Grade 12. "However," he said drunkenly, "I did not screw her until the day after she graduated." This made some sense to me at the time but, of course, I was drunk too.

I could see his problem. There had been a Professor at my University in Toronto who was notorious for perching at a table in the cafeteria each September to grade the new crop of women in First Year for later exploitation. He resembled a brilliantine tree frog, had bad dandruff and was squat, bow-legged and almost repulsively ugly. First year women were his downfall, and he theirs. Each year he preyed upon these 18 year old girls, who were often away from home and in a school with male teachers and male students for the first time. Each year he scored with three or four of them, leaving all the male students baffled.

However, these two teachers were not child sexual abusers. They were heterosexual men engaging in sexual intercourse with women over the age of consent.

Most men I know would grudgingly envy both of these reprobates, and while the women they took advantage of were of legal age (barely), the men had nothing to be proud of.

Well, you may say, this is all ancient history. This kind of reprehensible conduct between University Professors and their students must be strictly forbidden by now.

Not so's you'd notice.

Allow me to present Greg Bird, a psychology teacher at Lethbridge College in Alberta. Professor Bird admitted in 2006 to having had sexual relations with three of his female students.

So they threw the book at him, right? Fired him? Well, yes and no. Yes, they fired him, but no; he was reinstated, in part because the College had no rule that said he could not have sexual relations with his students. And you cannot fire a teacher for breaking a rule that doesn't exist, can you?

Lethbridge College is presently re-thinking its rules on faculty-student relations.

Few colleges and universities have a rule in place prohibiting sexual relations between faculty and students. And, as the students are mostly over the age of consent and universities are supposed to be venues where individual experimentation and growth are thought to be generally beneficial, one can see why governing bodies might be reluctant to impose strictures on the freedom of the students to have sexual relations with their professors and vice versa.

The line for teachers and students having sexual relations becomes worse than problematic, however, when the student is 18 or under. The age of consent (when you do not require a note from your parents to have sexual intercourse and where your partner will not go to jail for statutory rape) is 16 in Canada.

And 16 is a fine age of consent if your partner is 17. Or 15. Or 21.

If your partner is 47, however, problems arise. A 17 year old and a 47 year old having sexual intercourse when the 47 year old is a teacher is not a partnership. It is a hostile takeover.

A secondary school teacher touching a student's breast or penis or vagina is a pedophile in my book (and this, don't let's forget, IS my book). No matter the age of the student, there is power imbalance between the two that is not normally part of the sexual equation. A teacher has massive amounts of power over any student. This is Teacher power. No matter how sexually active or precocious the student may be, teachers have the upper hand in the power relationship. In the classic case where a student provides sexual gratification to a teacher in return for better grades, the imbalance of power between the two is readily identifiable.

More subtle is the teacher who gives a student at his school (not a student of his) a ride home every night, say, and drapes his arm over her shoulder, finally touching her breast as if by accident, in order to see how far he can go, and how far he can go the next time before the girl says "No!".

In my opinion, any teacher who sexually touches a student of any age should be fired, lose her pension benefits – yes, I said "her" – and never again be allowed to teach. Judges often do not share my concern.

In the fall of 2006 a 32 year old basketball coach in British Columbia who had kissed and touched a 17 year old female student was thought by a Judge to have suffered enough, and was not required to go to jail for what he had done.

In the same year, a teacher at my former school, who had touched the penises of two of his male students, aged 12 and 13, but not, according to the Judge, with an animus of such "moral depravity" as would require him to go to jail, 3as not only sentenced to no time in jail, but, in part because he was a member of a church, avoided having his name added to the national sex offender registry. His lawyer did a good job for him.

Yet another teacher at my former school was required to do no jail time for anally raping an 18 year old male student. The teacher has admitted to the rape in court. The student has not done quite as well. He has attempted suicide on a number of occasions, the last by jumping out of a fifth floor window. His troubles started with the anal rape. The teacher, however, has recently received a full Pardon from the National Parole Board. Legally, it is now as if this pedophile never had a criminal conviction. Thus, the teacher has escaped both jail time and the bother of not being able to go shopping in the United States. His lawyer did a good job. The boy the teacher raped should be so lucky.

When I was at school there were more instances of intended and actual pedophilia I witnessed than anyone should, because one is too many. I attended Upper Canada College in Toronto, an all-male private school which was then, and is now, one of the most expensive and exclusive schools in Canada. And one of the best.

When I first went to the school I was 7. I had to wear a uniform and to get that uniform I had to go to a tailor. The tailor, who was about 20 and therefore knew more than me, said to me as I was being measured for the distinctive blue blazer: "Do you know how they separate the men from the boys at Upper Canada?" "No," I replied.

"With a crowbar...." he said.

I puzzled over this comment. I knew it was said in jest, but I had no idea what it meant. I was 7 and was not looking for wisdom, just a jacket and a pair of pants. A crowbar. It was a vivid picture, but it meant nothing to me.

Once I had my blazer and gray flannels, I walked home from the tailor and ran into a friend who lived two doors down from me. He was about 14. He recognized the school uniform. "Ahhhhh hah!" he said. "Upper Canada, eh?" "Yes," I said, sort of proudly because it had been difficult to get into the school. Frankie then recited a poem for me:

Crumpets and tea,
Crumpets and tea,
We're the boys from UCC
We're not rough
And we're not tough,
But oooooooooh,
Are we sexy!

I was 7. I had had the school uniform on for twenty minutes and I now knew about crowbars and crumpets and tea and being sexy.

What the hell did all this mean?

For a few years I had no idea. I just went to school.

At UCC, there was a teacher with some seniority – he was the Vice Principal – and one day he began to teach us French by sitting down beside some of the 12 year old boys in class and slipping his hand under their blazers to feel their "breasts". I was in the class. I watched as the old pedophile worked his way down the aisle next to mine, feeling up all the boys as he went. I knew my time was coming and knew that what this old man was doing was wrong. But he was the Vice Principal.

I was frightened that I would not tell him "no" when he got to me. And he was going to get to me soon. I remember thinking "You can't say no to the Vice Principal. You can't tell the Vice Principal to stop. He has all this power..."

As Fate had it, I was literally saved by the bell. The class was dismissed and off we went to the next class. I often wonder what effect the abuse had on the boys who were not as lucky as I was. As sexual abuse goes, this hardly gets on the scale. But make no mistake, it IS sexual abuse and even this near miss had a definite effect on me.

The other kids and I talked about his behavior later and discussed reporting the old poof to the Principal. We all decided this would get us in even more trouble, and capped off the conversation by saying that the Vice Principal seemed to have us confused with the girls who went to the private school down the street, Bishop Strachan School.

We thought, in our rapidly diminishing innocence, that if he wanted to feel breasts he should go teach at Bishop Strachan. This was not very politically correct, but it was 1958.

So, that was how a bunch of 12 year old boys dealt with the problem. We made a joke of it, but we all knew it was something bad, not something funny at all.

Many years later I encountered another teacher from UCC at his cottage down the lake from a friend's place, while on summer vacation, three hours north of Toronto.

This teacher had brought a companion with him to the cottage. A male companion. I took our boat down to their cottage on a social call and was surprised to see the teacher (whom I had known to be homosexual, but not a pedophile) emerge from his cabin with a 17 year old football player whom he had taught at Upper Canada College. It appeared that they had both just rolled out of bed.

This was the tail end of the '60s and everyone was pushing envelopes.

I am ashamed to say I walked away only slightly astonished from this encounter and took no steps to protect that boy or any other children at my old school who might be victims of the thirty-two year old teacher. It later transpired that he had been using much younger children at the school for his sexual gratification and I could have stopped some of that if I had reported him to the police. But it never occurred to me to report him.

I would certainly do it today.

And so we learn, and the more quickly we learn the better. Because the longer it takes for us to learn, the more victims are created.

We know that all teachers have Teacher-power over kids. This is power that derives from the student-teacher relationship. It involves fear on the part of the student, and wanting to please and to ingratiate himself to the teacher. This is a powerful combination. Fear of not doing what the teacher wants and falling into his bad books is a constant with most young students.

When a child is told to obey a teacher and does obey the teacher every school day for five years with the approval of the school hierarchy, the approval of his parents and the approval of society, think of the conflict in that child when his teacher excuses him from class to go to the bathroom, then follows him into the washroom while he is standing alone at the urinal and says "Let me show you how to shake your penis dry."

Well, okay.

What 10-year-old boy would say no to that teacher?

EVERY THREE-YEAR-OLD BOY SHOULD SAY NO TO THAT TEACHER.

This is a true story, however. It occurred in the 1980's. The teacher shook the eight year old boy's penis off, then took him into the washroom stall and put his penis in her mouth. The boy was terrified and began to cry. The teacher continued to suck his penis, then told him that he had been a bad boy and that she would tell his parents he had been a bad boy.

And then she did just that.

At the next parent teacher meeting, she told the parents that the boy had been acting up in class, lying, making up stories about other students. Meanwhile this teacher was performing oral sex on the boy once a week now, in the washroom, in darkened stairwells, or simply by keeping him after school because he was a "bad boy."

The boy lived through this hell for an entire school year. By the end of the year he was sleeping in his closet at home so no one could get at him. He never told his parents about the abuse. He pretended to sleep in his bed every night, but he felt safer in the closet. Sometimes he would sleep in between the bed and the wall, again, so no one could get at him.

I was his lawyer.

He is over 30 now. After counseling he has recovered from much of the emotional turmoil the sexual abuse caused him. He has difficulties forming and keeping relationships, suffers from depression, has been suicidal and, on bad nights, he still sleeps between the bed and the wall. His teacher is still able to get at him emotionally after all these years, even though he never saw her after school, until her trial. His parents, nice people whom I met, blame themselves for not picking up on the abuse, for not stopping it. And so they should.

When your child has a personality shift, particularly one which occurs over a brief period of a month or two it is your duty to learn the reason why. This boy became extremely shy and withdrawn, almost overnight, when the abuse began. His parents asked him what was wrong. He said nothing was wrong. The parents let it go. Shame on them.

The macho male ethos would have it that, had he been 14, say, instead of 8, this was a very lucky boy. Inculcated into sexual relations by a horny teacher, given blow jobs once a week. The reality is that this horrible woman pedophile, this sexual ogre, took this boy's childhood and turned a nice, pleasant young kid into a suicidal, depressed emotional wreck of a boy and now, man, who occasionally drives through red lights at 90 miles an hour just to cheat death. Or not.

No macho man would want to walk a mile in this boy's shoes, or stand in them at the urinal while he was being victimized by his teacher.

How many other boys did this woman cripple emotionally over her twenty five year teaching career? In all probability she did the same thing to at least one boy each year.

How many teachers are there like her?

Well, most of us have heard of the teacher Mary Kay Letourneau who enjoyed a "relationship" with her twelve year old male student beginning when she was 34 years old. Letourneau showed remarkable restraint for a pedophile because she first encountered her victim at school when he was 8, but she held off using him for her sexual needs until he was 12.

Nevertheless, the Seattle area teacher subsequently spent seven years in jail for raping the boy.

Letourneau did "the right thing" by him in the end, however, by marrying him in 2005 after giving birth to two of his children.

What's going on here?

Why are women – and women teachers at that – preying on young, young boys?

There are probably at least nine reasons I can think of. Let's see:

1. The women enjoy the power imbalance. They have had men in their lives who have had all the power in the relationship. Now it's their turn. Kids have no power that can ever compare with Teacher-power.

2. Maturity. The women do not have it sexually or otherwise. The student they victimize is like an anatomically correct doll with a working penis. Or the boy is like a long-lost playmate, reminding the teacher of an earlier, less complicated, happier life in childhood. The teacher is a child again, playing dolls but this time the dolls have penises and vaginas and can be taught how to use them.

3. The women can imbue the child with any characteristic they wish. The child is their tabula rasa, and can become their small dream man.

4. Uncomplicated sexual gratification with no fear about whether he'll call tomorrow, what to wear or how much to eat. Physical attractiveness is not a prerequisite for a pedophile. Often a pedophile is physically unattractive in the extreme.

5. Inability of the woman teacher to relate to the adult male emotionally or physically, but preferring males to females as sexual partners.

6. Romantic delusion. This may be true, pure love in the twisted teacher's mind.

7. The ability to rape the children and then to cast them aside, moving on to new victims with no emotional attachment.

8. The need to have sex with a guaranteed virgin, not some guy who's been sleeping around.

Well, I could only get to eight. A psychologist could probably get to twenty without breaking a sweat. The most important thing for our purposes is that this is a trend and a trend which must be acknowledged, then stopped before more of our kids are harmed.

As usual, women are more complicated than men. Even women pedophiles. Male sexual abusers seem to be interested only in their short-term sexual gratification where female pedophiles seem to require a backstory, or a devised emotional underpinning to the "relationship", so that it makes sense to the women. Men do not care that the sexual abuse "makes sense". Most women seem to have a need to be able to rationally explain the relationship to themselves, as if the sexual abuse of the child were a storyline in a soap opera. Male pedophiles want to reach orgasm using a child. The context in which the orgasm is reached is irrelevant for a male pedophile. But not so with these females, apparently, to whom orgasms are probably of a secondary or even lower concern.

Women pedophiles seem to be about power, about control, about making up a storyline which they can inhabit. Not so much about sex for the sake of sex, but about sex as a tool through which to wield power.

When Janay Wilson a 31 year old teacher in Texas was arrested for having sexual intercourse with a 16 year old male student in 2004, it was after years of rumors about her pursuing him and other boy students in her school.

When Melissa Deel, a 32 year old teacher in Virginia was arrested in 2005 for having performed oral sex on a 13 year old male student, the woman had been calling and emailing the boy regularly.

When Sarah Salorio, a 28 year old teacher in California was arrested in 2005 on 20 counts of performing oral sex on two 13 year old male students, her husband, a local politician, was distraught at the existence of this side of his wife, which he claimed to have known nothing about during their marriage.

When Toni Woods, a 37 year old female teacher confessed to having had sexual intercourse with 5 of her male students at a Middle School in West Virginia in 2005, School Board officials said they would take the allegations "seriously". Given that the woman had already confessed, the School Board damn well HAD better take the allegations seriously because they were no longer allegations, they were FACTS and the School Board is responsible for the misdeeds of its employees. Or it should be, don't you think?

When Sarah Vercoe, a 25 year old female teacher in Sydney, Australia was sentenced in 2005 to four years imprisonment for having had sexual intercourse with 5 male students aged 14 to 16, she said in her defense that her marriage was falling apart. Yes. I wonder why?

When Laura Findlay, a 30 year old female teacher in Saginaw, Michigan was sentenced in 2006 to seven years imprisonment for having had sexual relations with 6 male students, all under the age of 17, a case involving 22 counts of sexual assault on which she faced up to life imprisonment, she admitted to the charges on the understanding that she be sentenced to no more than 7 years incarceration. The parents of her underage victims agreed to this plea bargain, in part so their sons would not be required to give evidence at her trial.

When Debra LaFave, a 23 year old woman teacher near Tampa, Florida performed oral sex on her 14 year old male student and then had sexual intercourse with him in the back seat of a car being driven by the boy's cousin along a highway, in 2004, she admitted she had "crossed the line" in the teacher/student relationship. Ms LaFave had driven 100 miles to the boy's home to have sexual intercourse with him. The husband of Ms LaFave was astonished when detectives told him what his wife had done. The police in Florida named her conduct with the boy "lewd and lascivious battery," just so everyone was totally in the dark on what she had done to the student. Ms LaFave did not go to jail because the boy's mother refused to let him testify against his former teacher, and he was only 14, so he had to do what his mother told him.

Female teachers abusing students is a real and current issue in western civilization, and one that appears to be gaining momentum. Look, for a moment, to Hillsborough

County, Florida. In March, 2008, Stephanie Ragusa, a 28 year old teacher in Tampa was arrested for allegedly having sex with a 14 year old male student in the back seat of her car. Seven days later, the Tampa Police were busy again, arresting Mary Jo Spack, a 45 year old teacher for allegedly having sex with a 17-year-old male student. Barely recovered from these two forays, the Tampa police were called out again 4 days after that to arrest Lisa Marinelli, a teacher aged 40, for allegedly having sex on 10 occasions with a 17-year-old boy. The assaults occurred on multiple occasions, mostly in Marinelli's car.

Tampa, already infamous for having given us the predations of Debra LaFave in 2004, was a bit shell-shocked, but not overly so. Because, between 2005 and March, 2008, there have been TEN similar cases in Hillsborough County. The Hillsborough County School District is said to be conducting a review of its criteria for hiring teachers…

In almost all of these cases, as in the Letourneau case, the female teachers had spent time "wooing" their male victims. They had not so much "groomed" them in the classic sense of a male abuser preparing a chosen victim for the abuse to follow, but had for the most part worked at building a notional "relationship" with the male victims.

It is for psychologists to plumb further these murky depths of the female psyche.

I just call 'em like I see 'em.

I also want to say this again. Many untutored people, men and women both, often say, "Well, weren't those boys lucky. Isn't that every boy's dream, to have sex with a woman. And a woman teacher! What could be better?"

For people new to the study of sexual abuse this is a very tough issue to wrap one's mind around. Sexual assault is the dehumanizing of the body of one person by another. There is no love, no matter what these women pedophiles concoct in their minds. These women are as twisted as members of NAMBLA are when they speak of the natural romantic and sexual love between an 8 year old boy and a 60 year old man. No such thing exists, as loudly as the North American Man Boy Love Association (NAMBLA) proclaims that it does, as if the volume of their voices could make it so.

When a boy aged 5 or 15 is beset by an adult female seeking sexual gratification, the effects of the attack on the boy are equally as devastating as if he had been raped by a man.

Rape is rape.

A woman can and will manipulate a boy until he attains an erection, if his body permits an erection at his stage of development. She can and does make use of this erection for her own purposes, and the result, often, is that the boy has an orgasm. Boys who are masturbated or raped by men also have orgasms. Even if they do not have orgasms, boys' genitals are sometimes engaged during sexual abuse.

This does not make the abuse any less painful or any less psychologically damaging to the boy. As with young women who are raped over a period of time, it is part of the inherent shame of the sexual abuse that for a brief period of time the defiling of a child's body may result in stimulation of the genitals.

These are dangerous waters. Few psychiatrists or psychologists have noted or dealt with this aspect of sexual assault. The child whose body betrays him by sensing pleasure in the act of being sexually debased feels all the more guilty because the receptors in his brain cannot distinguish between the caress of a lover and the self serving manipulations of a pedophile.

Psychologists must help those children who carry lingering guilt over feeling sexual excitement – perhaps for the first time – in the commission of the abuse.

Genitals have no memory. Genitals have no eyes. Genitals have no mind. Genitals have no conscience. Genitals have nerve endings which can be stimulated by a tender touch or by a brutal rapist. If a child's first experience with genital stimulation is an act of sexual defilement perpetrated by a rapist, a violation of the physical and emotional self at the hands of a pedophile, the child's mind knows that what is happening is all wrong, but the genitals may be transmitting a different message to the brain.

This is just one reason why sexual assault leads children to a future of depression, self-medication, sexual confusion, anger, guilt, shame, and sometimes suicide.

Adults tend to be slow to acknowledge something they have forgotten from their youth: children don't know what sex is. They pee through their front parts, they poop through their anuses and they have no idea at all why an adult would be interested in touching, sucking on, penetrating or enveloping in flesh those parts of their bodies which excrete. Children do not yet know The Rules by which the rest of us live. They are innocent of any knowledge or desire having to do with sexual contact. And we forget that.

But the children are aware when their genitals signal pleasure. In even a violent sexual assault there is a possibility that the genitals become "engaged" and transmit a feeling of pleasure to the brain. Not always, but sometimes.

This is not the only reason that guilt ensues from childhood sexual abuse.

Another reason is the inherent intimacy of the act, which, although violent, is an act between someone in authority and a powerless kid, someone ordinarily unapproachable, who, for the first time, displays a need to be in close proximity to the child. However, the child does have some power in this situation. She is the focus of attention. The abuser needs her. Even rape can be an intimate act, in the sense that "intimacy" connotes two people of whatever age and standing in society, involved in a private but mutual undertaking. That one party to the rape is unwilling does not discount the intimacy of the act, even if force and brutality is used by the pedophile.

Even if the child is raped with a knife at her throat, even where there is disgust, fear, pain, blood and physical injury, the element of intimacy may be one which she has never before known.

When the rapist goes on to say that this is to be kept THEIR secret, when the rapist gives the child a gift, when the child shares this horrible knowledge with no one, there exists the certainty that psychological damage will ensue because, at the very least, the pedophile has driven a wedge between the young boy and the people he trusts most, and at the same time has formed a bond with the boy that few things have the power to sever.

This may be what is in the subconscious mind of women rapists – especially women teachers – who require that a relationship exist before they rape their victim. In seducing their victim, they fill their own sexual needs. At the same time, these women make the sexual abuse result in even more far-reaching psychological harm being done to the victim.

Here, and elsewhere in this book, psychiatrists and psychologists may be of the opinion that my marbles are, at the very least, chipped, if not lost altogether, and that I should be blown out of the water as an armchair psychologist.

Good.

Fire away.

Let's get a discussion going.

Let's drag all of this out of the closet and into the open, where it can do nothing but help the kids.

There is an epidemic going on and society is tiptoeing around as if not to awaken knowledge. This ignorance plays right into the hands of all pedophiles.

But before we leave the sexually aggressive female teacher, a note to School Boards:

Open Your Eyes.

One way to do this is to increase the number of video monitors in schools.

Another is to have a program of education for schoolchildren and for teachers which specifically addresses the issue of teachers and other adults who sexually abuse students.

A third is to heavily lay down the law to your teachers. Let them know that any sexual impropriety with a student will result in their being terminated immediately with loss of pension benefits and their never again being hired as a teacher.

Finally, in almost every jurisdiction I know of, School Boards are not liable in damages for the pain caused to students by pedophile teachers. In the case I spoke of, where my client was fellated by a woman teacher on numerous occasions, I might well have convinced a Court to award damages of more than $500,000 for pain and suffering and for the loss of wages and opportunity to make income that was caused by the teacher's misconduct. I might have been able to collect half of that amount at best by selling the teacher's house and relieving her of her pension. The balance should have been paid by the School Board that employed the woman.

But the law says that the School Board is not responsible if it hires a pedophile who sexually assaults a child.

I believe this law is wrong.

All School Boards should be held to account for failing to weed out these people or, having hired them, for failing to keep children safe from their actions. Making the School Boards pay damages would go a long way to insuring that School Boards are more concerned about saving the children than they are about protecting the teachers and themselves. It would make the School Boards more alert.

So far, School Boards have been able to dodge the bullet of their liability by saying "Well, gee, we could hardly have imagined any sexual abuse would go on between our Kindergarten teacher and that little boy."

They can't say that now.

They've just read this.

Let's make this small change. Your local legislature has the power to do this and you should require them to do it.

Just recently in British Columbia, a teacher employment registry has been published. It may be made available online, enabling parents and others to keep a watchful eye on problem teachers and red flagging teachers who have been suspended or dismissed for sexual misconduct with students. It is a step in the right direction, and other jurisdictions should give strong consideration to implementing a similar service, as soon as possible.

The more parents know, the better.

I suspect that most people reading this book will be surprised by the prevalence of women teachers who sexually abuse their students. The problem is symptomatic of western society on a larger scale.

In Colorado a 41 year old mother, not a teacher, was sentenced to jail for 30 years in late 2005 after holding drug parties at her house and having sexual intercourse with two teenage boys. She admitted that she wanted her teenaged daughters and their friends to see her as a "cool mom".

In Connecticut a 30 year old mother named Tammy Imre went to jail for 6 years in 2004 for having repeated sexual contact with the 8 year old male playmate of her own 8 year old daughter. She had sent the boy a love letter saying, in part, "I want you," and "I don't want anyone but you. Now tomorrow it's supposed to rain. You can come over and we can (you know what). Love ya!" This woman's conduct was exacerbated when her daughter was forced to watch as her mother had sexual contact with her playmate. I have not been able to learn what the "sexual contact" was in this case because of the fuzzification by the press, but it goes without saying that any repeated sexual contact between a 30-year-old woman and an eight-year-old year old boy will likely permanently damage the boy and the daughter of the woman who watched her mother violate the young boy.

But wait.

This one may have a happy ending.

Ms Imre, a divorcee, told the police that she thought of the 8-year-old as her "boyfriend" and said she planned to marry him someday.

Well, sure.

After she gets out of jail in the year 2525, I'm sure the boy, by now a man, will want to marry a 100 year old nutbar of a woman pedophile who wrecked his life when he was eight.

Sorry. I guess I was too quick trying to find a happy ending there.

If sexual aggression on the part of women toward children is on the rise – and it is – all mothers are required to do everything in their power to ensure that the women her child spends time with – teachers, sitters, mothers of friends, caregivers, nuns and nurses – do not have a sexual screw loose. This stricture presumes that the mother herself does not have a sexual screw loose.

In that case, there's not much to be done.

For example, a woman in Martinez, California was arrested in November 2005 for offering her four-year-old baby to a pedophile on the Internet. When 22-year-old mothers are allowing people to rape their four-year-old daughters in return for $500, there is not too much we as a society can do except to take that woman's children away and make sure she never again has custody of a child.

I am not finished with women yet.

Later I will spend some time talking about nuns.

However, for the time being, it seems to me that the societal view of women as being benign when it comes to raping children, or, at most, as those who will be complicit but not active in raping children, has gone the way of the dodo.

Women may not yet be as aggressive as men$in raping children, but they have declared themselves, and it would be folly to ignore them or to think that they will somehow come to their senses. All the indicators suggest that the opposite is true and that for reasons which can only be guessed at by me, women in the 21st Century are potentially dangerous sexual abusers of children and they should be seen and treated as such by all of us. Women do not yet sexually abuse children with the same frequency as men do, but they are catching up to men in this unholy category where equality is the equality of shame.

Chapter 6

NICE PEOPLE WHO ADOPT SMALL CHILDREN

A tall, good looking man of about thirty came to see me one day. He had no appointment, but that is not unusual in my work. People want to talk about this stuff when they want to talk about this stuff.

I asked him how I could help him, and he began to cry. Unfortunately, that is also not unusual in the work that I do. His name was Dave and for twenty minutes he sat with me – a stranger – and sobbed his heart out and said nothing. My secretary had overheard and brought in some coffee for Dave and she sat with me while Dave did what he had to do, which at that moment was to cry. During this time I said a couple of things every few minutes. The first thing I told the man – I did not know his name at the time – was that he was safe here, that no one could hurt him here. The second thing I told him was that crying got the poison out of his body and that crying was an important way to help him get better. The third thing I told him was that I would do everything I could to help him.

As he wept, loud, deep, wracking sobs, I thought for a moment about the other lawyers who work in my office and the other staff and what they must think goes on in my office. I waited until Dave was ready to talk, and when he began he was well spoken, intelligent and had a quick wit and a dry, self-deprecating sense of humor.

He had been adopted when he was 6 days old by a professional family – father a well known accountant, mother a nurse – and had had a horrible upbringing by any standards. Both his parents were alcoholics and both beat him regularly, sometimes strapping him with a belt, sometimes with the buckle end, sometimes on his genitals. This mistreatment had started, as far as he could recall, when he was about 6 or 7. He remembered going to school one day in the 1970's, having been so badly beaten the night before by his mother that he could not sit at his desk. His teacher had the sense to send him to the school nurse. The school nurse asked him what had happened. He said, as he was always told to by his parents to say, that he had fallen down. He looked at me and said "I should have told her I fell off the roof three times. That's how bad it was."

The school sent someone to the house to "check on things" and everything must have checked out fine because that was the last he heard about it, but after that the physical beatings stopped and he was more emotionally abused. His mother called him "runt", made him eat his parents' leftovers if he wanted dinner, and often went for days without talking to him. He had no friends because his parents wanted no children playing in the house. None of the other kids ever invited him to play at their house, either. Probably because he was a bit "different."

He became even more different from the other kids when he was 14 and his mother sat him down at the kitchen table and gave him a glass of what she was drinking – vodka and orange juice. He became drunk almost immediately. His father was away that night – attending another one of his meetings – and his mother took him upstairs and told him to take his clothes off and lie on the bed. He did. She strapped his buttocks with a belt, then told him to turn over. She strapped his thighs and genitals with the belt. Then she took her clothes off, got into bed with him, rubbed his penis until it was erect then put his penis into her vagina.

After that, this same thing happened quite a bit. Dave got to like it. He enjoyed drinking with his mother and having sex with her because "it was the first time she'd ever been nice to me, the only time she ever held me."

I sued his mother.

Dave had become not so much a member of society as we know it as an observer. He lived by himself in a shack he had made of reinforced paper – like tar paper – in a forest where no one went except him. He ate cold food from cans. He had no electricity. He traveled by hitchhiking. He lived on welfare and on money he made from occasional jobs cutting up trees for firewood. He had never had a relationship with a woman, or with a man or, after he left his mother at age 17 when he realized how wrong "it" was, with any living creature.

I was frankly surprised that he had come to see me and that he was able to appear so pleasant and easygoing, but he had decided that he wanted to straighten out his life and make it count for something. The way to begin to do this, he thought, was by confronting his mother not with violence but with the law.

We spent a lot of time preparing Dave emotionally for Court. It is a big step for a healthy person to sue someone, an even bigger one for someone who has lived outside the system both physically and emotionally.

With the help of a good counselor, Dave started to make progress. His depression eased. He saw some potential in his future instead of the bleakness he had lived with since he was 17. He told me one day that his goal was to get enough money from his mother so that he could by his own log splitter. I asked what that was and he told me it was a machine that had a large four-way axe head that was driven with great force onto a block of hardwood to split it into four equal pieces so the wood fit into a fireplace. I asked if he could get me a load of firewood and he said he could, but first he needed to rent the splitter. He said he was going to do that soon, but that his goal was to buy his own. They cost around seven thousand dollars. I said he could probably look forward to buying his own and then he would have a source of income for the rest of his life. Everyone needs firewood, after all.

Sometimes Dave cried when we were preparing his case, and sometimes he thought it was all hopeless, but he was having more good days than bad and his psychotherapist said he was making huge strides.

His father had died and his mother denied everything he said. To his credit Dave did not wither up and blow away. He kept on with his lawsuit.

When I got his mother on the witness stand in Court I asked her about the first time "it" happened. She denied "it" had happened, even though she had just heard Dave describe it in detail, down to what she was wearing.

I asked her if she could possibly have forgotten that she had required her son to have sexual intercourse with her. The mother's mind appeared to wander when I asked that question, as if she was not all there. She replied she never had required her son to have sexual intercourse with her.

I asked her if it was possible that she had and she had forgotten.

She said that that was possible.

Dave had just won his case.

I looked at the Judge and I looked at her lawyer and the case was adjourned at that point at her lawyer's request.

Afterwards I congratulated Dave on having the courage to do what was right for him and to come so far so quickly. I said his future looked bright, and we laughed about how much he had changed since the first time he came into my office in a torn shirt and boots with no laces and now here he was in a suit.

It was as good a day as you get in Court.

The next Monday, when I was about to try to settle Dave's case out of Court I got a call from the Police. They wanted to know if Dave was my client because they'd found my business card in his shack.

Dave was dead.

His head had been smashed in by a log splitting machine he had rented.

No one would have chosen that way to kill himself, the Police said.

Dave's death was ruled an accident.

But you and I know his mother killed him as surely as if she had put Dave's head in that log splitting machine.

Foster parents are wonderful people, selfless, who go out of their way and dedicate a large part of their lives to raising children whose real parents are not in the picture.

Foster parents are also people who are more likely than most to be pedophiles. Not all foster parents are pedophiles.

Some are.

Right now I am in the middle of a case where twin brothers were abandoned by their mother and father at the age of 6 and went to live in a foster home. These children were treated like slaves by the father and mother in their new family. They were fed very little, kept locked in the basement and were periodically tied to a chair, when they would be anally raped by the 18 year old son of their foster parents. Today, because of the frequency and severity of the rapes, one of the boys has a prolapsed anus and leaks feces. He wears two or three pairs of underwear to soak up the discharge. Emotionally, both brothers are basket cases. They trust no one, not even each other, they hoard food, and they suffer from massive depression. They cannot work with counselors because the pain of remembering the abuse is too great. Each day they wake up they are uncertain they will make it through without killing themselves.

When they had been through this horrible life for a couple of years, they were smart enough at the age of 9 to go to the local office of their social worker. The social worker had always thought things were going fine in the house and had never spoken to them outside the hearing of their foster parents. So the boys went to the social worker. He wasn't in. They told their story to another worker. The next day they left the foster home.

Too late, too late.

Now I have a problem. The foster parents are dead, the boy who raped them is long gone. The social worker who was supposed to care for them failed them miserably.

In 2004 the Supreme Court of Canada, than which there is no higher, said that under these circumstances the kids cannot successfully sue the government that hired the social worker because that would put an unfair burden on foster parents, social workers and governments.

I do not think so, for the same reasons that I mentioned earlier when I was talking about how to keep School Boards on their toes.

As it is, these kids will never have a decent chance because they will never have sufficient funds to turn their lives around. They are both smart, but so emotionally fouled up that they live from one welfare day to the next. They are a drag on society instead of being able to contribute. The major reason for this is what they were forced to endure while under the care of the government.

The law should protect kids like this from predatory foster parents and governments would be more inclined to scrutinize their foster parents if they knew they would have to pay for damage inflicted on children in their care.

Not all children who live in foster homes are sexually abused.

Many are.

Chapter 7

DOCTORS AND BOY SCOUT LEADERS AND OTHER POWER PEOPLE

One of the tenets of this book is that sexual abuse increases proportionately with the amount of time the pedophile spends with the child, the level of trust that the child and his parents have in the pedophile and the physical proximity of the pedophile to his or her victim.

An uncle may be a pedophile who is highly regarded in the family, but until he is left alone with his nephew, it is unlikely that the boy will be raped.

Doctors who are pedophiles have no problem gaining proximity to their victims.

Indeed, in no other situation is the victim of sexual abuse required to present herself to the abuser, disrobe and submit to personal questions and physical touching, including touching of the breasts and vagina.

Medicine has always been a magnet for those who wish to do well by humanity. The most highly regarded profession, medicine attracts intelligent men and women who have the admiration of society because most doctors seek to do good.

Occasionally, a doctor with a foot fetish will become a chiropodist, but fetishists of this nature are mostly harmless and if a chiropodist is aroused by playing with your tootsies unbeknownst to you, well, little enough harm done. This is almost a victimless crime.

Almost.

Far more destructive are the doctors who perform gynecological exams on young girls, or do breast examinations not for the health and wellbeing of the child but for the sexual gratification of the doctor.

How often does this happen?

Based on a reading of Disciplinary Hearings of Doctors in Canada, it happens far too often, even now when the light of public scrutiny shines brightly on a profession that has traditionally closed ranks around its miscreant members.

Anyone who has ever worked in a hospital will tell you that there is an aura of omnipotence about a doctor. Not that he IS omnipotent, but rather that he believes he should be treated as if he were.

Arguably, his doctor is the only person who annually grabs the President of the United States by the testicles and tells him to cough. And what do you think that doctor tells his wife about his day at work when he gets home? Damn straight. "Guess what I did today, honey?"

This power over people is heady stuff. Especially over people who have most of their clothes off, or are wearing those large wraparound lobster bibs that never quite close in the back. Doctors invented those.

They could have made them close in the back, but where's the fun in that?

Say, then, a developing 14-year-old-girl comes into a doctor's office for a physical, the first time without her mom being there. Say there is no nurse present. Say the doctor is a heterosexual pedophile. How does the 14-year-old girl know how long a breast examination is supposed to take? Or how long a vaginal examination is supposed to take? Theoretically, any pedophile doctor can take as long as she wants conducting an examination simply by muttering "hmmm, that's interesting. How long have you had this…" and scaring the bejesus out of her frightened young patient.

There have been instances – far too many instances – of doctors raping their patients while those women were as vulnerable as they could possibly be – naked form the waist down, their legs apart on an examination table to facilitate a vaginal examination and unable to see what the doctor is doing.

Sometimes a doctor masturbates while performing the examination. Occasionally he will insert his penis into the young girl and, if she asks, explain that it is his finger or a speculum or, in one case I am aware of, a thermometer. How is she to know?

And young women are not the only ones vulnerable to pedophile doctors.

In 1997 a man and his wife came to see me. He was a tough guy type, a man of few words, a self made businessman. Or so it appeared to the world at large.

Within minutes the man's wife explained to me that her husband often had bouts of severe depression, could not leave his bed, let alone his house, could not go to work and could not earn money in the face of bills cascading through their mailbox. Her job was to try to prop him up emotionally while keeping the creditors away from the door, but she was getting to the end of her rope. I asked her how long this had been going on and she replied "Since we were married – twenty-five years now."

She began to cry. Her husband sat looking at me numbly, a look of helplessness on his face.

I asked the man if he had been sexually abused when he was a child. He said nothing. His wife stopped crying long enough to say "Tell him."

With the help of his wife, prompting, filling in details, he told a story he had never before told anyone but her.

He had been a child of privilege who was sent to a private boys' school when he was ten years old. When he was thirteen he was in a gymnastics event and hurt his neck. A teacher drove him to the hospital and in the hospital a diagnosis was made and the boy was put in traction. His legs and arms were immobilized in an attempt to rectify the damage done to his neck.

On his first night in traction in the hospital, a doctor he had never seen before came into his room, made some adjustments to his bed then anally raped the boy while keeping him quiet by putting his hand over the boy's mouth. The pain of the rape was intense. The boy could not cry out for help. He was tied down and unable to resist. He suffered this torture for perhaps twenty minutes, which seemed like forever. The doctor left, telling the boy to say nothing or he would be back and he would bring a friend and he would do it again.

Later a nurse came into the room to check how he was. The boy said nothing. The nurse checked under his sheets and said "My God. What happened?"

The boy said nothing.

He watched as two nurses cleaned him with damp cloths. The pain from his rectum was intense, but he could not see anything except the wash cloths the nurses had, which were covered with blood and feces.

The doctor never returned and the boy was discharged from the hospital a week later.

The incident took control of his life. He began to suffer deep depression, and he became suicidal. Although he had been a bright boy and still was, his grades sank and sank. Instead of going to university as he would have done, he ended up in a mechanics course at a community college, and then did not finish that. He thought he must be homosexual, and that thought caused him untold pain.

In the 1980's and before, most boys feared being branded a homosexual. Those boys who were raped by men all believed that they had given off a homosexual signal to the pedophile, or that the pedophile had chosen to rape them because he knew they were gay. After all, he had come to rape them and as far as they knew he never raped anyone else, so they must have sent a powerful signal to the older man that they were homosexuals. Kids have no idea about their sexuality, but back in the day before we became enlightened, most boys thought being a homosexual was about the worst thing that could happen and chances are, if we were raped it was by a homosexual who somehow knew what we did not know – that we were homosexual.

This boy, too, thought the doctor had seen something in him that made him sexually attack the boy. He thought it was his fault that he had been raped. Why else would a doctor so badly want to have sex with him?

The boy was not a homosexual and has never had a homosexual experience in his life. Like so many boys, he was raped by a pedophile and lived in dread that his sexuality was defined by that rape.

The story this boy settled on to tell himself about the event so that he could better live with the memory of it was that the doctor found him sexually attractive because of the way the boy looked and because the boy had made the mistake of looking that way, the doctor had raped him.

So the boy was guilty.

And the boy felt guilty when, as a man, he came to see me. That guilt, and shame over that guilt, was one of the things that made it so difficult for the boy – forty years later – to tell me what had happened. He had convinced himself that the whole thing was his fault. Many times while he was trying to tell the story he interrupted himself and said to me "I don't know why I am even telling you this. It was probably all my fault."

I told him, as his wife said she had been doing for years, that the rape was definitely not his fault and that the doctor who had raped him was a pedophile. But these were just words that fell away from the man and did not reach their mark.

I asked him if he had any feelings of anger toward the doctor. He seemed puzzled and said he had never felt anger toward the doctor, only toward himself for leading the doctor on.

We had many meetings after that. I convinced the man to start meeting with a therapist, to try to lift his depression and to put some meaningful perspective on the sexual attack that had changed his life because he had been tied down in the wrong place at the wrong time.

In time he came to understand intellectually that the rape had not been his fault, that the doctor had committed a violation of the young boy's physical and emotional integrity in the worst possible way. The man had this concept in his mind. But his emotions would not obey his mind. It was rational that the doctor was at fault. He understood. But emotionally he continued to be guilty for what the doctor had done. His mind could not convince his heart of the truth because so many years had passed when his emotions had been beaten down by his misperception of the truth.

Most victims of sexual abuse know in their minds that they were not a willing partner in the sexual abuse that was done to them. Most know in their minds that the sexual assaults were not their fault. But in their hearts, most victims cannot shake the fear, the shame, and the guilt. Their mind cannot force their heart to obey what their mind now has come to understand. And this is where the need for a good counselor comes into play.

Most victims of sexual abuse tell themselves a version of the truth that they settle upon in their minds so that those memories of the abuse, when they return, as they always do, have as little terror in them as possible. Therefore, the memories of the sexual abuse almost always return in the same way. The pain is still there, but the pain is managed by the memory that the victim creates and the story that goes with the memory is painful, but familiar. When the memory returns and the story unfolds in the victim's mind, he knows it will be painful again, but no more painful than the last time.

The victim of a sexual abuser reduces the story he tells himself to one where the pain is not so great that he will kill himself or hurt more than usual, but hurt just as much as the last time. And he lived through it the last time, so he will live through it this time. He has taken that much control back from his abuser: he defines the story of the abuse to himself in such a way that he can tolerate it.

Or, as John Lennon would have it, "Whatever gets you through the night, it's alright, it's alright…."

I agree with John Lennon on this one.

Occasionally, though, a sight, a smell, a sound will trigger a new memory of the abuse – a memory never recalled since the abuse happened.

The sharp horror of recalling being anally raped because you see a man who looks like your abuser walking down the street is something most of us will never know. Those who have memories waiting to explode into their minds as if by accident carry a burden none of us would want.

It is important that these men and women know that they are not alone, that this happens to others, and that it can be made better.

But there was very little I could do for the man who had been raped by his doctor.

Unlike doctors, lawyers don't pretend to be gods.

We could never get away with it.

I found a good counselor for this likeable, severely traumatized man. I next investigated the records of the hospital from thirty years before – there were few records remaining – and I found pictures of the staff doctors at the time. I could find no information about any staff nurses who might have been witnesses.

Positive identification of the pedophile doctor was not possible. If I had sued on the basis that an unknown doctor at the hospital had raped my client, the Court would have heard my client's evidence then heard a lawyer for the hospital arguing that there was no proof of the assault, no proof that the assault was done by anyone connected with the hospital even if it did happen and no reason why the hospital should be held responsible in any event. That lawyer would probably have won the day.

The meetings I had with the man and his wife became further apart. I explained that the law was imperfect, that if I had the name of the doctor there would be something to work with. The man took it upon himself to search out the doctor. His wife spent weeks trying to find a paper trail that would disclose the name of the doctor. She wanted her husband whole. She wanted to save their business and their marriage. He became obsessed with tracking down the doctor.

But the doctor was not to be found.

One day we had a final meeting. I went over the law as I had done many times before. I said we could sue the hospital, but would almost certainly not succeed. I asked whether it would help if the hospital were found to be responsible for the rape that had ruined this man's life.

He replied "Somebody has to be responsible."

Because if we could not find who was responsible, HE would always be the one responsible.

In very many ways the law is an imperfect tool for helping victims of sexual abuse. However, the law changes to accommodate new information, new proof and new evidence.

As more cases of sexual abuse are brought to Court, the law will be modified to enable victims to have their stories fairly weighed. But this is a subject for another day.

The story of the boy raped by the doctor in hospital is an extreme one. As far as doctors go in general, children have no reference points for what is proper medical touching and what is improper.

All doctors should be required to explain to any patient under 18 years of age the nature of the examination that is about to be done, why these steps are being taken, and what sensation the patient will likely feel.

The doctor should always have a nurse present during any examination of a person under 18.

There should be a video camera in every examination room and every hospital room and all video recordings and paper records should be kept by the doctors' governing body for a minimum of thirty years. At the present time, many hospitals and doctors are allowed to destroy patients' records after seven years have passed. Why?

Preservation of these records would help many people in many ways.

These steps would help safeguard patients but would go a long way toward safeguarding innocent doctors as well from spurious claims of abuse or misunderstandings. In the past, storing records was a big problem, requiring a great deal of time and space. Now, records can be copied onto a computer and quickly stored forever. There is no reason why medical records should not be kept this way. This was one of President Obama's first announcements.

A doctor's office should be a place of supreme safety and comfort for all children. A hospital should be a place where no harm is done to a patient.

These suggested changes in medical procedure are not earth shattering. They are benign and relatively inexpensive. Considering the social and other costs of sexual abuse of children by medical professionals, when can we look forward to seeing these changes implemented?

Is there any reason why these policies cannot be in place by this time next year?

Is there some issue more important to doctors than the sexual integrity of their young patients?

Possibly.

A psychiatrist in Ontario was reinstated in 2005 after he had lost his licence to practice in 1998 for having sexually abused a patient. The patient was not a child, but the lesson is salutary. The Ontario College of Physicians and Surgeons heard evidence that the doctor was "no longer a threat to patients".

Possibly not.

In any event, he is now back to being a doctor and seeing patients again.

In a world where our children are at risk of being sexually abused by certain groups of people I believe we owe it to the children to do what we can to keep them safe when they are with their doctors.

Nor do I suggest that all doctors are pedophiles.
Some are.

Which doctor is your child safe with?

When children under 16 are supervised by coaches on a sports team, Priests or pastors in church, scout leaders on a camping trip, nuns or teachers in a schoolroom or on a field trip, stepfathers or babysitters or grandparents while mother is away from home, the klaxon of propinquity should resound in the mother's ears. She should grill the supervisor like a well done hamburger, if for no other reason than to put the fear of god into him before entrusting him with her child.

She should make certain that no child will ever be left alone with only one adult during the entire period of time her child is vulnerable. If such a situation occurs, the supervisor should know that he or she will be fired.

The mother should review once again with the child – for the thousandth time, if necessary – the rules about being rape-proofed. Remember, 2 is not too young and 16 is not too old to have the message drilled into your child so that his behavior becomes automatic when an abuser reaches for him.

Some may say that this is unduly tough on doctors or teachers or pastors or scout leaders. Aren't the stories about scout leaders sexually abusing children just a myth?

Maybe.

Let's see.

In Toronto in 2005, a man named Thomas McKnight had some pictures on his home computer. These were sexually explicit pictures of boys and girls aged 7 to 12. He sent these pictures to another pedophile via the Internet. Except that, in this case, the other pedophile was a police officer. Oh, and McKnight had been a volunteer with Scouts Canada for 15 years.

Barry Hardaker, Executive Director of Field Services for Scouts Canada said the arrest of McKnight was "very disturbing."

I guess Mr. Hardaker would have said the same about:

Frank Kense, a Scouts Canada leader in Edmonton who was arrested in 2004 when child pornography was found in his home

Scott Faichnie, a Scouts Canada Cub leader who was also arrested in 2005 for having pornographic images on his computer

Ian Mole, a Scouts Canada Troop leader who was arrested in 2005 in Toronto for having pornographic images on his computer

Trevor Harvie, a former Scout Leader for 12 years who was arrested in 2002 in Lower Sackville Nova Scotia for having possession of pornography on a computer at a Scout Camp.

Question: Do pedophiles flock to these places of propinquity, such as the Scouts, or do places of propinquity breed pedophiles?

Answer: It really doesn't matter. They're there in droves and we all must work to stop them from ever hurting a child again by making their superiors equally as responsible as the pedophiles for sexually abusing our children.

More Complex Answer: It's probably a little of both, leaning toward the notion that those with a propensity to abuse children go to where children are more easily abused, just as alcoholics go to a liquor store and drug addicts go to a dealer.

Those with a pre-existing propensity to have sex with children should be winnowed out by groups which hire employees or take on volunteers who will interact with those children. The burden is a three-part one: it is on the parent and child first, the pedophile second and the employer third. We cannot count on the pedophile to pitch in and do his part, so if the rape-proofing of your child fails for whatever reason to safeguard her, we must lay the blame on the person or organization that hired the abuser or took him on as a volunteer.

The weeding out of pedophiles before they can damage children is not rocket science but it does require a little labour on the part of those who put the pedophile in a position of propinquity with the children.

Right now there are few laws which hold that person in that organization accountable.

Citizens must elect politicians who make laws that children need to make employers more diligent in ensuring that no pedophile uses his employment or volunteer status to rape children. Life being what it is, society must make the employer pay with the loss of his liberty, the loss of his money or both if he hires a pedophile.

Not to enact legislation of this nature is to put our kids at greater risk when they are already at a high level of risk from things we cannot control. We CAN and SHOULD control the vetting of pedophiles who may now or in the future be taken on to raise, teach, coach, lead or minister to our children when we are not present.

Such a needed change in the law, people like Mr. Hardaker of Scouts Canada might find, would be "very disturbing" indeed.

Chapter 8

UNCLE BOBBY AND THE BACHELOR

If you have read this far, you already know what this chapter is about. I'm going to tell you anyway; because I know things you do not know.

One family's "funny" uncle is another neighborhood's pedophile. Their age is immaterial. Anywhere from ten to a hundred-and-ten. Gender, as we have seen, is also immaterial. But here is what Uncle Bobby and the Nice Man across the street have in common.

They like children.

They like to fondle children, feel their genitals, put their fingers in their anuses and vaginas and, sometimes rape children. They like to have children suck their penises.

They like children.

They love having children around. At a family gathering they will show great interest in Jason's Little League statistics or Jasmine's doll collection. They may prefer to eat with the children, go on long walks with them, or take them for treats when all the other adults are busy.

These predatory pedophiles will have stories to amaze and amuse children, magic tricks to show them, supplies of candy, soft drinks, chips, or the dollars to buy them with. They will sometimes bring their own toys to your house. They will be endlessly fascinated by all the children, especially the most attractive ones or the ones who are easily led or the ones whose parents aren't around much.

Dirty Uncles are very good at ferreting out the vulnerable children because that is what pedophiles do. You may have a Dirty Uncle in your family. He could be a brother, of course, or a nephew, or he could be your husband interacting with his nieces and nephews or his sons and daughters or his grandchildren.

Or you could be the pedophile I'm talking about.

A word of caution, though. There may be a man in your family who exhibits all of the behavior I have set out, and even more. He may love to be with children, have never had a wife or girlfriend, like to do magic tricks, and so on, and NOT be a predatory pedophile.

It's possible.

But it's not very bloody likely, as my father would have said.

So if you have an Uncle Bobby in your family, here's what to do.

Separate Uncle Bobby from the children, sit down with him in a quiet room and have a chat with him. Chances are this happens infrequently, so he will likely be suspicious.

Tell Uncle Bobby that you are concerned about him playing so much with the children and say that you and the other relatives want him to stop spending so much time with them.

Uncle Bobby, if he has half his wits, will sputter and protest that he is just keeping the kids happy and doing what the parents ought to be doing.

Tell Uncle Bobby that from now on, whenever he is with a child there will be another adult relative present. And then do that.

Uncle Bobby will become angry/petulant/dismissive and ask if you are accusing him of anything.

Your answer: "Not yet."

Speak with all the children. Mothers will want to speak with their own kids. Have a chat about Uncle Bobby and all the fun things he has done with them. Be alert. Granted, you are no trained professional, but you should know your own child and when your child is dodging a question.

Do not suggest to the child that Uncle Bobby has hurt him. Rather, ask the child what he and Uncle Bobby play at when they are alone, where they go, whether they LIKE Uncle Bobby.

If the child volunteers that Uncle Bobby has touched him for a sexual purpose, phone the police. You may or may not wish to lay charges against Uncle Bobby but you owe it to other kids – to MY kids – to have the police open a file on him.

It is not your job to say whether Uncle Bobby is guilty or innocent – that is the job of a Court.

It IS your job to save your children and other children from harm. It may turn out that you know Uncle Bobby put his fingers in your daughter's vagina but the Court says he is not guilty of that. That happens more than we would like. But from the minute you know the truth, you and your family will decide what to do about Uncle Bobby.

You will want to think hard about getting therapy for your daughter. Depending on the nature of the sexual abuse, therapy may just draw more attention to something already on its way to being forgotten.

In my family, an eight year old girl was set upon by a flasher in a park. He gave her the open overcoat, hanging penis treatment. She went home and told her parents who reported it to the police. The police arrested the flasher. The parents asked the girl if she wanted to talk about it, trying to gauge whether therapy might be indicated. The girl had already moved on, and though she never forgot the incident, it left no deep psychological scar. But it did leave a scar. Any incident like that would bother any child. And for a long time to come.

But every child is different. Probe gently and if in doubt, a trip to a good psychologist probably never hurt anyone.

In 1993 a boy came into my office and asked me if I handled sexual abuse cases. I said yes. He was twenty-eight-years old and told me that between the ages of 9 and 12 he had been sodomized by his Uncle. The story was new to me then – way back in 1993 – but all-too-familiar now.

The boy's parents, knowing their son had always been a bit withdrawn and socially awkward, thought he might benefit by spending some time with his Uncle in the big city rather than spending another summer holiday on the family farm.

Right away, if you've been following along, you know this is not going to end well. You see, we're all learning at the same pace here. Look how much we know already about how this isn't going to end well for Carl. If his parents had read this book, Carl's life would have been a lot better.

You see, we're all in this together.

And we're getting somewhere.

The Uncle picked Carl up at the airport, took the eight year old home and gave him the run of the house. There was a swimming pool. There was pizza and Coke and no bedtime. When bedtime came, eight-year-old Carl was homesick and asked his Uncle if he could sleep in his bed. The Uncle replied in the affirmative and the boy was surprised but not terrified when, in the middle of the night, he felt the Uncle's hand down the front of his pajamas. The boy asked what his Uncle was doing. The Uncle replied "I'm just checking to see if you wet the bed." Carl said he never wet the bed and that was the end of that.

The Uncle pulled his hand out of Carl's pajamas.

The next day the Uncle and Carl were playing together in the swimming pool.

The Uncle kept swimming underwater and coming to the surface under Carl with one hand between Carl's legs. Carl knew this was wrong, too, but he said nothing to his Uncle.

That night Carl was relaxed enough to sleep in his own bed but his Uncle got into bed with him anyway, to "keep him company" in case he got lonely.

It was a hot night and the Uncle suggested they both take their pajamas off and "sleep in the raw, like men." Carl had never done that before, but the whole trip was one of new experiences and he really liked his Uncle and wanted to please him.

The next thing Carl knew his Uncle was fondling his penis and asking Carl if it "felt good". Carl said it did not feel good. His Uncle said "I bet you'll like this," and put his mouth on Carl's penis and began to suck on it. Carl got an erection for the first time in his little life. And it DID feel good.

But Carl knew it felt more wrong and dirty than it felt good.

He told his Uncle to stop and he did stop.

But the Uncle had two weeks with Carl before he had to send him back to his parents. He took Carl for trips in the car and on a boat he rented, they went to kids' movies together, they swam and they laughed during the day.

And at night the Uncle would always be in bed with Carl and after a week he took a tube of some kind of ointment and put it on Carl's anus and put his finger in Carl's anus. That hurt. It hurt more when the Uncle put his penis in Carl's anus.

There was some blood, too. The Uncle said he did that kind of thing with lots of little boys and Carl would soon come to like it.

Carl did not want to disappoint his Uncle and, besides, what else was he going to do. He was far away from home and the only person he knew in this City was his Uncle.

After that, his Uncle sodomized Carl every night except the night before he was to fly home. When he got home, Carl's parents asked him how he had enjoyed his vacation and he said "Fine", but he seemed more subdued than he was before he left. They thought that was strange, but, as I have said, he was a socially awkward boy and they thought no more about it.

At family gatherings over the next three years, the Uncle arranged to be alone with Carl and Carl, whether in a tent, a car, or one time in the bedroom next to his parents, was anally raped by his Uncle. This behavior was their dirty little secret, not the Uncle's – the Uncle AND Carl.

They were in it together. As with most children, Carl hated it but felt he was at least an equal party to the rape, that he had done something to deserve it, that it was somehow his fault, and although he felt guilty, he had a bond now with his Uncle and a secret life with him which he was part of. He could not disclose this life to his parents or to anyone. His Uncle had told him not to. He had said to Carl: "No one understands people like us." Carl believed that. He knew, much as he hated it, he was part of the "us" with his Uncle, and he was ashamed of himself.

Imagine, a little ten-year-old boy being ashamed of himself for being sexually abused.

ALL little boys and girls who are sexually abused are ashamed of themselves.

Do you remember when you were a kid and you were playing doctor with that friend who lived down the street? Have you ever told anyone about exactly what you did and what your friend did to each other when you were playing doctor?

Why not?

Are you, perhaps, a little bit ashamed of what you did to your little friend and what your little friend did to you?

Why?

But if you know this feeling, you can almost begin to imagine the secrets that the kids who were sexually abused must keep.

Carl would have taken his dirty secret to the grave, and he told me he would have and I believed him.

But one day, years after the rapes had stopped, the Uncle showed up at the farm with another ten year old boy in tow and Carl knew immediately what he had to do. He went to the police, told the police what his Uncle had done to him a long time ago and said he thought his Uncle might be doing it to this new boy. Then Carl told his parents.

To their credit, they believed their son, although they were shocked and frightened by what they had heard.

But mostly, they were angry.

They confronted the Uncle that night with Carl's story. The Uncle denied it. Carl called him a liar. Carl's father told the Uncle that he had better leave the farmhouse "while you can still walk." Farm folk are like that. I like farm folk.

The Uncle left, taking his ten-year-old companion with him. The police had no grounds to detain the Uncle or to apprehend the child.

In the fullness of time, after Carl and his family and I became quite close through criminal and civil trials in two jurisdictions, the Uncle went to jail for an extended period of time, but only after he had spent his considerable life savings, including his pension, paying for lawyers to defend him and paying for the pain and suffering he had caused Carl.

Not all "weird" Uncles are like Carl's Uncle. Not all "strange" grandfathers or cousins or stepbrothers are like Carl's Uncle.

But there are enough pedophiles out there that it is likely every family has one somewhere.

Mothers, don't let your children spend any time alone with a man like Carl's Uncle. He may be the nicest, kindest, most gentle man in the whole world. He MAY be.

Do not take the risk. It can never be worth it.

What about the nice old man across the street who offered to sit for us that time? That's Uncle Bobby when he's at home. He likes nothing better than to have his house a mecca for neighborhood kids, the more the merrier. Or for one special kid.

When no one else is likely to come around.

I was about to write here that I do not want to frighten you, but I thought better of it.

Of course I want to frighten you. I want to frighten you so badly that you will never, ever make the mistake of turning your child over to a predatory pedophile.

Let me tell you about Ross, a fine young man I know. He is thirty two now and is a professional making good money, married, has a couple of healthy kids and he is always alert to the possibility that those kids may be hurt as he was hurt.

When Ross was ten he had a paper route in his own upper middle class neighborhood. His parents both worked and every day after school got out, Ross delivered 60 papers. One day it was raining and cold and the nice old man across the street who always gave him a nice tip when he collected for the paper offered to drive Ross around his route. The man was about 65, the same age as Ross' grandfather, and he had an old English car with a gearshift and when they were about three-quarters of the way through the paper route, the old man was explaining to Ross how to shift gears. Any ten year old boy would want to know stuff like that. And the old man shifted the gears a few times and every time he did his right hand would brush against Ross' left thigh. Which gave Ross the creeps, but he could understand that, you know, that must be how your hand goes when you shift gears on an English car.

When they got back from doing the papers Ross had time to kill and his mom and dad were still at work so the old man asked Ross if he wanted to come in and see his workshop and maybe they could build a model airplane in the workshop.

Ross thought that sounded great.

Ross and the old man walked into the old man's house and the old man's old wife was there and she looked "sort of funny" at the old man and the old man didn't say anything to her and she didn't say anything to him or anything to Ross and so Ross and the old man went down to the old man's workshop in the basement.

(Later, I thought of suing the woman because she knew or ought to have known what went on in that house and in her husband's mind and might have saved Ross but failed to. Perhaps I should have sued her. I would have had to prove that she had actual knowledge of what happened next. Many women know or ought to know that their husbands are sexually abusing young kids, even their own kids, but they say nothing because they do not want to lose their husband. These women should be ashamed of themselves.)

The old man took Ross down the basement and, sure enough, he had a nice workshop with lots of tools and wood and they started making a design for a model plane and the old man would occasionally brush against Ross with the front of his pants rubbing the front or behind of Ross' pants, but that was probably just a mistake, Ross thought, although it creeped him out.

Those of you who googled "frottage" a while back will know the exact word for what it was that the old man was doing to Ross that creeped Ross out.

The old man continued to help Ross do his paper route two or three times a week after that and they would spend the time they saved making model planes and kites and boats and one day the old man touched Ross' penis through his pants, but that was probably another creepy mistake and later he put his hand down the front of Ross' pants to see if he was "getting to be a big boy yet."

Ross knew that was no mistake.

Then one day Ross had to go to the bathroom and the old man asked Ross if he could shake off his penis for him and Ross thought it was a creepy thing to ask and he felt uncomfortable, but the old man just did it and then put his mouth on Ross' penis to "lick the drops off."

That was weird and creepy and if his parents had been home from work, Ross would have gone home right then.

When spring came the old man took Ross out on his boat and they cruised to an island, just the two of them and slept in sleeping bags and that night the old man sucked Ross' penis again and then put his tongue in Ross' anus.

Then the old man kissed Ross and told him that he loved him.

Time passes.

We are in a Courtroom now. Ross is thirty-years-old. The old man is in his mid-seventies. He is in the witness box. He turns to Ross with tears in his eyes and says "But Ross! I loved you."

And Ross, breaking all the rules of Courtroom decorum, stands up and yells at the old man: "I can still taste the shit from when you stuck your tongue in my mouth you fucking bastard!"

Well, good for Ross.

Court's adjourned.

Ross wins.

He wins some dignity back from the old man, some of his self is reclaimed from the man who stole his youth, some power returns to Ross that had been taken from him by two years of degradation and humiliation.

Some breakthrough that his therapist had been aiming for is achieved by Ross in that courtroom on that day. Some closure is reached. Some healing is done.

But it was all so unnecessary.

Oh, Ross' parents were in the Courtroom with him that day. But where were they when they should have been keeping him safe from the old man?

Maybe I should have sued them, too.

However, as I often tell my clients, you can sue anybody.

It's winning that counts.

And Ross won that day. He got some money for the emotional pain he'd been through, but that wasn't the most important thing he won.

Chapter 9

THE WICKED STEPFATHER

Propinquity.

Almost all of the sexual abuse cases I have been involved in find their root in propinquity, or the familial or hierarchical proximity of the perpetrator to the victim, or possibly the kinship between them.

Where old men who help boys on newspaper routes have to work a bit at getting close to their victims, stepfathers have their victims handed to them along with a marriage license.

I know.

I have been a stepfather and here is a bullet I cannot dodge.

Here is another place in this book where I can speak from knowledge and experience.

There may be stepfathers of young girls who watch their stepdaughters blossom into a young woman who never have carnal thoughts about the girls.

It may be true that somewhere a heterosexual man has lived under the same roof as a young girl as she transformed from a child to a woman, and never had a moment when he viewed his stepdaughter in a new and sexual way.

This is not something we talk about at our Stepfathers' Meetings held in the high school gym every Tuesday at 7:00. This never gets on the agenda.

Although I have many male friends who have stepdaughters and from whom I thought I had no real secrets, THIS topic of conversation has never arisen and I know the reason why.

Of course it is shameful, unacceptable, improper, and disgusting to think that all stepfathers at some time think of their stepdaughters as sexual beings.

That does not make it any less true.

The stepfathers we do not hear a lot about fall into two categories: the ones who do not act upon these sexual impulses and the ones who do, but who "get away with it."

Stepfathers who have access to their stepdaughters seven days a week 52 weeks a year, who eat, sleep, bathe, talk, laugh, cry and play under the same roof as their stepdaughters, have two aspects of propinquity working against them. The first is physical nearness and the second is kinship.

Stepfather Jack and his high-spirited 15-year-old stepdaughter spend the afternoon painting the porch. On a warm day, the stepdaughter wears her new bathing suit. Jack paints vigorously, averts his eyes and hopes for the return of his wife from shopping.

Jack and his stepdaughter talk about his work, her school, her friends that he knows and his friends that she knows. She laughs. He laughs. They like each other.

I do not believe Jack is as sick as I believe Priests who rape young boys are sick, but society deems Jack to be sick.

If Jack were to act on his impulses toward his stepdaughter, and many stepfathers do, he would be a child sexual abuser as much as any pedophile.

So in THIS case, where I see that there is something capable of being understood in the man's desires, and where I cannot say the same about a Priest and a young boy, I cannot let myself and other stepfathers off the hook.

Just as the Priest ought to have done, just as the woman teacher ought to have done, the horny stepfather – for at its basest, that is what he is and all he ever will be – must rise above his animalistic urges.

I use the word animalistic advisedly.

Throughout nature, the male in a family unit tends to assert his pre-eminence when he is newly arrived on the scene. Lions are a good example. When a male lion takes over a pride of lions – a female and her cubs – after the natural father has died or disappeared or been vanquished in a fight, his first order of business is to kill those cubs. They are not his. He will not raise them. The female, seeing her cubs destroyed, goes into heat and the result is that the newly-arrived male impregnates the female and new cubs, belonging to each of them, are born and cared for by their two biological parents.

Nature is brutal, animals are animals and humans have a measure of humanity. But some stepfathers have less humanity than others in dealing with their wife's offspring.

The damage done to a fifteen-year-old stepdaughter who is raped by her stepfather is as great as that done to a young boy raped by a Priest or nun. It may even be worse, because of the breach of the trust which the stepdaughter thought existed between her and her stepfather.

The stepdaughter inevitably feels guilt, shame, and depression that she was raped by her own stepfather – by the man her mother chose to keep her and her children safe. That this man, the provider of safety, could remove that safety from the child is a breach of the most fundamental duty that society bestows on us – the care of our children.

This concept flies in the face of how men are raised in western society: The love 'em and leave 'em lone wolf, who works his way through dozens of women before marriage and who knows that marriage isn't necessarily forever and that there are plenty of women who still want him even though he's married and who has an eye for a nicely-shaped woman even though she's thirty years younger than he is and who still believes he has a shot with such a woman, must run away when that "woman" turns out to be the teenage daughter of his wife.

It goes against most things Jack has ever believed or has learned, and happily most stepfathers manage to pick their way through the sexual minefield and come out the other side with the love and respect and maybe even admiration of their stepdaughters.

Of course the stepfather finds it a bit easier to function in a house where hormones are bouncing off the walls and ceiling if his stepdaughter has been rape-proofed and if he has taken part in her sexual education.

If the stepdaughter and the stepfather, along with the mother, have had periodic and appropriate discussions about inappropriate touching, and inappropriate conduct, and those twists and turns in a conversation which should alert a young boy or girl to the fact that the agenda of the older person may have just changed to a sexual one, the stepfather has then become part of the good guy team and it is next to impossible for him to then go over to the dark side, to sexually use his stepdaughter whom he has had a part in rape-proofing.

In a household where propinquity is a given, it is the urgent task of the mother in the early days, along with the stepfather in later years, to make certain that the stepdaughter has a clear understanding of how and when to say "no!" and that no one, not her stepfather or her brother or her teacher is permitted to seize control of her body. She is the only person who controls her body and she must learn that fact from her mother.

Her body is inviolable.

She should know that that means her body – her physical integrity – cannot be compromised by anyone and that any touching of her body by an adult is wrong.

Again, it is far better to err on the side of caution and to have your daughter begin screaming "No!" at an innocent touch than to have her raped.

If the touch is an innocent one, we can work it out later.

If the touch is a prelude to rape, there may not be a "later".

The daughter must always know, and the knowledge must be reinforced when it is appropriate to do so over time, that if some person tries to touch her vagina or her breasts, that person is not her friend and whether she or he is a relative or a teacher, she is always to say "No!" as loudly as possible, to bite, kick and scratch where she can and then to run to safety if she can.

If she cannot escape, she should continue to yell "No!" and to kick, bite, cry and, if possible, throw up on the attacker, to urinate, to defecate, and to make things as difficult as possible for the attacker. If she knows that her body is not to be touched and that she SHALL protect herself at all times, at all costs, nine times out of ten the pedophile will leave her be.

Pedophiles are professionals at what they do. They want no muss, no fuss and a compliant victim. If the intended victim becomes a "troublemaker", the pedophile moves on.

The mother and daughter, as part of the rape-proofing exercise, should act out what the daughter must do when a man or woman touches her. This should not be a "fun" exercise. This is serious business, and your son and daughter will know it is serious business if you are serious in your approach to the exercise. Have your daughter hit you hard, show your daughter where it hurts to be hit for a man and a woman, and practice the exercise regularly.

And remember, during all her fighting back, your son or your daughter should continue to yell "No!" at the top of their lungs.

It is important to make no distinction between men and women as the potential perpetrators of sexual harm, just as it is equally important to rape-proof both your young son and your young daughter.

If it is financially possible for you, your son or daughter should be enrolled in a self-defense course at an early age. Judo, karate, tae kwon do and other martial arts emphasize not only the skill of being able to physically protect oneself but the importance of the self, how it should be guarded and nurtured spiritually as well as physically. All kids would benefit from such courses.

Because, as you know now if you did not know before, pedophiles are everywhere.

By my reckoning, stepfathers account for most of the sexual abuse of children in our society.

Priests and teachers may get all the bad press and Internet pedophiles are growing in numbers, but day in and day out, stepfathers are always there and always a threat.

I have said that mothers often turn a blind eye to what their husband is doing to their sons or daughters. In the case of a stepfather, the mother is on at least her second marriage, usually dependent on her husband for money, and without making a moral judgement, perhaps, or even forming the concept in her mind, would rather "not know" what her husband does from one to two in the morning in her daughter's bedroom. Maybe they're just watching Conan....

They're not watching Conan.

Stepfathers rape their stepdaughters, sometimes starting with newborns. By the age of 16 some girls are so inured to the abuse that it just goes on and on as if it were normal. For years longer, even after the girl has married and has children of her own, the rape can become such a part of the girl's life, and the stepfather has so cowed the girl and made her complicit in the rape, that she feels helpless to stop him. He has turned her into a zombie, a psychological slave.

Until her secret is out, she will remain enslaved.

Once her secret comes out – for whatever reason – the stepfather's spell is finally broken and the girl is finally freed. If this sounds a fantastic scenario, it is not.

If this sounds as if the stepdaughter is stupid, she is not. The power of ongoing sexual assault which began at an early age, where the girl has been convinced by her stepfather that she is to blame, or that she is responsible for keeping the family together, or that she is helping her mother because her mother won't "do it" for her stepfather, or for any of the other lies told by stepfathers to gain the complicity of their stepdaughters, is a power so great that it can continue for decades.

You may not think that this rings true.

If you were sexually abused as a child, you have no doubt that this is the truth.

If there were one category only of sexual abusers of children which I could stop dead in its tracks, I would be forced to choose to stop stepfathers. The very number of sexual assaults on children by stepfathers in our continually fragmenting society demands such a choice. And for every instance of abuse by a stepfather we hear about there may be ten times as many or more that we will never hear about.

Let us be clear about one more thing. Little boys and girls do not "ask for it." A seven-year-old, a nine-year-old, a twelve-year-old does not have a clue how to "ask for it" from his stepfather or anyone. He does not know what "it" is. But his stepfather does.

No matter how many gangsta rap videos the boy has watched, he does not know what "it" is.

There are no sexually precocious pre-teens.

Even If there were 12-or-10 or 6-year-old Lolitas, morality and human decency dictate that the adult male take control of the situation. He is the one who ought to be in control.

He is responsible.

If he feels the need for extracurricular sexual contact there are thousands of places outside the home he can find it instead of debasing his little stepson or stepdaughter.

Here, in black and white, this all makes sense, and the reasonable ones among us – stepfathers included – will nod and say, "He's right, you know. Absolutely right."

And everyone will mean it and feel good and self-righteous.

But there is a truism that has existed probably since the dawn of man:

"An erect penis has no conscience."

Mothers: rape-proof your stepchildren and watch your husband like a hawk.

Remember the male lion, and act accordingly.

Most stepfathers do not start out as pedophiles that prefer to have sex with children.

Some stepfathers – a relatively large number of stepfathers – become situational pedophiles who WILL have sex with children, if those children are not rape-proofed.

Please do not automatically think "That could never happen. Not Jack. Jack has a Ph. D. in child care… He loves my kids…"

Why not ask Jack if he has ever had sexual thoughts about your children? Watch his eyes when you ask the question.

Then have a conversation about what he is going to do and not going to do to keep your children safe.

Watch Jack like a hawk. And keep the lines of communication open with Jack and with your kids.

And I mean no offence to Jack.

I was Jack once. Most stepfathers are Jack. You can either be a good Jack or a bad Jack.

Nor is it just stepfathers who play on the wishes of the child to keep a family unit together in order to have sexual contact with their children.

I have acted as a lawyer in cases where a child's natural father – her biological father – will rape her using the same blandishments and threats a stepfather would. This happens less frequently than sexual assault by a stepfather, but it happens enough that everyone, especially wives and mothers and daughters, should be aware of it.

Fathers and husbands too should be aware of the fact that occasionally a mother and wife will have sexual intercourse with her son. A rarity, this happens nonetheless.

In our society.

In the 21st Century.
No child is ever completely safe, even in his own bed in his own home.

In most cases, however, the rape is done by a father to a young girl, a girl who has not yet reached puberty.

The sexual assault by a father on a young girl is not something "low class," not something "they" do. It happens across socio-economic and racial lines. It happens because children, when the chips are down, do not want to displease or incur the anger of their father.

Allow me to depress you just a little bit more.

I'm on a roll, here.

Molly came to my office in 2002. She was thirty and had just finished her studies to become a nurse. She had also just given birth to a young daughter and it was that which prompted her to come and see me. She wanted to make sure that her baby was safe.

Many people who disclose their sexual abuse do so for altruistic reasons – to protect others, especially in their own family, having long since given up on thoughts of making themselves better. The heartening thing is that when someone discloses the sexual abuse they went through, the perpetrator is nailed, the likelihood of his abusing other children is greatly diminished and the person who discloses the abuse finds it liberating to talk of the abuse. She may go on to get counseling or otherwise be#in to look at the abuse in a more realistic and far less painful light. The fact of the abuse no longer holds so much power over her.

So it was in this case, where Molly told me the story of growing up in a house where her father would come to her bed each morning about five or five-thirty, get into bed with her and begin feeling her breasts and vagina, before putting his penis in her rectum and raping her until he ejaculated.

This went on between the years Molly was 9 to 13.

This story turns out sort of okay. Molly works helping kids today. She is a strong woman and has a good sense of humor. She goes to counseling regularly so she can continue to do her best at helping kids.

Molly's father would leave her bedroom and she would next see him at the breakfast table where he would ask her how she had slept and ask her to pass the milk. Molly never said anything to anyone, and her father would then drive her and her sister to school.

Where he was the Principal.

Molly kept the secret form the world for 17 years until she came to my office. She had learned to live with the pain, but now her baby had a grandfather and Molly was forced to admit to herself that the baby's grandfather was a pedophile. In all the world, Molly wanted most to keep her little baby safe from that baby's grandfather, the Principal.

So we did.

And the grandfather of the little girl stopped being a Principal and his wife divorced him and he went to jail.

And, as I say, Molly got counseling and I ran into her and her husband at the supermarket last month and I saw her happy, healthy little daughter and she's doing well and Molly's doing well and Molly thanked me.

And I said "For what? You were the brave one."

And she was.

And she is.

Chapter 10

GROOMING

Let me emphasize that the repetition of the message to your children that they never be touched is important for many reasons, not least of which is that the pedophiles are so good at what they do.

Pedophiles lie in wait. They have time and they have a plan. And they have motivation. Planning and waiting is part of their "fun."

Just as couples go through a courting process, a phase of getting to know the other person, hardwired pedophiles will take as much time as necessary to strike up a relationship with your child.

Unlike doctors or Priests or teachers where the need for grooming is supplanted by the overwhelming power of the pedophile in the relationship, a hardwired pedophile from outside the family group has to work at getting close to a child, both emotionally and physically.

Pedophiles will take infinite time and trouble to set their trap.

I have told you about the Uncle I sued who had put a swimming pool in his backyard to attract more children to his house. All the local children wanted to come by for a swim and he was always happy to have them come. He often joined them in roughhousing in the pool. And he had no wife or family around, so he was always free to be with the kids in the neighborhood.

Another pedophile, one I encountered in my own youth, was less elaborate. Perhaps he couldn't afford a pool. He told me he had a pet mouse and he put his hands together and made a squeaking noise, by expelling air from between his hands.

He asked me to go into his house with him to see the mouse.

I went.

He was just about to show me more than an imaginary mouse when, as if by magic, the front door flew open and my mother was standing in the entrance hall, looking daggers at old Mr. Sheppard and his imaginary mouse. She told me to get my jacket and come home with her.

I did.

She had never told me that Mr. Sheppard was a pedophile, but she clearly knew. I think I could have handled the information, but those were different times. I'm glad she was around, though. I stayed away from Mr. Sheppard after that.

I would have stayed away from him if she had told me before, too.

Grooming: the accidental touch. If the nice man across the street is teaching your child how to fly a kite, he may accidentally-on-purpose, brush up against his penis or her vagina or their buttocks or nipples. At that time he may or he may not say that he is sorry and excuse himself, depending on how your child reacts.

Your child should react immediately. Even if the touch is a glancing one, a momentary one, your child should loudly say "No! No one touches me there!"

The child should then leave quickly.

Again, presuming it is the one case in a thousand where an innocent man with no ulterior motives has touched your child inadvertently, there is no harm done. In all other cases, the pedophile will quickly lose interest in sexually touching a child who knows what is right and what is wrong.

Look at the example of the Uncle who built the swimming pool. With a backyard full of children, he will not select a child to abuse who has told him "No!" He will move on to find a more likely target.

Our task is to rape-proof every child in that yard so that they are all as safe as can be.

Say, however, the glancing touch on the genitals is not remarked upon by your child. The pedophile has now effectively succeeded in his undertaking and he simply ratchets up the experience. The next time the touch is more prolonged – his hand lingers for a second or two on the penis or vagina.

Plausible things may then occur. Your child has spent an hour at the house of the pedophile, who is babysitting while you are doing errands. The child has been given soda pop or chocolate milk in quantity and needs to go to the bathroom. The pedophile offers to help your child in the bathroom. Or stumbles into the bathroom by accident when your child is using the toilet. Or comes into the bathroom to get something.

Ever smiling, ever solicitous, ever friendly, the pedophile offers to show your son or daughter how toilet matters are dealt with in his family and before they know it the pedophile has his hand on your son's penis or your daughter's vagina, and is fondling your child.

Once this last barrier is down, once the pedophile has breached the physical integrity of your child's sexual identity by touching his or her sexual organ, the next step is to make the act (which is always unpleasant for your child, creepy, icky, and a violation that your child cannot put into words, but feels deeply nonetheless) something closer to pleasurable, or something associated with pleasure.

The pedophile will seek to overpower the creepy, icky, WRONG feeling with a major reward: a twenty dollar bill, a video game, a trip to the zoo, anything to take the child's attention away from what just happened and make the next time easier for the pedophile.

Over time, the pedophile, who has nothing but time and who is good at being a pedophile and who has done this hundreds of times and who knows just where and when to up the ante with your child, increases the sexual contact in such a fashion that it appears to your child that each step is equally abnormal as the first touch was, even though the child knows each succeeding escalation is wrong.

Each escalation in sexual touching leads to an escalation in rewards or positive reinforcement from the pedophile.

The pedophile praises the youngster as a good boy, a smart, attractive, and interesting boy, a boy who is so magnetic a person that the pedophile will drop everything to be with the boy and devote his complete attention to making the boy interested in what they are doing while they are together. This is a relationship the boy has never had before, certainly with his father, or his brother, males with whom he should be bonding.

Instead, here he is bonding with a pedophile.

Shame on the mother and father who allow this to happen.

There is a price, the boy recognizes.

Occasionally, when the man's wife is out, he has to take a nap with the pedophile. In his 'sleep', the pedophile puts his hand down the front of the boy's pants. In his sleep, the pedophile takes out his own penis and puts the boy's hand on his penis moving it up and down. In his sleep, the pedophile undresses the boy and puts his penis between the boy's legs. In his sleep, the pedophile puts lubricant on his penis and sticks his penis into the boy's anus.

The pedophile does all this while pretending to sleep, and after a while the boy catches on and he pretends to sleep as well.

So when they "wake up" it's just as if nothing ever happened.

And it only happens once or twice a week, and the rest of the time the pedophile and the young boy are building a surfboard in the basement and going out for pizza or playing on the new PlayStation with the latest game that the boy's parents think is too violent for the boy to have.

And after that they go out for ice cream, or to a movie.

And it's their secret what happens in bed.

The pedophile tells him that it's their secret and that they are special friends.

And the boy never will tell anyone, because he feels dirty and guilty and ashamed and is sure he has done something to deserve this and is sure that it is all his fault and he has somehow made it so that this nice man is doing these things to him and even the nice man knows they are wrong, so it is all the boy's fault.

Who would the boy tell?

What would he say?

It's all his fault anyway.

Why doesn't he run away, stop coming to the man's house?

Well, the man is so nice to him almost all the time, and his parents know he is over there, so it must be alright. Maybe his parents even know what the man is doing to him... In that case it would HAVE to be alright, wouldn't it?

And after the first two or three times, well, it's not the worst thing in the world although it was really gross when that white stuff squirted out of the end of the man's penis and the man asked the boy to lick it off.

But that only happened once or twice so far.

It has been said with some truth that life hinges on a couple of seconds that you never see coming.

Every child should be made aware that sexual abuse is coming right at him, and sooner or later someone will, not may but WILL attempt to sexually assault him.

When that attempted assault takes place, in those two seconds, your child will know what to do because you will have enabled him to see it coming.

And his life will not hinge on those two seconds because he, with your help, will have defeated the pedophile.

But only you can make this happen.

I am putting a large burden on the shoulders of this boy's parents, aren't I?

Do you think I'm wrong in doing that?

Chapter 11

THE RULES

When does a boy or girl finally "get it?"

When does he become aware that he was sexually used when he was a kid and that none of what happened was his fault?

The short answer is: never.

The usual course of events is that the pedophile moves on to another victim after some change in circumstances in the relationship – someone moves away or the boy changes schools. Or begins to go through puberty. Some pedophiles don't like children with pubic hair.

The boy who lived through the abuse then tucks all the sexual assaults away in his mind. He may have nightmares about things from time to time, but often he cannot trace those nightmares to the pedophile.

He may want to ask questions about the abuse - in school or with his parents - but he never does because he was the guilty one.

No, he thinks, it was his fault and he was wrong. The pedophile was right. He and that pedophile are alike and no one else will understand him. What kind of monster is the boy now?

Does he like men like other boys are supposed to like girls? Is he a fag?

He must be a fag. Maybe worse. What's worse than a fag? Whatever it is, he's worse.

He's the worst boy who was ever alive and he has no one to talk to about it because he is so very ashamed.

So the boy buries the memories and tries not to revisit them in his mind. He learns as he approaches the age of 12 that he appears to be interested in girls and kisses one when he is thirteen and that's the first time he's kissed anyone outside his family since the pedophile put his tongue in his mouth. But kissing the girl was nice. And he sometimes thinks about kissing boys, but he's pretty sure he's not gay. And when he thinks about kissing other boys like the pedophile kissed him, he becomes afraid all over again that he's not normal.

Maybe he IS gay.

What if he's gay?

Every kid wants to be normal.

But male kids are much more worried about being – or becoming – gay than female kids are.

To prove he's not gay, he has sex with a girl when he's 15. She has sex with everyone in class so it was no big deal for her. He believes he is as male as anyone, but after that, every time he has a chance he has sex with girls he dates.

And not just oral sex like the other kids.

He has sex where he puts his penis in the girls' vaginas, like manly men are supposed to do.

The boy does this until one of his sperm hits an ovum and sticks and by the age of 19 he is working and supporting a wife and child.

He drinks. He does drugs. He is depressed. He is sometimes suicidal. His doctor puts him on anti-depressants. The man is depressed because his high school friends have gone on to college and he's married with a kid and he screws around on his wife and he's turning into a juice head and a pothead and he never goes home and he's been fired twice from his job as a laborer.

He thinks about suicide.

One day he buys a gun and checks into a motel and writes a note that says he's tired of this shitty life and he's sorry to his family and especially his wife and daughter and none of this was their fault, he's just a fuckup.

He sits on the edge of the bed drinking vodka out of the bottle and puts the gun in his mouth.

He sits there like that for a long time, waiting to pull the trigger, thinking.

His life is such a fucking mess.

He can't even pull the fucking trigger.

What a fucking loser. He can't even kill himself.

He is crying, now.

He passes out and wakes up in the psychiatric ward of the hospital.

The doctors are solicitous. They've read his history of depression. They've seen that he was married young – had to get married, girl was pregnant, and has addiction problems. His wife isn't very helpful – says they never talk much. He is no longer in touch with his parents.

The doctors determine that the man is going through a rough patch at twenty four years of age and they prescribe a new anti-depressant which has been advertised heavily in all the medical journals and may just do the trick.

They recommend he see a psychiatrist.

They discharge him with no plan for a follow-up.

The guy's just another one of the walking wounded, and there's only so much they can do. Plus they need the bed in Emergency for that gunshot wound that just came in....

Now, the important thing is that at no time in the last five years, not when he has been trying to set records for sexual conquests to prove his manliness, not when he was drinking, not when he was depressed, not when he was writing the suicide note, not even when he was sitting on the edge of the bed with the gun in his mouth, did the man know that being raped when he was a child was the thing that put him on the edge of the bed with the gun in his mouth.

Those rapes have made him the man he has become.

If he had not been raped, he would have joined his cohort in college, met a girl, gone steady, got a job and settled down.

The rapes took all those prospects away because they took his internal compass and broke it to smithereens.

A bundle of low self esteem, confusion, dysfunction, depression and anxiety, the boy limped through his teens into manhood without grappling with the ugliness of his sexual abuse and how that had impacted on his psyche.

Now he was indeed one of the walking wounded.

As John Lennon, again John Lennon, famously said – probably because he spoke from personal experience - one thing you can't hide is when you're crippled inside.

Until about the year 2000 it was extremely unusual for doctors treating people for depression, family doctors in particular, to question their patients about whether they had been sexually abused. Even psychologists and psychiatrists treating men and women for depression will sit and listen for a seemingly infinite number of fifty-minute hours without asking their patient whether he or she was sexually abused.

It is a rude, demeaning, intrusive question. No matter that sexual abuse is the root cause of the depression, it is a dirty question for a therapist to ask a patient.

So why don't they ask it?

This seems all the more strange when it is clear that probably one in five children in North America – boys and girls alike – has suffered some form of sexual abuse.

Either the doctors are ignorant, or they are unaware of what kind of Pandora's Box they might be opening when they delve into their patient's sexual abuse.

Most doctors still do not have the tools to effectively counsel people who were sexually abused as children.

This is a major failing and one which must be addressed with intelligence if we are to overcome this scourge.

Until about 1990 the need for this type of counseling rarely arose because it was only around 1990 that people started to learn The Rules.

I am not suggesting that all caregivers are stupid or unlearned or both. Only that some of them are. Perhaps a preponderance of them. Certainly not all of them.

It is part of my job to read the medical records of my clients who were sexually abused. I have read hundreds of reports from hundreds of treatment centers where counselors, psychologists and psychiatrists have treated my clients for drug and alcohol abuse and depression.

Rarely, if ever, is the caregiver aware that my client was raped as a child.

My client often has no desire to impart this information, feeling guilty or complicit in the abuse as he or she always does, but that does not lessen the onus on the caregiver to dig out the truth. Otherwise it is like attempting to treat a patient for a headache without first ascertaining that the patient has been shot in the head with a gun.

The caregiver can make appropriate noises and apply a bandage, but three hours later the patient is bleeding again and still has the bullet in him. The doctor has failed to ask about the gunshot wound and the patient has failed to disclose it.

Many of the medical records I have seen go on and on about what a patient says today and how a patient is feeling today and what a patient is thinking today and how a patient is getting along with her spouse today and what dosage of antidepressant a patient will get on a trial basis starting today. Almost never is there an entry in the medical records of a patient being treated for depression that says: "I asked Ms Smith if she has ever been sexually abused. She said she has. We spent some time discussing her feelings about this, and her belief is as follows…"

More often than not, when a caregiver sneaks up on the question of the possible sexual abuse of a patient, he or she will make a notation in the notes to this effect, or one similar: "Patient denies being sexually abused."

That would be about right.

I know – and now you know – that almost every abused person denies having been sexually abused in response to a question starkly put.

Why don't all doctors and psychiatrists know this?

A good doctor, unafraid of an answer in the affirmative, can and should winkle out the history of her patient's sexual abuse. Otherwise the good doctor is treating her patient with two hands tied behind her back.

It helps, then, if the patient has discovered The Rules.

It would help immeasurably if the doctor knew The Rules and could make educated inquiries of his patient as to whether she knows The Rules.

Put simply, The Rules are the rules of sexual abuse disclosure, its timing, its progressive nature and the maturation of the concept in the mind of the individual who was sexually abused to the point where he or she, having walked for many years with the solitary knowledge of having been raped as a child, is prepared to begin giving voice to the nature and extent of the sexual abuse because he finally suspects the abuse was wrong and was not his fault.

The first of The Rules is that most people do not become acutely aware that the rapes they were subjected to were wrong until they reach their mid-to-late twenties. This seems bizarre, even unimaginable, but it is nonetheless true.

The person of average intelligence who was raped as a child has nothing to which he can compare his experience and so must journey on his own toward finding an accommodation with the knowledge that only one other person – his abuser – carries with him.

I hope that this book will promote dialogue between various members of society so that children who have been raped no longer need to carry that knowledge themselves but have someone whom they can turn to in order to help them share the burden.

All victims of sexual abuse are astonished the first time they learn that this same thing happened to someone else, that someone else feels almost exactly the same as they do. They each think they are unique in the burden they carry, and knowing that there are others in a similar psychological hell helps them because there's someone else they can talk to.

Not that they would talk about it.

But they could.

That is a bit of power that they never before had. That is a good start.

For the time being, however, it is not until the age of, say, twenty-five to thirty that the average person amasses sufficient life experience from what he or she sees or reads or discusses with others, to know that his childhood rape was a wrong done to him by an evil person.

This is because society has locked sexual abuse in a closet and no one wants to open the closet door unless they absolutely must.

Memo to the world: we must talk about sexual abuse if we wish to prevent sexual abuse.

This seems plain on the face of it, but it poses a problem, doesn't it?

Who wants to talk about sexual abuse? You're having a hard enough time just reading about it.

No one WANTS to, but it is better to talk about it than have our children suffer from it.

This is a message that bears repeating.

Until the day dawns that the boy or girl learns The Rules, she is frozen in time with the story that she has chosen to refer to in short form when thinking of the abuse. When the trigger is pulled and thoughts of the abuse come unbidden to her mind, the story begins to unfold again.

The smell of semen may be a trigger. Or a trip to McDonald's. Or the sight of a windsurfer, or a suggestion by someone that a nap is in order. Or, most sadly, in one case I know, the words: "I love you".

Whatever formed the backdrop to the rapes – say they happened on a chenille bedspread – has the potential to trigger a memory of the rapes.

Trigger.

"Oh god, that reminds me of the sex. I feel pain, I feel dirty, I feel guilty, I am ashamed, I am a child, I am alone. I hurt."

This is one possible mantra the victim will repeat. Each boy or girl carries his own mantra and hopes that as quickly as the memory is triggered it can be shut back up.

But occasionally the memory will stay on for a while and the victim of the rape will examine the pain, the depression, the isolation, and then think of his abuser and wonder where the abuser is now. The next step may be to wonder if the abuser is still hurting little boys.

And that question, put by the victim to himself in the darkness of his emotional night, is a breakthrough question. Once asked, that question cannot easily be filed away with the old memories of the abuse. This is a new thought, and a powerful one, because for the first time since he was a child the victim has made a leap from thinking about himself and his abuser to bringing another, unidentified person into the unholy duality that was the rape.

Now there may be someone for the victim to worry about other than himself.

And now, for the very first time the victim perceives what happened to him as being wrong because it would be wrong if it happened to another child, if it was happening today.

This, for the victim, is like the sun coming up, but it comes tentatively, and the victim is still far removed from absolving himself from the blame, the shame and the guilt.

Although it may be too late for the victim, he thinks, perhaps he or she can save another little boy or girl from the same fate and then something good will have come from the abuse the victim suffered.

And with this thought two things happen simultaneously. First, the victim begins to crawl out of the hole the pedophile has dug for him. Second, although he doesn't know it and might not know it for a while, the pedophile is on his way to losing his freedom to rape children.

The dawning of knowledge about The Rules does not always occur in this fashion – that would be too neat and would belie the complexity of the tricks sexual abuse plays on young minds. However, I have seen the beginnings of healing take on this guise on a sufficient number of occasions to know that a process like this is possible for most victims of sexual abuse and that the process might be readily guided by trained caregivers, once caregivers become aware of the process.

Indeed, in the majority of instances where the person who was abused finally feels the tumblers click into place, the proximate cause of the revelation is fear that the newborn child of the victim will suffer the same fate as he or she did. It is an extremely altruistic and all-too-human reaction to try to protect one's children from a predator before one confirms that he or she has been the prey of that predator.

This speaks to the better side of our humanity and is a defense mechanism worthy of deeper exploration by doctors who, in the past, have spent too much time on the sidelines in the war against sexual abuse.

Chapter 12

THE GOOD PRIEST

One of the reasons why doctors may not have the knowledge they should about treating victims of sexual abuse is that the subject is such a difficult one to study. There are not enough sexual abuse victims who are willing to speak about their abuse in order to provide a database for those who want to help them.

My knowledge of the effects of sexual abuse on kids and adults grew because of the accident of history that confined Aboriginal children in Residential Schools in Canada where they were raped in their thousands.

One of the first stories I heard confirmed that the work I would be doing for the rest of my days had been chosen for me. I could not run away from this work if I wanted to.

It was the story – My Truth, she called it – of a little Aboriginal girl named Mary. She was named after the Virgin Mary, the one who gave birth by Immaculate Conception. "Immaculate" means, of course, "clean" and the phrase Immaculate Conception implies that other forms of conception, earthly forms, the ones we mortals employ to conceive, are dirty.

Mary, like all the rest of us except You Know Who, was dirtily conceived by her mother and father.

Because Mary's mother and father were good Catholics, even though they lived on an Indian reservation, conceived dirtily and had been pagans until they converted to Jesus, the Priest in the Village took a shine to them. He brought them used clothing. He brought Mary and her brothers and sisters candy. Both were enormous luxuries for Mary's family in the 1950's on an island off an island off the coast of North America.

Mary's mother, who had been known by the name Smiling Face – before she accepted Jesus into her heart - often invited the Priest for lunch.

One day Mary went over to the church and found the Priest in the sacristy and the Priest said he had a bag of candy for Mary and he gave it to her and as a good big sister would do, she began going through the candies picking out which ones each of her brothers and sisters would get. She probably committed one of the sins here – the Catholics have so many sins, it's hard to keep up with them – perhaps greed or avarice or coveting or something, because she may have chosen to keep the best piece of candy for herself when she was mentally going through the candies the Priest had given her. She wondered for years if this sin was what triggered what happened next. She knows she must have done something horribly sinful.

After all, she was a six-year-old girl. She should have known better than to sin with a bag of candy, picking the best piece for herself.

Well, sins have a way of catching up with you in the Catholic Church and Mary's sin caught up with her right away because the Priest said they were going to play a game for a minute and the game was called "horsie."

Mary was only six, but she wasn't stupid. Even though she used to be a pagan and had been dirtily conceived, a game of "horsie" with the Priest sounded fishy to her.

Still, the Priest coaxed her up onto his lap, offering her a piece of candy, candy that Indian children only rarely got, and said that this wasn't going to hurt.

In my experience, and possibly yours, and certainly in Mary's, when someone tells you something is not going to hurt, it usually hurts quite a lot.

The non-hurting began when the Priest took off Mary's jeans and her panties. The "horsie" game started when the priest bounced Mary up and down on his lap, which somehow had developed an erection which kept tearing into Mary's vagina.

She screamed.

The Priest put his hand over her mouth, and told her she was a bad girl and told her to shut up and stop screaming.

The Priest continued to rape Mary until he ejaculated.

Mary knew he ejaculated because when he threw her off his lap she saw blood and white goo coming out of her vagina.

The Priest cleaned Mary off with her panties, threw those panties away and gave her a fresh pair from the bag of clothing he was about to take to her mother.

The Priest told her that she had just done an evil thing, evil in the eyes of God.

The Priest then began to instruct Mary in the Catholic religion and explained the concept of Hell to her.

Six-year-olds probably still today don't know much about Hell, but the Priest helped Mary figure it out by lighting a candle. Not a candle to pray with, but a candle to instruct with. The Priest held Mary's hand over the candle flame until it hurt a lot and then told Mary that hell was like that pain only worse, and forever.

The Priest then said that if Mary ever told anyone what had just happened, the horrible dirty non-conception she had just engaged in with the Priest, she would die and go to Hell.

Well, Mary was six. The Priest was coming to lunch at her mother's house in a minute. Mary loved her mother and her mother loved the Priest and looked up to him as the representative of Jesus Christ in their village.

So Mary believed him.

The Priest said that if she told anyone she would never see her mother and father and brothers and sisters again, and the Priest would make sure of that.

And Mary believed him.

Then the priest told Mary that if she told anyone what had just happened, after she had been taken away from her family, he would do to her little sister Margaret what he had just done to her.

And Mary believed him.

Although it was difficult and painful for her to walk, Mary took the bag of candy in one hand and the Priest's hand in her other hand and they walked together to her house in the village and she sat with the Priest and her mother and said nothing all through lunch and her mother thanked the Priest three times for the clothes and the candy and when the lunch was over Mary went down to the beach by the ocean all by herself and threw up her lunch and began to cry.

After that, the Priest came for lunch many times that summer and every time he came Mary's mother made her go to the church to get him because that was the polite thing to do. That was the Aboriginal way. And every time she went to get him, the Priest raped her.

Mary thinks it happened ten times, but she agreed with the lawyer who asked her the questions that it could have been more. All she remembers is that it happened many times.

The Priest is dead now.

If I understand the teachings of the Catholic Faith and if the Priest confessed the sins of what he had done to Mary, then the Priest is in Heaven.

Or perhaps the Priest neglected to confess this particular series of sins.

None of which matters to Mary, who has spent the last fifty years going in and out of depression and in and out of hospitals for treatment of that depression.

That she hasn't killed herself is astonishing.

Perhaps she has a lingering fear that she will go to Hell like the Priest said, and perhaps that fear has kept her from killing herself.

The Lord works in mysterious ways, His wonders to perform.

You have to marvel at a religion that has so many fixed positions on such important matters as eternal life and eternal damnation, makes edicts to billions about homosexuality, birth control, abortion and marriage and yet can still produce a Priest who has a fresh pair of panties to give to a six year old girl he just raped.

Chapter 13

RESIDENTIAL SCHOOLS

On the far west coast of Canada is the most beautiful place in the world. Lying at the edge of hundreds of miles of rainforest full of majestic fir trees, bear, deer, and cougars is a sand beach dividing the forest from the high, crashing surf of the Pacific Ocean. In a fit of lucid thinking the Government of Canada has turned part of this beautiful wilderness into a National Park and, until the world is down to its last tree, this park will remain accessible to all and untouched.

I am happy to say that I am writing these words smack dab in the middle of this lovely spot, looking at the surf that was made for children to frolic in, and thinking black thoughts.

The spot I am now on was once home to a Residential School in British Columbia. The proper name of the School was the Christie Indian Residential School. The children who attended the school from 1900 to 1982 did not get to play in the surf and laugh as children should do. Rather, owing to a policy of the Government of Canada, the children were taken from their parents at the age of 5, 6 or 7 and transported over great distances to be purposefully isolated from their families in an attempt to force the (bad) Aboriginal culture out of them and force the (good) western culture in.

The school was one of 20 in British Columbia, one of 200 in Canada which had the same goal for over a century - to take the Indian out of the Indian, to give the children a rudimentary introduction to western ways and a minimal education and to alienate the child from his parents and culture, to make him ashamed to be a dirty, stupid, pagan Indian.

This was cultural genocide on a national basis.

The Residential School system was Canada's darkest hour.

Put another way, I cannot think of a time in the history of Canada when Canada has acted in such an un-Canadian way. Canadians will understand this. Others will have to take it on faith.

The damage done to innocent Aboriginal families can never be undone or forgiven. Brothers and sisters were turned against their parents and each other; children who had been fluent in their native language were strapped or humiliated at the schools for speaking anything other than English; Aboriginal spiritual practices such as dancing, singing, or praying to The Creator were dealt with more harshly, with more severe beatings from nuns and Priests.

It is difficult to believe that as recently as the 1980's the staff at these schools physically beat five year old boys and girls for speaking their own language, often just minutes after they first arrived at the schools, and hours after they had been taken from their parents by subterfuge, or force, or threats that their parents would be put in jail.

Terrified, confused and alone, separated from their siblings, these children were strapped for the first times in their lives by white men or women who were dressed all in black and who worked for a church that represented the white man's God.

Where did Canada find such people who could treat little children so cruelly?

Canadian churches vied for the opportunity to manage these schools for the Government and chief among these was the Roman Catholic Church which operated the majority of the Residential Schools in Canada. In return for being paid a stipend for each child, a battery of Priests, nuns and religious Brothers in various Catholic Orders migrated across Canada to bring civilization to the Aboriginal children and to win their souls for Jesus and the Church.

And it came to pass that near Tofino, British Columbia, Christie Indian Residential School rose up on that beach of sand near the ocean meant for children to frolic in. When they looked out the window of the school, the children could only imagine escaping across that ocean to be reunited with their parents.

Many of the brave and terrorized children did manage to escape, often floating on logs or borrowing a canoe that was never meant for ocean travel. And when those brave children finally made it home - and some did - and some drowned - their parents brought them right back to the school. Why? Because the Government of Canada, thinking that even pagan Indians might feel something like love for their children and want them to stay at home, again threatened the parents with jail if their children did not come back to the schools. That was the law in Canada.

Well, that worked, because if the mother and father were in jail, the children could easily be snaffled by the Government because their parents were no longer there to care for them.

The whole system was rather well thought out.

Adolph Hitler would have been impressed at how smoothly it all worked.

Other books have been and are being written about this Residential School genocide, and I commend them to those of you who wish to safeguard the rights of minorities and ensure that this kind of horror – dare I call it a holocaust? - never occurs again.

Because we are, each of us, part of some minority, the interest level should be high.

My purpose in presenting a thumbnail version of the Residential School experience here is to let the reader know how it was that children came to be in a setting much like a prison where their movements were overseen by Priests, nuns and religious Brothers twenty four hours a day, seven days a week, fifty-two weeks each year from the age of five to fifteen.

Lord Acton penned the phrase: "Power corrupts. Absolute power corrupts absolutely."

The "caregivers" to these Aboriginal waifs were absolutely corrupted. They had control of every function of their small charges and had control, as well, of their small souls. Once the children had learned about Hell, understood Hell, feared Hell, the religious staff at the Residential School made certain the children knew that they were going to GO to Hell, because they were pagan, dirty, worthless, stupid redskin Indians.

And, of course, the children believed this.

Why would they not?

All the white people in the black robes and gowns at the school told them about Jesus and Hell and they all seemed to be telling the same story, and so the children believed the story and did what the staff told them to do.

Some tried to scrub their skins until their skins became white like the Priests and the nuns. Standing for an hour a day by the sink, one boy in particular scraped first one arm then the other trying to wash the Indian color off.

Spiritually, the children began to say white man's prayers, crossed themselves like Catholics do, went to chapel, served as altar boys, and sometimes got into the communion wine, got giddy and fed the host (the little crackers) to each other.

Until they were caught, stripped naked and strapped.

Adults who have proximity to children, absolute power over children and are isolated from the rest of society and answerable to no one will, nine times out of nine, sooner or later abuse those children.

The adults at Christie Indian Residential School were no different. Sexual abuse of the children by the staff was rampant and went on from decade to decade.

The Catholic Church may wish to dispute this. Let them fill their boots, as we say on the West Coast of Canada.

They know where the Courthouse is.

Other churches oversaw the Aboriginal children at different Residential Schools in Canada. The United Church, Anglican Church and Presbyterian Church were three such entities. In their turn, members of these churches, whose job it was to care for the children, did more damage to the children than their job descriptions called on them to do.

The level of sexual abuse of the children by adults in authority seems to have increased with the isolation of the children and the institution.

And where children were so very young, were without the tender ministrations of their mothers, fathers and siblings, where they had no friends and where the only adults who dealt with them did so harshly and generally by meting out punishment in the form of physical and emotional abuse, some children were surprised to find a caregiver sitting on the edge of their bed, speaking to them in quiet tones in the middle of the night, comforting them if they were homesick and crying, telling them that things would be alright, that they would see their parents soon.

How much an isolated and terrorized youngster must have been surprised and grateful such kindness and human warmth that came from out of nowhere in the middle of the night. The child would have been even happier to hear from this now kind man that the man had a surprise for the little boy or girl, and that the treat was waiting in the office of the Priest which doubled as his living quarters.

Taken from his bed by the Priest, led by a large, warm hand which had previously only strapped and smacked the six year old boy, what a delight it would have been for the little boy to find a chocolate bar waiting for him in the Priest's bedroom. The six-year-old had never had a whole chocolate bar to himself before.

And when the Priest sat on his own bed and motioned for the child to join him, that was icing on the cake. And when the adult patted the little boy on the head and murmured that everything was going to be fine, the child might even be feeling happy for the first time in months.

When the Priest began moving his hand down the child's front and back, asking if it felt nice, well it did feel nice to the child. It was human contact and it was not punishment.

Yet there was something wrong with the touching that the child had never experienced before. He was only five, but he knew it felt wrong.

When the Priest told the little boy to lie down beside him and go to sleep, things were looking up again. He finally had an adult to comfort him and he felt safe.

Until he felt the hands of the Priest undoing the string on his pajama bottoms. Until he felt the hand of the Priest playing with his penis.

Until he felt the finger of the Priest poking into his bum hole.

The little boy knew that this was wrong, and he wanted to tell the Priest to stop, that he did not like what was happening to him, but he could not and did not say stop.

The Priest kept saying that everything would be alright, and when he put his mouth on the little boys penis, he said that everything would be alright and when he put his penis in the little boys anus and raped him until he ejaculated inside the little boy while covering the child's mouth with a pillow, the Priest said this was God's will and everything would be alright, even though the little boy was screaming in pain into the pillow.

Now the little boy was bleeding from the skin being broken around his anus and blood mixed with semen was running out of his rectum and down his legs and even though the little boy would not be able to walk or get out of bed the next morning, the Priest said everything would be alright and this would be their secret and the little boy was to tell no one, because if the little boy told anyone at all, the Priest would make it so the little boy never saw his mother and father again.

The next time the Priest came to the little boy's bed, a week later, it was much easier. The tear in the anus had not quite healed yet, but the anal muscles had been stretched, so it was much easier.

And after three or four months, while the little boy was by now truly living in a world of his own, trying to think of some way to avoid being raped once a week, he was at a loss.

He was more alone than ever, but the only human contact he had was with the Priest who raped him.

And it didn't hurt so much anymore, as his anal sphincter had stretched to accommodate the man's penis, and there was hardly ever any blood now.

He had even learned how to go to the bathroom and pretend to have a bowel movement to expel the semen from his anus and then clean himself up with soap and water and get back into his own bed by himself.

He had learned quite a bit for a six-year-old little boy.

And what he had learned stayed with him, in some form, every day for the rest of his life.

So, never let it be said that the Residential School system in Canada never taught the children anything.

It taught them to confront stark terror in the night; it taught them self-loathing; it taught them to live in a private world which they shared only with their rapist, where they were always on guard and never felt safe. It taught them to question their own sexual identity, and it taught them that white men wearing black dresses and singing the praises of Jesus during the day, abandoned the teachings of Jesus in the night for their own sexual gratification.

Note this please, and please remember it for the rest of your life: this horror happened to little Aboriginal girls and boys thousands and thousands of times over the years.

If someone had sat down and said: "Let's make a plan to ruin the lives of five generations of Aboriginal people in Canada," they could have done no better than to invent the Residential School system.

But why wasn't Canada alive to the potential for such abuse?

Canada, the forward thinking Country which never said boo to a goose and was highly thought of by most other countries in the world when it was thought of at all?

What went wrong, here, to Canada's undying shame?

Canada failed to care for the children. Having abandoned them to the mercies of the churches and their hirelings, Canada sent the occasional inspector around to the schools to ensure that mayhem was not taking place. No child I have spoken with recalls ever seeing an inspector from Canada, and only one inspector seems to have ever unearthed the travesty of the sexual mistreatment of his charges.

Canada has a special relationship with its Aboriginal people. By custom and by law the Canadian Natives must be treated with the utmost of good faith by the Government. For most of our history, these have been empty words or words viewed as only guidelines. In recent decades, however, some Prime Ministers, notably Trudeau, Chretien and Martin have attempted to live by the spirit and letter of the law. They have failed, but they have tried, none more than Paul Martin who established the Kelowna Accord in November 2005, just weeks before he lost the 2006 election to Stephen Harper's Conservatives.

In the 1960's and before, however, the special relationship with the Aboriginal people was mostly words. The Aboriginal people could not vote until the 1950s, nor could they hire lawyers.

So, when Government inspectors went to the Residential Schools to have tea with the Priests who ran the place, do a head count and check the kitchens for rats, the last thing they expected to find was a nest of pederasts using the boys and girls as their sexual playthings.

Even in an ideal world, a visiting Inspector, closeting himself with the senior boys and girls without religious staff around to hear, would have met with silence when he asked the children how they were being cared for. The inspector, after all, would be gone in a few hours whereas the children had their own hides to worry about (and those of their sisters, brothers, mothers and fathers) if they ratted out the Priests. Things were tough enough at the school without the Priests getting word that little Mary had told an Inspector that the Principal had put his thing in her bum.

However, a Police Commission investigation into the aberrant behavior of staff members in 1939 found serious misconduct between one of the staff members and students at Kuper Island Indian Residential School in British Columbia. The problem was dealt with by transferring the miscreant and after that was, to all purposes, dead, buried and forgotten. Instead of approaching Inspection with more vigilance, Canada tootled merrily along as it had done before, leaving the sexual abusers in place for another forty years and ruining the lives of two more generations of children.

A stark example of an Aboriginal child's chance of getting through to authority, compared to a snowball's chance of surviving Hell is to be found in the story of two kids I know, aged ten and twelve, who rode a log to freedom over six miles of choppy winter ocean, hightailed it to their grandmother's house and holed up for three days in the late 1950s. Their grandmother opened her door on the fourth day to a team of two Priests and three police officers. At first she denied the children were there, but the team of runaway catchers cracked her like a nut and she gave them up, shedding tears as they were taken into custody.

To teach the boys a lesson, the police drove them to the nearest jail, locked them up for the night and brought them in front of the Judge the next day. Their father had been summoned to Court too, to explain these shenanigans. Both of these boys had been sexually abused by nuns – one made to have intercourse with a nun, the other made to rub a nun's vagina over her panties – and they had stories to tell but could not get them out, not to their granny, not to their father, not to the police, not even to each other.

When the Judge asked them why they had run away from the Residential School, a place well heated where the rain did not come in and where they were fed three squares a day, the boys were silent. The Judge was probably thinking that the boys were homesick, and of course they were, but he did not know about the nuns. The eldest boy said that "bad things" were happening at that school.

That was as far as that brave twelve year old boy would go.

The Judge, to his credit, heard the boy.

The children were then dispatched back to the institution with the judicial stricture that they be good boys from now on and do what their teachers told them to do and then arranged for a police officer to make a "surprise" visit to the school.

There is no surprising a group of Priests and nuns on an island six miles from land, especially when the police boat drops anchor for an hour before Officer Michael rows his boat ashore.

A meeting of all students was hastily called in the recreation room and the Principal told the children the truth: that they knew what was good for them.

When the police officer met with a small group of boys and asked them as a group and then individually if anything bad was happening to them at the school – and one of the runaways was in this group – all the students stood silent. The children knew what was good for them, as the Principal had pointed out.

The police boat returned to base, never to return again to the Residential School.

And things at the institution returned to normal.

Had the police boat dropped by even once a month on an irregular basis after that first visit, the incidence of sexual assault of the students likely would have plummeted as the children became more emboldened to speak and the religious staff became more fearful of being caught out.

And if wishes were canoes, all the children would have escaped.

But it was not to be.

Well, then, why was it that the Bishop in charge of these religious orders wasn't on the ball and cracking down on pedophiles in his schools?

When Bishops came to the institution, as infrequently as it was, they came in their regalia and welcomed souls to the Church and had tea with the Priests and staff and left. If a Bishop making a procession through a school ever spoke informally to any Indian child, the event has not been recorded for posterity.

Occasionally a religious Brother would be cut loose from one school and spun off to another one for no obvious reason. There may have been legitimate staffing problems, and there may have been need of a certain kind of expertise at a certain school, but it seems to me that the more egregious the behavior of a pederast, the further west he ended up, the more isolated he became.

This may be a coincidence, but I have reached the stage in life where I have too little time left to believe in coincidences.

The worst pedophiles at the Residential Schools appear to have ended up in the most far flung of those schools, preferably on an island, preferably on an island off the coast of another island, far from any city, or town or, indeed, any village, unless that village was inhabited solely by Natives.

Later on I will be discussing the attitude of the Roman Catholic Church hierarchy to sexual abuse done by its clergy. The short version is that where a pedophile is found within the clergy he is to be protected and sent to another job in another part of town, or another country.

If that was the method by which the entire Catholic Church removed the threat to children of ongoing sexual assaults, and it certainly appears to be, why would a similar method not be employed in the case of those at Residential Schools who were found to be "taking liberties" with some of their pupils?

And if a pedophile had been abusing children at school after school, is it not likely that he would be further and further removed from the possible prying eyes of authorities outside the Church?

Would such a policy ultimately end up with all of the rotten apples finding their way to one or two barrels?

Possibly.

It is likely that we will never know the truth because it is unlikely that the Roman Catholic Church, in a fit of openness and full disclosure, will ever divulge the history of the inner workings of these horrible schools.

Suffice to say that the sexual abuse of children was rampant, that Roman Catholic and other church authorities knew or ought to have known that it was going on and that they failed to stop it.

The Principals, Priests, nuns, Brothers and other holy men and women who had dedicated their lives to God and the teachings of Jesus, who used children under their care for their own sexual gratification, committed sins that cannot be washed away.

In defiling the most innocent in society, they defiled their own vows and their religious beliefs.

By acting in such a heartless, soulless, animalistic manner, they ruined the lives of many children at the same time as they ruined their own chances of ascending into whatever Heaven they aspired to.

Their sins toward these little children are unforgivable.

Chapter 14

I KNOW SOMETHING ABOUT NUNS

I know what nuns wear underneath those black habits.

If you do not want to know what I know, and I can't really blame you, please skip this next bit.

I suggest the Pope do the same. It may be information that will blow his big pointy hat off.

Nuns wear layers of cotton shifts, one, two or three depending on the climate and the time of year. They wear girdles with fasteners on them to hold up their stockings. They wear plain, white cotton underwear with elastic at the leg openings. They wear industrial-strength brassieres. And if the nuns have particularly large breasts, the kind that are inclined to protrude, these breasts are flattened against the chest wall by a brassiere that acts like a pair of pie plates that squish the breasts against the body.

As an aside, nuns do not wear deodorant, wash with plain soap and water, employ no hair care products and have sexual fantasies, which they act upon.

I wish I did not know all this but I do and now you do as well. I have learned this information from children who were sexually assaulted by nuns in the 1950s 1960s and 1970's.

Nuns may have changed their habits since then.

The nuns who hurt the boys I know did so with the same tenacity and the same absence of regard for the wellbeing of the children as their male counterparts in the Catholic Church.

Generally speaking, a nun would pick a time when she was alone with a boy. If she was a teacher, it might be that the boy was kept behind after class. If a boy was sick, she might come to his bed, under the guise of caring for him.

One nun was a chaperone at a movie held at a Residential School. She asked one of the senior boys, a boy of about eleven, to sit by her during the movie to help her run the projector. When the lights went down, she took the boy's hand and put it up her habit until his hand was on her vagina. He remembers the nun's vagina was wet through her underwear. He remembers the feel of the elastic in the leg openings of her underwear. Today he has recurring memories of this incident and requires women to wear to bed underwear with elastic in it. This guarantees that he will become aroused.

Because of this incident when the nun rubbed his hand back and forth on her vagina, the boy developed into a man with an unusual fetish. But he was really quite lucky compared to others.

Another boy at the same institution was visited by a nun while he had the flu and was confined to the infirmary. The nun made certain the doors were locked, stood beside the boy's bed, took off her wimple and her habit, then the layers of undergarments and finally, when she was naked, got under the covers with the boy. He was twelve years old at the time. He had had no experience with women, or sex, or even with white people being close to him. He was frightened, but he soon had an erection as the nun continued to manipulate his genitals.

Remember that genitals have no ethics.

The nun straddled him, inserted the boy's erect penis into her vagina, and raped him.

The boy lost his erection.

The nun, unsatisfied, dissatisfied, began to pound on the boy's chest with her fist and said that he must get his erection back. She said that otherwise he would never please a woman.

The boy, not surprisingly, was unable to produce an erection and the nun, after masturbating him, left his bed in disgust, only to return later that same day when she again raped the boy.

This occurred approximately ten times over the next week and was always the same, the nun pounding on the boy's chest, telling him to concentrate on maintaining an erection, and saying when he lost the erection that he would never please a woman.

The boy began to look forward to the nun's abusive conduct and spent the time when she was not there with him trying to manufacture and hold an erection.

Among all the other factors at play was the important tie between the two that now existed. Because he had been at the institution for over six years and because during that time no adult had held or hugged or kissed or praised him but, to the contrary, had beaten him with belts or sticks, punished him scolded him or ignored him, the pleasurable contact with this nun was something the boy craved.

He wanted to please her.

In later years this boy married five times and had numerous sexual relationships with women. He told me one day: "What that nun said was right. I have never been able to please a woman." He paused, and then he said "I want to feel women hit me when I have sex but I'm afraid to ask them."

Certainly the nun had put these thoughts in his head and, under the circumstances of his hearing the nun over and over again while she was astride him and urging him to keep his erection, he developed a condition by virtue of which he was so concerned about maintaining an erection that this became the sole focus of all his future sexual encounters.

The needs of his partner were secondary; his own desire was secondary; if he did not meet his erection requirement, the intimacy was a failure and often the man blamed his partner, even though he knew that he was to blame for imposing on himself requirements the nun had first imposed on him, because when he was having sexual relations, he could still hear the nun repeating "you'll never please a woman."

And there were even worse nuns, even nastier nuns, although it is always a mistake to attempt to compare one sexual assault with another – they are all hurtful and they all scar the individual who is abused.

There was a nun of about sixty, less than five feet tall, over two hundred pounds, who taught nine year old children about God and Jesus and Mary and Joseph and oral sex.

One of her pupils needed to go to the bathroom during class. He raised his hand. The nun ignored him. He raised his hand again with the same result. Finally he stood up and peed beside his desk. The pee formed a puddle at his feet.

This humiliated the young boy but caused no end of mirth to his fellow students. The nun was incensed and told the boy to stay behind after class.

In his soggy underwear and jeans, the boy was uncomfortable and now he was punished by the nun for peeing himself. She told him to hold out his hands and she strapped him with a barber's razor strop on the palms of his hands and on his lower inner forearms.

Because he peed in her class.

Then the nun took the boy over to the door of the classroom, put her back against the door, raised her habit and made the boy lick her vagina. The boy gagged at the odor. He vomited. The nun smacked him hard on the side of his head and told the boy to go into the bathroom, get a mop and clean up the vomit and the urine. He did as he was told.

The nun told the boy to return to the classroom where she again stood with her back to the door and lifted her habit.

This time the little boy managed to lick the nun's vagina without throwing up.

He continued to lick the nun's vagina until the nun told him to leave her, but not before she told him that he had the devil in him, that he was a pagan, and that he would never amount to anything. She said that no one would ever believe him if he told anyone what the nun had forced him to do. She told him he would go to hell. He believed her.

So the little boy never told anyone, not even his parents, not even his wife, until he told me in my office one day.

And that day he cried just like the little boy would have cried if the nun had allowed him to. He let himself cry for the first time after all those years, and it was part of his walk along the path to healing.

For children who are sexually abused, crying releases some of the poison from their system that sexual abuse put in. As the crying continues and the story is told, so the healing takes place and step by step the memories of the sexual abuse lose their power to control the minds and lives of the survivor.

Many nuns took their sexual satisfaction from the little children, but one in particular reached depths that made me wonder what humanity might ever have been in her.

The nun was also large, perhaps two hundred and fifty pounds. She had gray hair. She liked to have the little boys come to her room two at a time. She would get naked and would then dress one of the boys in girls' clothing.

She made the boys have pretend sexual intercourse with one another on her bed.

Then she would take one of the boys and lay him on his back on the bed and straddle his face with her vagina on his mouth. She sat on the boy's face with her full weight.

One of the boys who watched this happening to his friend knew what it was like under that big nun – he had been under her as well – and he saw his friend kicking and struggling and then all of a sudden go still. The boy remained still under the big nun for a long time.

His friend thought the nun had killed the other boy, but he was terrified to do anything. Finally the nun rolled off the boy and he lay on the bed gasping for air. Although he did not die, his life after this was never the same and, among other things, he became a transvestite with severe emotional difficulties that were caused by this treatment.

This happened to the boy many times.

And it happened to other boys many times.

Yet another nun had a sexual preference for young girls, aged about eight or nine. She would have them to her room while she was in her nightdress, brush their hair, remove their clothes and insert the handle of her hairbrush into their vagina.

Afterwards she would lick the girls' vaginas and put her fingers in their anuses.

She stretched their anal sphincters, visit after visit, making their anuses more accepting of something larger than a finger.

That was where one of the Priests came in. The nun stretched the muscles of the anus of the young girls to more easily accommodate the penis of the man who would anally rape them next. She would pass the girls along to the Priest after she had broken them in and then select another girl from the dormitory for her attention.

The Priest would anally rape the young girls.

We will never know how many girls the nun and Priest did this to. Most of them are dead now, many by their own hand because they could not drink away the guilt and the shame or live with the depression.

For the record, those nuns who are still alive deny that anything like this ever happened and say that all the children were properly cared for at these schools.

I invite them, or their Bishop or their Pope to sue me if they take issue with the truth of any of the stories of sexual abuse I recount in this book.

And that is all I care to write about nuns for the time being.

And I suspect that that is all you care to read about nuns for the time being.

Chapter 15

HOW DO I FIND OUT IF MY CHILD HAS BEEN SEXUALLY ASSAULTED?

Ask him.

There are three reasons why your child has not told you that she was sexually assaulted by someone, four if he's a boy.

First, she fears you will not believe her.

Second, she is frightened she will be punished because she believes she did something wrong to cause the sexual assault.

Third, the person who abused her told her to never tell anyone and threatened her or her family with more pain if she told.

Fourth (if he is a male), he will fear you think he is a homosexual and he is probably not certain himself whether he is or not and really does not want to discuss this with mom and dad, and probably is terrified of learning that he is a homosexual.

Even in these enlightened times.

If you have not yet rape-proofed your son and daughter, they don't yet know The Rules that you and I know.

A girl or boy aged two to 22 doesn't know The Rules, doesn't know where she stands in relation to the sexual abuse she has had done to her. It was probably done a while ago. She has learned to live with it in her way. She certainly is not likely to volunteer the information, but she has become inured to carrying the abuse consciousness as part of her psyche.

With one exception.

An older girl, say one over 8, may hear the story of someone she knows is admired and respected having been sexually assaulted as a child.

In the past, such celebrities as Roseanne Barr, Oprah Winfrey, Ellen DeGeneres and Terri Hatcher have disclosed that they were sexually assaulted by men when they were younger and that the assault severely affected their lives.

This knowledge may prompt your daughter to begin to piece together some of The Rules in her own mind and venture the comment while watching the story on television with her family: "I think something like that happened to me."

This first disclosure will be tentative. The child waits with breath abated to see what your reaction will be. She believes that enough time has passed that she is free from her abuser – at least for that moment – and she ventures a comment that aligns her with a celebrity, a person who is on television and therefore has power, is more normal than normal and is admired by society.

She believes that if the celebrity was sexually assaulted and can speak of it openly, like it was not her fault, like she was not guilty of anything, well, maybe she can too…. But she's not sure of any of this, so she awaits the response of her parents to her confession. Please remember that she believes with all her heart that she has done something wrong to have been sexually abused. Boys think the same.

A pre-eminent example of this catalyst to disclosure is found in the life of Sheldon Kennedy, a Canadian hockey player who had good skills and was much admired as a player in a sport where all the players are "tough guys". Kennedy had been sexually assaulted by his hockey coach when he was 14.

Coaches of young boys and girls – boys and girls generally too young to know The Rules – fall into approximately the same category as Boy Scout leaders.

Not all are pedophiles.

Some are.

When Sheldon Kennedy was 14-years-of-age and had not yet pieced together The Rules, he was raped by his hockey coach. His coach, who has had enough publicity and will go nameless here, held the key every young hockey player covets: the key to the Big Leagues. So when the coach approached Sheldon sexually, what was he to do? He went along with the coach as hundreds of kids had done with their coaches before and may still be doing today.

After he learned The Rules, Kennedy went public with the rapes and laid criminal charges against his former coach. He was in the Big Leagues then and even in the late 1990's it took a hell of a lot of guts to demand that justice be done.

Sheldon Kennedy has since written a book I commend to you, called Why I Didn't Say Anything. Thousands of men across Canada found the courage to come forward with stories of their own abuse after Sheldon Kennedy did. A popular and talented player, the idol of many kids and adults too, many kids who had been sexually abused, and some "kids" as old as 70, came forward with their stories of abuse at the hands of other men. Most were fearful of so many things, not least of which was being branded a fag, but they thought if a rough and tumble, straight-ahead guy like Sheldon Kennedy can talk, and HE'S no fag, I may be able to.

In his book, Sheldon Kennedy denies that he is a hero.

Sheldon Kennedy is a hero in my book.

The accusation was a first in Canada – a high profile athlete admitting publicly that he had been the victim of a pedophile's anal rape.

The unintended consequences of this revelation were a wonder to behold. Men everywhere said, in effect, "Hell, if it could happen to a tough guy like Sheldon Kennedy and he's not ashamed to talk about it, maybe I should not be ashamed of what happened to me."

Men who formerly thought they carried a gay gene or were pedophiles-in-waiting themselves, or thought they had enticed their abuser by giving him the come-on and were ashamed that a man had put his penis in their anus gave serious thought to coming forward to make the abuser PAY for what he had done to fuck up their lives.

They didn't care if he paid them MONEY. That was irrelevant. They wanted the son of a bitch to pay. And they thought that somehow this would make them feel better. Make them feel normal for the first time since they were raped.

They were getting angry now. It was not as bad a feeling as feeling guilty. Now they actually sort of half believed that someone had done something wrong TO them, not WITH them. It was a good feeling to start to learn The Rules. Maybe they were a bit normal after all...

There's that word normal again.

They didn't know the word "closure," or if they did, that wasn't what they wanted. They just wanted someone to lift the burden off their back a bit. Take a ten pound rock out of that thousand pound pack they'd been carrying around.

A little help here, okay?

That would be a good thing.

Someone to believe them.

That would be a start.

If Sheldon can do it, some of them said, I can do it.

One of the key things for parents – or caregivers or any one of us in society – to be aware of is that the victim of sexual abuse is terrified at the moment of first disclosure. It is a turning point in his or her life. He has chosen to share his dark and dirty secret with YOU. He has given you a sacred trust. He has, in essence, put his life in your hands.

What do you do with this information?

You will treat it as if it were precious diamonds, rubies and a bird fallen from a nest all at the same time. You treat the revelation with care. But you do not shy away from your task. After all, this child, or adult, has bestowed a great gift on you – the gift of his absolute trust – in the hopes that you will be the one who will know what to do to help him.

But he hopes, really, just that you'll believe him.

That's really all he wants right then.

So you cradle this information in your arms. You protect it. You shelter it.

Because now it is partly yours, and always will be partly yours. Now there's no turning back, even if you wanted to.

In those hesitant seconds between the time the disclosure is made to you and your response, a thousand things may flow through your mind:

Were you somehow at fault? How could you have been so stupid not to see it? Will the perpetrator go to jail? Sue you? Will this get in the papers? Will people at work find out? Is your son gay? Why pick me to tell? Will you have to go to court? Is your son going to kill himself? How horrible was the abuse? The poor little kid. What if he's lying? What if he's joking? What are you supposed to do now?

All of these questions will be answered in the fullness of time.

Your sole job, your only job on earth for the next little while, is to tell your son that you believe him and that from now on things are going to get better, because you are going to help him.

Then do it. Help him.

Hold him, hug him, tell him you can only imagine how horrible it must have been.

If he begins to cry, encourage him to cry. Tears are one way of getting the poison out.

If you start to cry, that's good too.

People worry too much about crying and looking foolish and not enough about children being raped.

Tell your son that you and he will deal with this together. Reassure him that his confidence in you has been well placed. Ask him if there is anything you can do right now, this minute, to help him? If you are a caring person this should all come easily to you. If you are not a caring person, it is unlikely this boy would have chosen you to share his burden. So do what feels natural. Resist the temptation to make this moment about you. All of this will ultimately have some impact on you, but that can be dealt with in the months and years to come. At this second in time, your job is to be 100% in the moment for your son.

But just in case you are a caring person who freaks out from time-to-time, and just in case this disclosure is in danger of precipitating one of these freak outs, here are some things NOT to do:

Do not tell your son you don't believe him. Words like "That's ridiculous, I would have known," or "Uncle Ralph would never do such a thing. He's my brother," or "We'll talk about this later when you've had a chance to settle down, and when your father gets home," may drive the secret back into your child, perhaps never to emerge again.

Remember, the disclosure is often tentative so that your daughter can withdraw from having said anything if the information is not well received.

So take a minute, take a breath and think.

After two or three minutes you will be surprised how things return to normal, even though there is a large elephant now sitting in the room with you and your son. The elephant is examining his toenails and wondering with interest what will happen next.

Make coffee. Give your son your full attention. You can ask questions about when, where and how the abuse happened. As long as your son is willing to keep talking, keep listening.

Listen carefully to what he says and be guided by how he wishes to proceed.

Take as much time as he needs.

Put on some more coffee.

Be there for him.

Be yourself.

The worst is over now. She has got the dirty little secret out. She did not die. You did not fall off a chair or call her a liar.

Tell her that.

Things will be better now. Things will never again be as bad as they were for her just this morning. Because now there are two of you working to help her feel better about herself.

Now you and she can begin to rebuild the areas of your child's psyche that have been damaged by the sexual abuse.

There is no moment in the life of a child analogous to the disclosure to his parents of having been sexually abused. The closest I can come is the moment when a gay child tells his parents of his sexuality. The analogy is supported by the fact that in each case the child fears the reaction to the revelation, but has a need to share the secret. In both cases the life of the child and his parents will never be the same again. In both cases the child is keenly aware of the fact that there is a stigma against his conduct and that the disapproval of his parents may be the result of his disclosure.

Still, he gathers up his courage and makes the announcement.

Neither in cases where children disclose their sexuality or their sexual abuse should society or parents condemn them. It is difficult to believe that at this stage of our progress as a species children still fear an assault upon them by their parents for telling the truth about their sexual orientation or about having been sexually abused.

As parents, we owe our children the respect of listening to and supporting them in their best and worst times.

We should all work to make the disclosure of sexual abuse a moment in a child's life that he knows he need not fear, a moment when he knows he can count on his parents to understand.

Above all, don't worry. It's not as bad as you may think. You can do it because your child has faith that you can do it.

Suppose you have children at home now. They are eight and ten years of age, a boy and a girl.

What do you do now, this minute?

Well, keep reading the book.

But at the end of the book I'm going to ask you to do you-know-what. You know, ask them The Question.

Has anyone ever touched your private parts?

THAT question.

You want to ask them in private, just you and your son or just you and your daughter. People don't want to talk about this to an audience.

But it's okay. We'll get through it together.

Don't bail out now after having come so far.

And your child may not disclose the abuse right away. Probably he will not. But at least she will know that you are open to talking about it some other time and that you love her and that you care about her and that you are trying to help her and not judge her. That is a good thing to happen on any day.

Once your child – and for our purposes, your child is anywhere from one to 60 years of age – has made a disclosure of having been sexually abused and you have had your coffee and cried together and kicked the elephant around and started to get back to normal, your next job as a parent is to find a good counselor for your child.

A good counselor serves the same purpose as a decompression chamber serves for scuba divers who may have surfaced too quickly. A counselor will help your child adapt to her new life post-disclosure, the life where the dirty little secret no longer has absolute power over her, where she is reclaiming her power from that secret.

Just as the decompression chamber prevents the scuba diver from contracting a potentially life-threatening condition, the counselor – the GOOD counselor - will walk your child through the miasma of the past, let him know he no longer stands alone but has allies at his side and will furnish him with a set of tools to help him manage the triggers, the flashbacks, the nightmares and the consciousness of the sexual abuse.

At literally any age a child or adult may decide he has long enough carried the weight of the sexual assaults all by himself.

He may "come out" to his mother or father, best friend, wife, or, as so many times in my case, his lawyer.

It really doesn't matter to whom the child or adult discloses the fact of his sexual abuse. What matters is that when the disclosure is made, the next step is one of belief and consequence.

"Right!" all and sundry should exclaim. "Let's get you in to see Dr. Fonebone next Friday at 11. She's particularly good at dealing with victims of sexual abuse."

If you are reading this and you were sexually assaulted and decide to come out on your own, phone through to your local Crisis Center and ask someone there who they would recommend you see to discuss your childhood sexual abuse. They'll find you someone. Your job is to go to see that doctor and assess him or her to see if she is a good candidate for you to talk to about it.

Phone 911. Ask for the number of your local crisis line.

You'll be okay.

(Although some people in society are still a little knotted up about how to get other people help, even on a Crisis Line. I was in a city in the United States last week and saw that in the front of the telephone book, the Crisis Line number to dial was 1-800-SUICIDE. Let's have a gold star for the pinhead who thought that one up and all the other pinheads who bought into the idea. It's like having the Hotline to Alcoholics Anonymous as 1-800-DRUNKBUM. Good intentions, bad execution...)

If you do not respect your doctor or do not believe that she cares about you, fire her.

Many doctors, like many lawyers, are inept at dealing with a patient or a client who has been through sexual abuse. It is, after all, a large burden you have carried and now wish someone else to share. Some will share the burden with you better than others. That's just human nature.

Most general practitioners are not the best choice to counsel people who were sexually abused. They lack training because most were given little at medical school. Not many people knew much about sexual abuse when most doctors were students.

All doctors can learn more about counseling victims of sexual abuse.

A General Practitioner or Family Doctor can be useful when it comes to talking about your sexual abuse. But they are usually working to a schedule. The best you can hope for from your family doctor is a referral to a psychiatrist who has her wits about her and who can help you.

It is not surprising that good, caring, intelligent therapists who work with people who have been sexually assaulted are not only difficult to find but have a high burnout rate. They can handle only so many patients with severe symptoms at the same time before their ability to help those patients becomes diluted and they subsequently lose it altogether.

This is a pernicious consequence of being too good at what you do.

However, with education and a fair tailwind we will arrive at a time when there are many decent therapists available for victims of sexual assault.

Once you find one you can trust, whom you know is smart enough and well-read enough to help you, you are on your way home.

You are on your way back to becoming the person you would have been but for the sexual abuse. That precise eventuation is unlikely to be achieved. Too much water has flowed under too many bridges to construct an exact replica of You Without Sexual Abuse.

I believe that what you can realistically hope for is to bring into being a new you who has grappled with the sexual abuse that the young you suffered from, and has throttled the effects of that abuse within an inch of their lives, giving you a new outlook on life, as well as a new INLOOK on who YOU really are.

The idea, then, is to work to become that you.

That you is one devoid of anger, low self-esteem, fear, anxiety, panic attacks, depression and sexual difficulties. This is a tall order. There is only one way to fill the order. Start as soon as you can.

And work hard.

We are all works in progress. We all carry baggage. Some of us have baggage as difficult to manage, or MORE difficult to manage than yours.

Time's a wastin'.

You're not getting anywhere sitting on your ass.

Get to work on yourself today.

Phone the Crisis Line, even if you have to poke 1-800-SUICIDE to do it. (Ask for Mr. Tact...)

What's the worst that could happen?

Chapter 16

PANTS ON FIRE

People never lie about having been sexually abused.

Man has never set foot on the moon.

George W. Bush is the smartest President the USA ever had.

There is a colony of Martians living under the Pacific Ocean.

Which of the above statements is true?

The only one I am certain of is that some people lie about having been sexually abused.

Not all, not many, not a majority, not a large minority, not a substantial number, not a significant number, but some.

People lie for all sorts of reasons about all sorts of things. Some people lie about having been sexually abused. I am sorry that they do and I truly hope their numbers are small.

I can say that of the hundreds and hundreds of people I have met I do not believe one of them has lied about having been sexually assaulted.

One or two may have fooled me, but I very much doubt it. Once you've seen one person who has been sexually abused spill their guts, there is a certain bar that all future victims must clear. No one in my experience has ever failed to clear that bar.

Some – indeed most – engage in what is called "progressive disclosure". Over a period of time – days, weeks, months, years – people will say that their abuser fondled – masturbated – fellated – raped them.

The reason for this progressive disclosure is simple. If the person who hears your initial disclosure about the abuse is not blown away by your disclosing the dirty act of fondling, in time that person may be worthy of hearing – may become a person you can trust hearing – about the masturbation he made you do to him – about having to blow him – about how he came in your mouth – about how he penetrated your anus with his penis or a broom handle or a hairbrush.

So people who were sexually assaulted remember the dirty deeds that gave rise to the dirty secrets, but very often they will not want to open up to anyone – because they have barely admitted to themselves – how they were anally raped twenty or thirty times when they were 13 and never fought back and always wondered why they were cowards and didn't fight back, or even tell…. And who will believe them now, after all these years…..?

Very few sexual assault victims tell their whole story of abuse the very first time they tell someone they were assaulted. They will go to some lengths to deny that more abuse took place than they have already said. They will tell you when they are good and ready, or they may never tell you. They are not lying. They just prefer not to tell you everything at once.

A favorite trick of lawyers I know who act for the Perpetrators of abuse is to go to the first time the Plaintiff disclosed his abuse. They will say:

"On January 33, 2008 you told your psychiatrist that my client, Mr. Fonebone, masturbated you and made you perform oral genital sex on him. Do you remember telling your doctor that?"

"Yes."

"Did you tell your doctor that?"

"Yes."

"Was that true?"

"Yes."

"Now today you say that Mr. Fonebone anally raped you."

"Yes."

"Is that true?"

"Yes."

"Did you tell your doctor Mr. Fonebone anally raped you?"

"No."

"Did you trust your doctor?"

"Yes."

"Why did you not tell your doctor Mr. Fonebone anally raped you?"

"I don't know."

"Were you lying to your doctor when you said Mr. Fonebone masturbated you and made you perform oral-genital sex on him?"

"No."

"Are you lying now when you say that Mr. Fonebone anally raped you?"

"No."

"Did you tell your doctor the truth?"

"Yes."

"Are you telling the truth today?"

"Yes."

"Would you agree that what you are saying today that Mr. Fonebone did to you is different from what you told your doctor, a man you trusted?"

"Yes."

"No further questions."

Now, some Judges listening to these questions and answers, knowing that the test for proving sexual assault in Court is a very high one, will be persuaded that this witness is a liar, is seeking to maximize his claim or has, at best, an unreliable recollection of exactly what Mr. Fonebone did to him.

Judges who have been properly trained about the nature of progressive disclosure, however, will know that this witness is not only not lying, but is telling the story as a truthful textbook Plaintiff in a sexual abuse case would do.

But, you see, it takes a lot of education before Judges become aware of certain truisms.

Fifty years ago, no Court had to deal with any law involving computer technology. Now it has become common in court to drag up mountains of information about technical differences between computer A and computer B. Judges, mere mortals, get up to speed by following the advice of experts. In cases where the parties to a case do not provide sufficient expertise, the Court can get its own expert. So, too, will Judges learn about "Progressive Disclosure", not so much from lawyers, but from doctors that lawyers bring to court to explain why their client did not tell the whole story the first time he decided to speak about his abuse.

Here, in passing, it seems appropriate to make a comment about doctors' notes.

Not every doctor writes illegible notes. Only 95% of them. The next time you are on your way out of your doctor's office, ask her if you can review the notes she has just made about your visit. Her first instinct will be to clutch the notes to her chest and give you *Such A Look*. Ask again. The notes are yours to see. Stand firm. She will ask why, she will look at them for a while, she may tear up, she may develop a twitch, but finally she will let you see those notes. Not that it matters. Because short forms, abbreviations, private code and generally bad, hurried handwriting make the notes almost useless to all but her.

Doctors also have an annoying propensity to listen with one ear while making plans for the evening, thinking about buying a new car or investing in a diamond mine. You may go to your doctor and say you were in a car accident on March 20th and your Honda Civic was rear-ended by a black Dodge Dart and you now have a pain in the back of your neck and it's been three weeks now and it's not getting better. The parts of the doctor's note you are able to decipher may read:

"Ap.15 pt c/o nk/bk pain. MVA Feb 20 car strk by whte drt. T-3 prn. 2/52"

Three years later a Judge, two lawyers and your doctor will be reading this note in a Courtroom. The lawyer for the person who hit you will ask if you complained of a sore back. No you will say, I said my neck hurt.

Well why did the doctor write that your BACK hurt?

Did he say that, Doctor?

Doctor: That is what I wrote, yes, nk/bk, neck and back pain. Yes.

Lawyer: "And did he say his car was struck by a WHITE Dodge Dart."

Doctor: That's what I have here, yes…

Lawyer: And did he say that the accident happened on February 20?

Doctor: That's right.

Lawyer: Not March 20?

Doctor: No, February 20.

Lawyer: So Mr. Fonebone told you on April 15 that his BACK was hurting because the car he was in was hit by a WHITE Dodge Dart on February 20, is that correct?

Doctor: Yes.

Lawyer: No Further questions.

Like many lawyers, I have both lost and won cases based on sloppy doctors' notes. In Court, these notes are regarded as The Sacred Truth. In real life, unfortunately, they are often merely a rough approximation of what transpired between the doctor and the patient during a visit.

It does no good for the lawyer whose client is getting the short end of the stick to ask the doctor if his notes might be wrong. She will allow they MIGHT be wrong, but that's highly unlikely and because this all happened three years ago, this is the best evidence we have.

If doctors wrote every note as if it would some day be they keystone in a lawsuit, justice would be better served and so would their patients.

All of this having been said, the Courtroom remains the place where the truth about an allegation of sexual abuse should come to the surface.

As I have said, some people lie about it.

Those who lie about having been sexually abused do so because they mis-remember or they want attention or money. There are no other reasons.

The ones who mis-remember may believe in fact that they were sexually abused – to the point where they could pass a lie detector test. In fact, they probably WERE sexually assaulted by someone in their youth, but their brains have put the assault in a box other than the one in which it belongs. There may be other things improperly wired in their brains, connecting things in television shows they have seen or books they have read or dreams they have had with the reality of their own lives, and with minimal or no distinction.

In many cases the mind blots out memories of the sexual abuse for the very good reason that to remember the abuse is to cause pain. Sometimes the mind will block out the memories for decades and decades and then, one day, something will trigger a memory – something like a smell or a song or a television program – and then, later, another memory will come. But most people are happy to have the memories not come at all and let their subconscious minds deal with the aftermath of the sexual abuse. When the memories do barge back in, however, a lot of people are taken by surprise, starting with the victim, of course, and going onward to the victim's family, his doctor and possibly, later, his lawyer.

But cases where people just stand there and LIE about being sexually abused are few, and even fewer when it comes to the laying of criminal charges. It is fair to legitimate victims of abuse to let them know here that there are people – misguided, troubled, cupiditous people – who will make allegations of sexual abuse against someone when those allegations are untrue.

The system sorts out the people who make spurious allegations.

There is a saying that the wheels of Justice grind slowly, but they grind exceeding small.

People who make false allegations of sexual abuse will either be chewed up and spit out by the Justice system or will be cart-wheeled over into a slough pile of people who have severe emotional problems that were caused by things other than sexual abuse, or by sexual abuse that they say X committed on them when it was in fact committed by Y.

The mind is a mysterious thing when it processes information on sexual abuse. Sometimes the victim tries very hard to access memories of the abuse, but finds those memories are wrapped in a dream-like phantasm that they just cannot penetrate. Rarely do people with this memory make any accusations against anyone because they are afraid they may mis-remember what truly happened. They just know that SOMETHING BAD happened, and they can access glimpses of it when they think hard about it, but cannot access the whole picture.

Judges tend to err on the side of caution. Before a man or woman is denied her liberty or her money for having sexually abused a child – in fact a sentence which will severely damage a defendant for the rest of his life – a Judge must be satisfied that it is far more likely than not that the sexual assault took place. This has always been true in criminal cases.

In civil law, where I practice most, the test is more onerous for a Court to find that sexual abuse took place than in any other area of civil law. The test is not "the balance of probabilities" but rather something higher. Expressed in percentage terms, if the balance of probabilities test is 50% + 1 and the criminal test of "beyond a reasonable doubt" is 95%, the civil test to find sexual abuse is something in the order of 80 to 85% certainty in the Judge's mind.

A Court must be satisfied WELL beyond the balance of probabilities that the abuse took place as alleged by the Plaintiff OR, and this is key to an understanding of the system, the Court may find that SOME sexual abuse took place, NOT NECESSARILY as the Plaintiff described it, but of such a nature as to require that the Plaintiff be paid damages.

In other words, a Court is allowed to waffle. The Judge believes the Plaintiff was sexually abused but thinks the story of the abuse has changed over the last fifty years or so since it happened. The Judge therefore decides in her own mind what the abuse PROBABLY was, and awards damages accordingly.

This is like being half pregnant.

In my respectful opinion, the Judge has a duty either to accept all the evidence of the Plaintiff or reject it all.

However, this is not the place to argue the issue. Suffice to say that anyone who lies about having been sexually abused will have her credibility tested again and again and again before she even sets foot in Court.

If her story holds up in Court so that a Judge finds that her complaint is valid, it is highly unlikely that an innocent defendant will be found to have committed sexual abuse which he denies.

No system devised by man is foolproof and there will be exceptions, but speaking generally, those who say that a person accused of sexually assaulting a child cannot get a fair trial are wrong.

Not only does the system require that the person sexually abused have a close to airtight case, but the system also gives an opportunity to the person accused to tell his side of the story. Often this is a simple denial, without more. "I didn't do it. I wasn't there. I never saw this boy before," the Defendant will say. There are only so many ways he has of saying no.

But if a person is truly innocent, a simple denial is all a judge would expect. In every way the onus is on the person who says he was abused to prove his case.

With all the devils and demons in his psyche that a sexually abused person brings into court with him, he must have become extremely strong to stand up under the dissection of his story – and every story can be hacked to little ill-fitting pieces by a competent lawyer – and to keep on fighting when he is made again and again to return in his mind to the scene of his abuse – the worst days of his life.

The lawyer for the pedophile, who has had access to all of the counseling records of the victim, knows the victims vulnerable spots, and attacks those.

Here is an example of what can happen in Court:

Bad Guy Lawyer (BGL): "Your mother died when you were six. How did that make you feel?"

Good Guy (GG): "Sad"

BGL –"Your father used to get drunk and beat you up. How did that make you feel?"

GG -"Frightened"

BGL – "The kids at school used to call you Elephant Boy. Why was that?"

GG -"I was fat and ugly."

BGL – "How did that make you feel?"

GG - "Sad."

BGL – "Sad. Is that all?"

GG – "Sad and worthless."

BGL – "When my client, Mr. Fonebone, befriended you, your mother had died, your father was a mean drunk who beat you up and the other kids at school mocked you and called you Elephant Boy because you were fat and ugly and you had no friends at all, is that correct?"

GG – "Yes."

BGL – "And you are asking this Court to believe that you are an emotional basket case simply because my client allegedly kissed your penis and for no other reason, is that right?"

(Here the proceedings were adjourned while the witness had an emotional breakdown...)

My hat is off to every child who was ever sexually abused who has decided to tell her story in Court.

And to those who think that "kids make up these stories of being sexually abused. They do it for money. It's easy to get money if you accuse an old Priest and you know how to cry. People get away with it every day..," my hat is on.

Chapter 17

A CURIOUS TIME FOR PEDOPHILES

What to write about pedophiles?

I'm tempted to say "Go find your own damn book." But it's unlikely anyone will soon write "How To Be A Pedophile For Dummies."

I can wedge pedophiles in here in the hopes that you want to change to become a celibate or non-practicing or retired pedophile.

The good news is that you probably cannot help what you are.

The bad news is that you probably cannot help what you are.

Pedophiles are usually hardwired that way.

They have sex with adults from time to time, but they prefer children.

Most pedophiles really have no choice in the matter.

There are only one or two things we can do, therefore.

We cannot kill pedophiles in most jurisdictions in the western world. Other countries have other laws, but these are the laws we have at the present time. So unless a pedophile rapes a little boy then kills him, and then only in certain countries, he will not be killed.

He will be imprisoned.

If he rapes a little boy and does not kill him, he may go to jail for three years, and be out in two. Or go to jail for eighteen months, and be out in ten.

Not enough.

But also too much, if you believe that no amount of incarceration or indoctrination or education will change a pedophile into a sexual non-deviant.

I have already drawn to your attention the perfectly legal group of pedophiles and would-be child rapists known as NAMBLA, the North American Man Boy Love Association. These deviants believe that love between a man and a young boy is perfectly natural and pure. Their motto is: "Get them by eight before it's too late."

I kid you not.

These guys probably have conventions in Vegas, but I would prefer they not be at my hotel.

I would prefer there not be an organization like this at all, but since it is legal, and since its membership is probably three-fourths FBI agents keeping tabs on the deviants, it is probably better to have it out in the open than underground on the Internet.

Let's review the options our society has for dealing with pedophiles.

We have the police monitoring deviants who are released into neighborhoods, having served their time. We have alerts to the media resulting in jerky television footage of a deviant getting out of jail and into a waiting car. We have pictures of deviants who have moved into the neighborhood so we can warn the children to keep an eye open for them. We have Amber Alerts for occasions when deviants take small boys or girls from their homes or schools to rape and kill them. We have special jails for the deviants when they are caught at it again so that the other prisoners – who regard "child molesters" as the lowest scum on the lowest shoe on the lowest rung of the ladder in any prison – do not annoy, harass, molest or kill them.

But we do not have an answer for the deviance (from the norm) or the perversion (of the act of love) in the first place.

I have looked carefully at the alternatives. I believe that anyone criminally convicted of touching a child for a sexual purpose should do five years in jail with no time off. For more debasing and detrimental crimes like child rape, the sentence should be fifteen years to life with no time off.

A second offence of a serious nature, demonstrating that the pedophile has no control over his sexual needs, should result in castration.

The odds are that the pedophile wasn't looking to procreate in any event or he would be having sexual relations with people other than boys or girl children.

Castration does a service to society by getting uncontrollable pedophiles out of circulation and a minor disservice to the pedophile, compared to the damage he does to the children he rapes.

As for women who sexually abuse children in their care, the same jail time should apply as in the case of their male counterparts, but in the place of castration a second offence should result in a sentence of true *life* imprisonment.

It's a start.

Finally, some people have asked about a possible connection between homosexuals and pedophilia.

We do not have sufficient data to prove or disprove whether homosexuals are more or less likely to be pedophiles. They probably are more likely to be pedophiles, with male homosexuals finding young boys sexually attractive. It seems to make sense that they are, but there is no proof that they are.

However, if we enact criminal legislation mandating the sentences I have suggested, the question is moot.

As in most other areas of human endeavor, there have been good and bad times to be a pedophile. The good old days for a pedophile were from the year dot until about 1970. I suspect that in the 70's pedophiles began to be more than a little concerned about victims' rights movements and women's rights movements and gay rights movements because somewhere in all of that, or as an adjunct to it, was bound to be a sexual abuse victims' rights movement.

Sexual abuse victims however, almost by definition, do not band together and take out full page ads in the New York Times and line up to go on Oprah to tell the story of how they have been persecuted by The Man and The System.

Victims of sexual abuse, as you will know by now, tend to be extremely guarded and inward-looking, unsure of their moral position and, even at maturity and being well read, uncertain of The Rules.

Rather than starting a massive societal movement, the people who were sexually abused began in the 1980's to take on their abusers on a one-to-one basis. A girl tells a social worker that her stepfather "touched" her; a boy tells his parents that his teacher "touched" him; an altar boy tells his cousin that his Priest is jerking him off. The reports in the 1980's were, to begin with, the word of one child against the word of one alleged pedophile. Few people except the professionals in the field noticed any shift in the firmament. Pedophiles, although still cautious, saw nothing to instill fear or panic. Certainly there was insufficient news coverage in the 1980's of sexual abuse of children to dissuade a pedophile from carrying on assaulting children. But change was in the air.

In the 1990's the landscape changed forever. Large groups of children began to come forward from places like orphanages or homes for the deaf or schools run by Priests in Ireland and Canada and the United States and France and Australia.

By the end of the 1990's there was hardly a week that went by when a pedophile could pick up a newspaper and not see that some other pederast either down the street or on the far side of the world had been thrown in jail for doing to children what he had been doing to children with impunity for most of his adult life.

In addition to the stories of the institutional abuse of children – schools, churches, orphanages and the like – there were stories in the papers every other week of men who sexually abused neighborhood boys or girls, or their stepchildren, going to jail and paying great sums of damages to the children for having wrecked their lives.

So I suspect, although I do not know for certain, that by the year 2000, every pedophile in the western world who could read or who had access to television had been put on notice that his victims from the past could come knocking on his door at any time of the day or night in the guise of a policeman or a Sheriff, serving Court documents which would effectively change the pedophile's life forever.

To lose one's liberty at the age of 50 or 60, to lose the house and savings one has spent a lifetime working for, on legal fees and payment for damage you have done to the plaintiff, is a crushing thing. It is no less than a pedophile deserves.

But there was more to come.

Because sexual abuse is such a deeply personal crime, committed by a sexual bully on a virginal, defenseless child, there is the theft not only of the child's innocence by the pedophile, but of his pride and his sense of self and self-worth, and his sense of safety and his bodily and sexual integrity.

All of these things are lost when a child's innocence is taken by a sexual predator.

Let's look again at the analogy of the child being shot instead of sexually abused. The comparison is apt. While a child of 6 may be shot in the shoulder by a 30 year old man wielding a gun, the bullet wound would be healed by the time the child was 30. There would be little or no animosity harbored by the child for the shooting incident that took place so long ago. The shooter would likely have already paid his debt to society. The life of the child would adapt to the wound, whose only reminder is a scar on the shoulder.

Not so with a six-year-old child whose life has been forever changed by a sexual assault. The psychological effects of the wound remain fresh; the ability to deal with the results of the wound may never proceed past a certain point; the animosity inspired by the actions of the pedophile may grow, rather than shrink, as the victim learns The Rules and comes to understand how deeply the sexual abuse has affected her whole outlook on life.

The depression – the hopelessness – in the heart of the victim of sexual abuse may be so overwhelming that no amount of counseling or alcohol or anti-depressants or therapy can change the mind of the victim – that he has lost his childhood, been alienated from members of the opposite sex and has lost the ability to love another human being, wholly or at all.

Where these wounds cut deep into the psyche of a victim of sexual abuse and there is a remorseless ache that will not go away, the victim in the past has often chosen to end his suffering by suicide.

Beginning in 2005, however, The Rules underwent a transmogrification which, in hindsight, was predictable. The victim of sexual assault by a Priest on the Eastern Seaboard of the United States determined that rather than kill HIMSELF, he would kill the Priest who had caused him so much pain.

He bought a gun, tracked down his abuser and shot him dead.

He was charged with murder. As the facts came out, the charge was reduced to manslaughter. As more facts came out and a psychological profile of the accused was reviewed, it was determined that he would be charged at the end of the day with the offence of the unlawful discharging of a firearm.

He was given a suspended sentence.

Well. One can imagine thousands of pedophiles sleeping with two eyes open the night that case hit the news.

Then in the Spring of 2006 a 20 year old man from Nova Scotia traveled south to Maine. There are many American states that have laws requiring the publication of the names, addresses and photographs of people who have been determined to be sexual predators or a sexual danger to children. Maine is one of those states.

The man from Nova Scotia went to the doors of five men whom he had apparently identified on the State's Internet website as being registered sexual abusers of children. Of the five doors he went to, two men opened their doors and were shot dead.

The other three failed to open their doors. The 20-year-old, Stephen Marshall, was subsequently surrounded by police near Boston and killed himself with his own weapon rather than be captured.

These alarming killings are a not unexpected outgrowth of years of repression of the sexual abuse visited on children coming into contact with The Rules as they now are, modified by more and more knowledge. This violent self-help was something that society should have been anticipating.

As people from any underclass become more empowered, as they try their wings or, in the case of sexual abuse victims and for the purposes of this book, as they modify The Rules to fit their particular bundle of grief and depression, they push the envelope of behavior.

As with the women's movement, the African-American advance, the Latino advance, and gay rights, the movement begins tentatively and ultimately finds its place in society by pushing and pulling societal mores and societal opinion along with it.

The people who believe they have been failed by society, or who believe society does not feel their pain as THEY feel their pain, are more inclined to take up arms to redress their personal grievances.

In a case where rampant technocracy was deemed the enemy, the Unabomber blew things up. His case was almost unique. Those who abhor abortions will, from time to time, kill doctors who perform those abortions, but, once again, those who feel so strongly as to kill to protect the rights of the unknown unborn are likely fairly small in number.

There are far more people who have been sexually abused as children than anyone in the west has ever dared attempt to put a number to.

Let's say, then, in North America there are about 350 million people. Let's be very, very conservative and say that one in ten has suffered sexual touching or worse as a child. If thirty five million people, in North America were sexually abused as children, and if only one per cent of those opt for self help in dealing with their demons, this constitutes a powder keg of 350,000 people in the United States and Canada who may become violent unless we take steps to ameliorate the pain these victims carry with them every day.

When these victims figure out that they were not at fault for the sexual abuse, but that their abuser was at fault, all hell could break loose.

I have said earlier that a lawsuit is an imperfect manner of means to settle a grievance that deals with one person stealing the life, heart and soul of another – the unforgivable sin.

Money cannot give one back his peace of mind or sense of normalcy or belonging; possessions cannot dispel a lifelong depression; counseling cannot always rectify the tremendous psychological damage done when the very sense of selfhood and sense of safety of a child is brutally ripped away from him at the age of 5 or 15 by an uncaring pedophile.

When a victim is confronted with suicide as a real and even apparently desirable and necessary option, one cannot truly blame the victim if, before he terminates his own life, he thinks: "Why should I kill me? I didn't do anything wrong? Why don't I kill the bastard who put me through all this? Then, if I feel like it, I can still kill me. But at least that bastard won't be raping any other kids."

In a situation where a victim of sexual abuse is left with no options, he truly becomes dangerous to himself and one other – the person who abused him, or maybe even to many other people – pedophiles in general. Who can say what conclusions the victims of abuse may arrive at?

There is a good chance that there will be a spate of killings of child abusers over the next ten years as more and more victims learn The Rules in a new era when victims have become more powerful.

In California, and in many other states, the law requires that all sex offenders be registered with a central government agency which keeps an updated website showing the residence of each abuser.

If you live at 123 Any Street in San Jose you can go to the website, click on your city, click on your block and all the local registered sexual offenders will pop up on the map on your screen.

You may then see their address and what they look like and read the sexual offences they have been convicted of.

And this is a good thing.

Or is it?

Unintended consequences, again.

If I had been raped by John Fonebone in 1965 and I decided it was time to pay Mr. Fonebone a visit to get even with him, mayhem is just a point and click away.

The idea of a central registry for sexual offenders is a good one. The unintended consequences of these central registries may be to make it open season on pedophiles.

Or, as is perhaps the case of the young man from Nova Scotia, MY Mr. Fonebone may have passed away or be otherwise beyond my reach. I may then form the opinion that if I cannot take out my vengeance on my own Mr. Fonebone, I can at least take out someone else's, or two, or three pedophiles who abused other kids. Sort of the same as the victims of pedophiles who become homosexual-bashers, but with the result being that the convicted pedophile ends up dead.

In Brussels, Belgium, in late 2006, a 12-person jury acquitted a man named David Bouchat, who was 26-years-old and had figured out The Rules. He was found not guilty of murder after he killed the pedophile who had repeatedly sexually assaulted him when he was a child. His friend who helped him kill the pedophile was also found not guilty of murder.

You must know that I do not condone the killing of pedophiles. No one should. But not to emphasize that this will likely become a larger problem would be a grave mistake indeed.

The rights of pedophiles are protected in our society and it may be that these sexual abuse registries will be modified for the protection of pedophiles if more and more victims make use of them in order to murder their abusers.

A strange phenomenon has begun to occur in the community of those who are registered sexual offenders. Finding life difficult with the modern equivalent of a Scarlet Letter on their persons, convicted sex offenders have begun to congregate in groups.

In Miami, Florida, 19 or more men joined forces in 2008 and began to live together under a bridge. There they had access to a common kitchen, gym and living room, lived in tents and played video games.

Stung by the opprobrium of society, they slept together in harmony until the local authorities broke up the group.

Some of the former communards fled to makeshift camps in the Everglades rather than return to be monitored by the police. This apparently medieval societal unit is another result of the mismanagement of pedophiles.

Again, society comes late to the problem of sexual abuse. There is a great deal we must learn, and the time in which to learn, so that we can assist all the victims, and protect the abusers, is growing shorter each day.

While roaming gangs of sexual abuse victims will never be seen in our streets, those choosing to take solitary action after having been forced to live a solitary life may be with us until we get a handle on how to defuse the powder keg.

And people who have little to live for generally may not mind taking the cause of their despair down with them.

My advice to all people who were sexually abused and who may be thinking about murdering their abusers or other pedophiles is to get help from a counselor and a lawyer you trust.

Let the system, as imperfect as it is, deal with the abusers. Get clear of the abuse and the abusers. Then live the life you were meant to lead. Don't get down to your abuser's level.

It will diminish everything you have fought for and won so far.

Chapter 18

THE EFFECTS OF SEXUAL ABUSE ON ADULT AND CHILD

From time to time I have spoken of how sexual assaults have affected the lives of the young people who have been hurt. It is important to know the range of difficulties encountered by these children as they grow older.

In the 1950's and earlier, it was probably a widely-held belief that there was little or no permanent damage done to children from childhood sexual assault, even prolonged and painful rapes.

In 1972, Mel Brooks, a comedian, not a well known authority on sexual abuse, but a commentator on life, uttered these words as his character The Two Thousand and Thirteen Year Old Man: "If God had thought the gentles (read "genitals") were the most important organ, He would have put a skull over the gentles. But He put a skull over the brain. Let's talk plain. What do you care if someone comes over and plays with you and your gentles. It's a momentary thing. But if someone comes over and strokes your BRAIN, then you get all confused and you write out the wrong check."

As it turns out, it IS a big deal if someone plays with you and your gentles.

It was only when people who had been sexually abused as children began to come forward with their stories that doctors became aware that sexual abuse had long-lasting psychological effects.

Judges used to say, and some still say in private: "Why doesn't she just get over it? Why doesn't she just get on with her life? How long did it take, that rape? Ten minutes? Come on, that was fifty years ago. Why is she still crying about it?"

And many therapists, as we have learned, are not well-schooled in digging out the root cause of their patients' depression and anger. If the doctors cannot come to Court and educate the Judges, the Judges have nothing to go on.

There is much work to be done, educating all these folks.

Most stories which deal with historical sexual abuse emphasize that the sexual assaults took place 30 years ago, or 60 years ago. The implication is twofold: first, the victim should just get over it and second, what possible good can come from pestering the poor old pervert who sexually abused the child all those years ago?

The media misses the point in putting this spin on historical sexual abuse.

The victim is clearly NOT over it, and in order to GET over it needs to take a stand of some sort.

And the poor pervert, to the victim, is a living menace who might at any minute injure some other child like he or she did fifty years ago.

The victim knows this, and that is one of the reasons she has come forward.

It takes people a long time to deal with the devils in the attic caused by childhood sexual trauma. That some never do is understood.

Those who do come forward have chosen to plant their flag on a hill they are willing to die on for the sake of trying to put the pain behind them, for the sake of, at long last, warning others and for the sake of attempting to get finality with respect to the most important event of their life.

Make no mistake: when a child is sexually abused, that abuse defines his or her life from that point forward. The victim may lock the memories away, but the effects of the abuse manifest themselves, either continuously or periodically, either hugely or to a lesser extent, and forever.

The degree of the harm caused by the abuse is mirrored by the degree of control the abuse retains over the child as he grows, by the number of days or hours he can go without recalling the abuse, or by the psychological contortions that the abuse has imprinted into the emotional core of the victim.

Generally speaking, the more severe and prolonged the abuse is, the greater the after-effects are on the child as she grows and matures into adulthood.

While it may be true that a child will cast off the emotional damage done by someone who touches his or her genitals, the memory will always exist in the child, always to cause a psychological shudder of pain and disgust when it is recalled, always to make the child feel dirty, ill-used, and diminished at having been treated like an object for the sexual gratification of a pedophile.

The child has a diminished value of himself, a loss of self-worth, a lower sense of self esteem.

Those children who are anally or vaginally raped in a brutal fashion over a protracted period of time have other, larger, more tenacious psychological demons.

In a paroxysm of muddled enlightenment, the medical profession became convinced in the late 1990's that what these children were experiencing was Post Traumatic Stress Disorder, and that syndrome became the touchstone for professionals for many years.

Once the caregivers had managed to name the disorder, to put it in a box, as it were, they began to attempt to treat it as they would have treated a veteran of Vietnam who had seen his best friend blown apart while standing by his side.

The analogy was appropriate because something horrible had happened to these patients many years ago, the horror revisited the patients and the patients displayed a bundle of symptoms which were similar to those of a veteran who had seen horrible death in a horrible war.

Some of these symptoms – by no means all – are:

Depression
Suicidal Thoughts
Feelings of Worthlessness and Low Self Esteem
Nightmares
Anxiety
Intrusive Memories of the Horror
Fear of all sorts of things, some having to do directly with the sexual abuse, some not.
Fear of Intimacy
Anger

Sleep problems
Panic Attacks
Obsessive/Compulsive behavior
Always being on guard and alert
Drug or alcohol abuse as self-medication
Problems being sexually intimate
Self loathing
Inability or Impaired Ability to feel or show love or friendship
Inability to Trust some or all people
Fear of People touching your Body
Fear of Doctors' physical examinations
Inability to Concentrate
Anger at your parents for not protecting you better
Wearing baggy clothes – attempting to be unattractive (women in particular)
Difficulty Taking Orders from People in Authority

(If you were sexually abused and did not find one of your symptoms on this list it is not because you are different. I just ran out of paper. Your symptoms will be on the next list if you send them to me.)

Like Vietnam veterans, childhood victims of sexual abuse, left to their own devices, coped with this basket of symptoms by self medication (abuse of drugs and alcohol), acting out (blowing things up or sexually abusing others), dropping out of society, failing to achieve positions of responsibility commensurate with their levels of intelligence and members of their family or school cohort, having difficulty in finding and maintaining close relationships, particularly familial, spousal and sexual relationships, with concomitant feelings of isolation, loneliness, leading to a desire to live and be alone. In addition, both groups were inclined to be easily angered, and often became involved in abusive relationships where their spouses and children were targets of physical and emotional violence. The anger they carry often finds its outlet in the victims hurting the ones they love.

The framework was there that tied Vietnam Vets with victims of sexual abuse, yet there was much more involved in sexual abuse cases, because where some Vietnam vets experienced personal guilt, not all did, and when some - but fewer - Vietnam vets felt complicity in the horror, far from all did, and NO Vietnam vets became resigned to accepting their horror when it was occurring. And no Vietnam vets had to get into bed with the person who caused the horror and smell his breath and kiss him.

There is a reason that our forefathers described sexual abuse as "perversion".

The sexual act is supposed to be a mutually pleasurable one, but it is perverted when it is done with children. This perversion of the act from its traditional procreative or romantic usage is what makes a pervert of the pedophile.

When the victim becomes part of the act, as she must essentially be once she has struggled and screamed and done everything she can to stop the horror, she becomes a pervert in her own mind because she could fight no more and she was "just waiting for it to be over."

No Vietnam vet ever derived pleasure from seeing his best friend blown apart in front of his eyes, but as we have noted, genitals have no memory, no sense of revulsion, no sense of discrimination.

A diagnosis of Post Traumatic Stress Disorder, which has served its purpose by acknowledging the depth of the effects of sexual abuse on the psyche of the child, must be modified to permit the caregivers to delve deeper into the problem, to wring the last drop of poison out of the victim's system so that he or she can begin to heal with few remaining impediments to that healing lurking in the attic of the mind, waiting to creak open a door in the dark and attack the healing process.

The perversion of the act of lovemaking by a pedophile scars the child with complicity in that act because the child was unable to stop the act and therefore, in his or her mind, must have been indifferent to of the abuse. The child will tell himself or herself the story in the darkness of night and generally end with the phrase "Why didn't I stop it? Why didn't I say no?" - again confirming the advice and actions of the abuser that the abuse was "their secret."

The adult believes now, now that he knows The Rules, that the child let him down by not fighting back more, by not running away, by not killing the abuser, because that is what the adult would do if the abuser came into his room tonight.

The adult blames the child within him for the years of shame and anger.

But the child was unable to stop the abuse because of the power of the abuser, his position in her life and his position during the rape. She is now an adult and, with an adult's perspective, wonders why the child simply didn't run, or get a knife, or alert the household.

This continuing question leads to guilt which, in turn, reaffirms the complicit behavior of the child in the act which then, in turn, makes the child more certain of his or her own ultimate participation in the act.

"If I wasn't PART of it, why didn't I stop it?" the adult asks the child. "If I WAS part of it, I am as guilty as – or MORE guilty than – my abuser."

I say this again now because the children who were abused, who read these words, will derive comfort from my certain knowledge that their secret may now be told. And the kids need to hear again and again the truth that they are not alone in their feelings which, for so long, they have carried alone. I know those kids will read these words over and over again to make sure they say what they say.

They do.

You are not alone anymore.

It is safe to tell your story now.

There is hope if you want to take the next step.

I hope that, when you are ready, you will take the next step, which is to see a psychologist or psychiatrist who knows what to do to help you.

In the numerous medical reports I have read, in the conversations I have had with psychologists and psychiatrists, in the expert reports prepared for Court that I have read, I have never encountered a caregiver who has made these breakthroughs in a patient's treatment: why didn't you walk away from the abuse? Why didn't you kill the woman who was raping you? Why didn't you tell anyone?

The reason that the doctors fail is clear.

As human beings first, and as doctors sworn to do no harm, caregivers must heal, not hurt their patients.

Treating sexual abuse is a lot like treating a limb that has set improperly: you have to break it first in order to re-set it properly.

No doctor relishes having to dig through the layers of a history of abuse to learn the details of the rapes, and why the child appears to have accepted those rapes, then to take his patient through the various levels of the ways in which the prolonged sexual abuse has affected the life of his patient, then to try to put together a plan to help build a NEW psyche, one untroubled by the$memories of the sexual abuse.

This requires an intrusion by the therapist into the innermost parts of his patient's defenses which for years have been the private preserve of the patient and which he has literally guarded with his life.

The doctor must find a way into the castle keep of his patient's sexual abuse.

The patient will go to almost any length not to break faith with the child who was raped. The patient will give up anything to heal, but is loath to break faith with the little child he represents in that doctor's office.

Now the patient can take this book to his therapist, open this book at a page he has chosen, circle some words, hand it to his therapist and say "This happened to me... And here, on this page, this is how I feel..."

That is the next step.

And that will be a happy day for the patient and the doctor.

Because now the doctor can do what she does best.

When a doctor takes her patient back to the abuse, the patient spends far more time thinking of it than she ever would of her own volition. Usually, no one save the victim has had any input into the story. It is his or her own private account – never before published and never really intended to be published – of what happened to change his or her life all those years ago.

Now a doctor is going to be poking around in the story.

And here is the doctor's best opportunity to heal her patient.

Because the story has never had an outsider edit it, or even comment on it, the most reassuring thing that a doctor can say to a patient who has determined to disclose consists of eight words:

"I believe you. You're normal. I can help"

For years the patient/victim/survivor has thought he was a freak in a world full of normal people. He has always wanted to be normal, not appreciating that there is no "normal," but knowing that whatever normal is, he's not it.

When she is told that for all of the abuse she has suffered she has reacted in a normal fashion, like thousands of others before her, that everything that flowed from the abuse was almost pre-ordained, that she is a textbook case, then perhaps for the first time in her life she breathes a sigh of relief over her sexual abuse.

Maybe there is hope. She is not a freak after all. The doctor said so.

The trouble, of course, is that there is no textbook because there are an insufficient number of case studies and those case studies that have been undertaken do not grasp the nettle of the nature and consequences of sexual abuse.

But we must begin somewhere.

For all of you who are reading this because you wish to learn the truth about what happened to you and how it has affected you, this is my truth to you.

I have spoken with your brothers and sisters – members of the same unwilling society – and if they could speak directly to you they would say: "The truth is here. Now go and get a good doctor to help you and begin the healing journey of putting this behind you. It is part of your past. It belongs in your past. It does not define who you are today. You have power over it and the more power you have over it, the less power it has over you. We are all on your side, just as you are on our side. Good luck."

Of course, that is another thing about people who have been sexually abused: they are unlikely, as a group, to have a convention in Las Vegas any time soon.

While they share so much, and each is normal in his or her way, the stigma they carry now for something that was done to them years ago is still so strong for now, at least, that they cannot break it.

They will in time.

There is no real difference between children who were sexually abused and children who were hit on the head by a brick dropped from a three story building. Each was in the wrong place at the wrong time, and bears no culpability for their injuries. Neither wanted the event to occur. Each suffered a long-lasting trauma, and feels the effects of the injury today.

It is far more likely as I write this that children hit on the head by a brick will have a convention in Las Vegas before children who are victims of sexual abuse do.

But why?

The shame, the stigma that is self-imposed, the stigma imposed by society, all attaches to the little ones who were sexually abused. No unkind defense lawyer ever suggested that some child who was walking underneath a building was "asking for it" when the brick fell on his six year old head.

But lawyers, and even other human beings, sometimes suggest this of little sexual abuse victims.

Even some Judges have made mention of this, to their shame.

One Judge spoke recently in a case where a 4 year old girl was raped by her stepfather and said that the girl had been "dressed provocatively". Judges like this we don't need anymore.

No child asks for "it". Children don't know what "it" is. Adults know what "it" is.

Shame on Judges and all adults who can think, let alone say, let alone say in Court, that a 4 year old girl can ask for "it."

And shame on all the people who do "it" to any child.

The pleasure derived by an adult from "itting" a child may last a few minutes. The damage to the child "itted" lasts a lifetime.

Really, folks, if we ever want to see these kids kicking up their heels in Vegas, we're all going to have to pull together.

And if you're not part of the solution, you're part of the problem.

Like that Judge.

A word or two on triggers, now.

The nature of the trigger is as individual as the sexual abuse.

I am acting for a group of women now who were fondled and forced to perform oral sex on a Priest who had a habit of masturbating in their presence while using Pam vegetable oil spray on his penis. All of these women immediately think of the sexual abuse whenever they see Pam. Whenever they see a can of Pam or an advertisement for Pam, the trigger engages the memory of sexual abuse that happened forty years ago and the memory is almost as real and painful as if the abuse had happened yesterday.

A man I worked with was anally raped by his stepfather in a room that had a cactus plant in it. Now, whenever that man sees a cactus he returns in his mind to the scene and pain of the child he was while being raped. He will turn off a movie about the old west because he fears he may see a cactus.

Another boy, forced to have sex with a nun, remembers clearly the smell of her garments, in particular the odor of the starch used on her wimple. This man was triggered back to the abuse every time he walked past a laundry in his town and smelled the starch coming from there.

If the sexual assault took place in a 1975 Ford, seeing that car may be a trigger. Music may have been playing during a rape. That music is a trigger. One man has worked diligently to insure that he never comes into contact with Beatles music – carefully selecting all his radio stations and avoiding stores with canned music – because the music is a trigger. Ave Maria is a trigger for one boy. Another was triggered by a Harry Potter movie.

Short men, bald men, fat men, women with moustaches, Priests, nuns, crosses, jangling keys, the smell of bread baking, a certain television program, the sight of an eagle in flight, all of these have been triggers to take some of the people I have worked with back to the time and place where they were raped.

Sometimes the victims spend only scant seconds remembering the abuse when they are triggered. Others, particularly where the trigger is a strong one, may spend days reviewing the sexual abuse in their minds. During the review these people are not themselves. They become the young victim again. They are withdrawn, moody, depressed and sometimes even feel the body memory of the abuse, feel the pain in their anus or vagina, taste the sperm or vaginal secretions in their mouths. One man, who had been forced to perform oral sex on a Priest, could not get the body memory of the taste of semen out of his mouth. He ate candies all day until his teeth rotted and had to be all pulled out.

The triggers may come by stealth in the form of nightmares. Many children grow up believing the nightmare is part of their lives and may experience a severe one monthly or weekly or nightly. It is natural for them to have terrifying dreams of being pursued, trapped, shamed, isolated and hurt over and over and over again. Often the person violating them in their nightmares is faceless or a stranger. Sometimes the abuser in the nightmare is the abuser in their earlier life. In any case the nightmares bring terror.

Many victims sleep with the lights on, the door to their room open, the television or radio on. One woman I know has spent every night from age 13 sleeping in a closet. She would get into bed at first, then when her parents were not about, would move her bedclothes into her closet and shut the closet door, only to reverse the process in the morning so her parents never learned her secret sleeping arrangement. For years she chose places she rented and finally the house she bought with the bedroom closet being the most important factor in choosing her new home.

Other victims sleep with a knife, gun or baseball bat close at hand.

In almost every case the victim is a light sleeper, alert to any sound in the house which might indicate he is about to be attacked. Many victims never lose the fear that they will be raped again in the night. Long after their abuser is dead, these people continue to live in fear that the rapist will come by night to hurt them again.

Because sleep is fraught with so many difficulties, victims of sexual abuse take extraordinary measures around their sleeping. Many turn to alcohol or drugs to ensure that sleep comes quickly. Alcohol is the drug of choice in the first instance for most victims of sexual assault. For many of these people the first time in their lives when they are "free" is when they first have one drink too many.

The freedom is illusory, is temporary and comes at a great cost. However, to the person who has carried pain all her life and has had no relief from that pain, the realization that alcohol can numb, dull or banish the pain is a sort of miracle.

On the one hand, the victim can live with the fear of nightmares, triggers and memories of the sexual abuse including that certain dull throbbing in the soul that never leaves completely; on the other hand, six ounces of alcohol – like a wonder drug – makes that pain go away. For many, the choice is easy. The alcohol always works, although more and more may be required to achieve peace as time goes by.

The victim, wounded in so many ways, finding it difficult to function on so many levels, is now at risk of becoming dependent on alcohol. Far too many do.

Others turn to drugs or a mixture of drugs and alcohol to create a temporary surcease from the pain. When consciousness is an unremittingly painful state, unconsciousness is something which is often deeply desired. When the emotional pain is remorseless, the victim will pay almost any price to steal a few moments where the memory of being sexually assaulted is banished.

Many choose suicide.

I have long since ceased being judgmental about choices people make in their lives, up to the most important choice of continuing to live.

Those victims who have carried the weight of their sexual abuse for many years and been unable to lighten their burden through therapy and understanding should never be condemned if they decide they cannot continue on their healing journey. Suicide brings the same result as an alcoholic blackout. The only real difference is in the duration of the period of unconsciousness.

I hope that no one reading these words who was sexually abused will choose suicide without trying first to walk the healing path that so many have successfully walked already.

I know that for some people, they feel they will never get over the abuse and what it has done to them.

My message to those people is that you CAN get better.

Thousands of people just like you have gotten better.

I have seen them get better.

You can start to hope right now and as soon as you start to hope, you'll start to heal.

Society can be a harsh environment for people who do not carry a daunting emotional burden and a profoundly guilty conscience. Those of us lucky enough to have had a "normal" upbringing have difficulty enough sorting out our place in society.

Victims of severe sexual assault have many psychological factors in common. They think very little of themselves as human beings because they carry a dirty little secret about the time they had sex with someone and they have never told anyone about it and they feel it was their fault that this dirty act happened. They know it. They have beaten themselves up about it for years. There is nothing they can do about it now. They just have to live with it.

They aren't like the other kids. They have this secret, you see. The secret makes. them dirty. Dirtier than the other kids. They'd never dare talk to anyone about it. Then people would know how dirty they are. No one in history has ever felt like this. So dirty. This has never happened to anyone else. Not like this. That sex that happened to them when they were 8. That was their fault. They ASKED FOR IT. It was the way they dressed, the way they acted, they did something wrong that made that sex happen. It wasn't that man's fault that he raped me. It was my fault. I AM SO DIRTY. I AM SO ASHAMED OF MYSELF. I HURT SO BAD.

WHY DIDN'T I STOP IT? I MUST HAVE LIKED IT! OH, GOD I AM SO BAD.

This child, the one who sleeps in the space between the bed and the wall, the one who sleeps in the closet, faces the world with both hands tied behind her back. Her chance of becoming a thoroughly successful member of society is hugely diminished because the intrusive thoughts of the sexual assault, the most important event that has occurred so far in her young life, never fully relinquish their hold on her consciousness. Unless she is drunk or drugged.

Perhaps at her first drinking party, when she gets drunk and for the first time in her life, banishes the pain, she is astonished at the beneficial effects of alcohol. And later that night when a boy wants to have sex with her, well, why not? She feels pretty good. She's had sex before when she was raped and she has no virginity left to protect. And it's probably all she's good for. She's already dirty. Sex is dirty. He wants her. Sure, let him have sex with her.

What difference can it make? She feels worthless, unwanted, unloved, misunderstood. At least the boy likes her.

She becomes pregnant, the father disappears. She drops out of school and takes a McJob so that she can care for her child and all thoughts of further education disappear with her parenting the child.

Years later she meets a man who moves in with her and her daughter. As a stepfather, he begins to sexually abuse the young daughter and the circle is complete.

This scenario does not always or even often happen as I have set it forth.

But it happens enough.

Women victims of sexual abuse tend to have psychological difficulties that differ from those of their male counterparts. Many women become sexually active at a young age and have a large number of sexual partners in an attempt to recreate the feelings of being wanted that the sexual abuse brought with it. Others fear sexual contact of any kind and either eschew it completely or endure it when they must.

Other women, consciously or unconsciously fearing further abuse, put on weight or wear baggy clothing in order to present a less attractive target to the world. Because they believe they were sexually abused as a result of something they did wrong – enticing the man who abused them – they go to great lengths to avoid enticing any man again.

In my experience men do not share this trait of trying to present a more unattractive version of themselves to the world to avoid further abuse. Men, however, carry the burden of attempting to understand their sexual selves once they have been used as an object of desire by an adult male.

In their mistaken belief that they did something to deserve the sexual assaults, many men believe that they must be homosexual themselves to have attracted homosexual contact from a pedophile. Some men who were sexually abused by a male become homosexuals. They may have become homosexuals in any event. The sexual abuse, however, may have acted as a catalyst in their sexual maturation.

Other men who were raped or otherwise seriously sexually abused by a male will turn to heterosexual activity as a way to purge themselves of their doubts about their sexuality. They take as many female sexual partners as they can, in order to "prove their manliness".

This mindset may also come into play in the choice of a career. Where I live, a disproportionate number of men who were sexually abused become loggers because, Monty Python notwithstanding, it is believed that the logging industry attracts only "real men" and that no gay male would ever be found making a living hacking down trees with an axe.

In the case of both men and women, intimate contact becomes a problem in their lives. A caress, a kiss, a touch on the body can become a trigger which returns the adult to his or her childhood sexual trauma. Lovemaking is difficult when certain areas of the body or certain touches cause alarm in the partner.

One man I know cannot abide anyone – his wife included – touching him near his anus. He has had one rectal examination from a doctor in his life and swears he will never have another, even though his anus leaks feces because it was so damaged when he was raped as a child.

A woman I worked for became physically ill when her partner tried to put his tongue into her mouth because that was the behavior of her abuser.

Many men and women cannot tolerate having their partners perform oral-genital sex on them because of the memories the action invokes.

Making love to someone who has been sexually abused is something that requires patience and communication. Almost by definition a victim of sexual abuse is wary whenever someone begins to fondle his or her genitalia. So, once again, the best manner of proceeding is by explaining what happened in the past and how that affects the present. By talking it through, accommodations can be made which lead to a satisfactory sexual relationship, but victims of sexual abuse and their lovers almost always have one eye open for the third person in the bed during sexual encounters – the abuser.

He is never far from the victim's mind no matter how many years go by.

Almost all victims of sexual abuse present a face to the world that is sadder than most. They are forced to be introspective and in their introspection and guilt most now have a persona which is emotionally vulnerable, melancholy and docile. It may be that these people were docile as children – something which might have made them a target for the pedophile – but as adults, these victims are inclined to spend a lot of time in solitary silence, not likely to fall about laughing but more likely to be withdrawn and depressed for no apparent reason.

Depression is the great leveler. It has the capacity to throttle the will to strive, to make that victim feel so empty of any emotion but sadness that the person will not leave her bed unless the house catches on fire – and even then she will take a few minutes to decide whether to stay or go. Depression saps the life and force out of all who suffer from it. Depression is the antithesis of happiness. No person suffering a bout of depression can imagine a time when he will ever laugh again – ever take an interest in anything again – ever care about anything again.

Every victim of serious sexual abuse suffers from depression to some extent. Depressed people are usually not leaders. Depressed people are usually underachievers, and sometimes their depression becomes so overwhelming that life is no longer worth living.

The healing professions are gradually getting a handle on treating depression and the drug manufacturers churn out billions of anti-depressants a year. Severe depression can now be reduced to moderate depression; moderate depression to mild depression and so on. For those depressed victims of sexual abuse, therefore, there is hope.

But let us be clear, here. Depression is not what you feel when your mother or your dog dies. That is sadness; that is grieving; that is natural, normal and even beneficial.

Depression is when you wake up in the morning and feel so sad and empty that one of your very real options is to put a gun in your mouth and pull the trigger. Except you don't have enough life left in you to go get the gun THEN cross the room to get the bullets.

That's depression.

Rare indeed is the person who suffers from this condition, or a lesser version of it, who goes on to become the CEO of Microsoft or the President of the United States. Or, indeed, anything where she must show up everyday with a smile plastered on her face, a cheerful outlook on the world and a "can do" attitude. No one who suffers from moderate depression or worse will ever be described as a "self-starter".

More likely, a self-stopper.

Not surprisingly, many victims of sexual abuse become angry. They are, of course, angry at their abuser, but very few return to confront the abuser because the abuser still has power over them. Instead they take out their anger on their spouses, their children, their parents who failed to protect them, on society at large. Most of this anger is vented by men, mostly in a physical manner, mostly by beating people up, sometimes homosexual people…

Absent a confrontation with the actual abuser, the victim makes do with the next best thing. He often develops a hatred of homosexuals – men who have anal intercourse with other men and, by inference, he thinks, with young boys like he was. Any homosexual who approaches this angry victim of sexual abuse suggesting that they engage in a homosexual encounter puts his life at risk, for he has set the match to a powder keg.

On occasion, this event will give the victim of sexual abuse the idea and the impetus to begin frequenting gay establishments with the sole purpose of "gay bashing" in mind. I have never known a woman to engage in similar behavior, but I have known many men who do.

Women, however, seem to suffer from panic attacks where men are less likely to.

A panic attack is variously described as an increased pulse rate, a fear that one is having a heart attack or losing control of one's functions, or living in an "unreal world", often accompanied by sweating, panic and fear of imminent disaster to the self. These episodes, which are normal for most victims of severe sexual abuse and other kinds of abuse, can come in a flash while giving a speech or driving a car or walking across a street or in a checkout line. They can happen once a year or once a week or once a day. They can last for hours.

Most men who were sexually assaulted as kids, and some women, have difficulty taking orders, difficulty with authority figures like policemen. They have been told to suck a man's penis when they were seven; the man ejaculated in their mouth. They are now 35. If someone tells them what to do now, they may react aggressively towards that person. This makes for a difficult relationship with the rest of society, especially if you are a man seeking employment. Pretty soon someone in authority is going to tell you what to do. If you react the way you are inclined to – and most do, sooner or later – there goes another shot you may have had at being CEO of Microsoft. And a lot of loggers, told what to do one time too many, may just pick up their axe and quit on the spot.

Most victims of sexual abuse – particularly males – do not play well with others. Some do not even care if they run with open scissors. They may appear socially retarded because they do not trust themselves with other people and they do not trust other people with them. They prefer to live an isolated, lonely, albeit safe life.

They drink too much, they often eat too much – or too little – they are aggressively antisocial, do not enjoy being the center of attention, are unable to let their emotional guard down and are unable physically and emotionally to give love.

Oh, and they're nervous. They often suffer from anxiety, which is a catchall word meaning jumpy, fearful, edgy, or terrified, depending on the circumstances.

Many men and women who were sexually abused as children develop a condition known as agoraphobia. Meaning literally "fear of the market place" in Greek. The condition manifests itself as a desire to stay in a familiar place where you have things under control – usually your house – rather than going out into the world.

If you are a person who is fearful of running into his abuser or is triggered to remember sexual abuse by men with curly hair, or if you have panic attacks when walking down the street, or if you are so depressed you cannot get out of bed for days on end, or if you drink a lot of alcohol and do a lot of drugs to numb the pain of your consciousness of sexual abuse, the likelihood may be that you will want to stay in the safety of your home rather than venturing far afield where you have given up control over your surroundings. This condition becomes so entrenched that it is no longer a conscious choice. The person sometimes simply cannot and will not leave his house. For anything.

On the other hand, agoraphobia may be a free-standing symptom of the consciousness of sexual abuse, arising in the psychological makeup of the victim all on its own.

Either way, agoraphobia is recognized as one of the bundle of major emotional difficulties suffered by many who were sexually abused. Agoraphobia may be mild, and may present as an unwillingness to be in a crowded place or a preference to do all of one's shopping on a single day to get it over with.

Not enough is known about agoraphobia and a lot of doctors treat it by throwing pills at it.

Without sedation a severe agoraphobic taken from his home against his will would suffer a massive panic attack, the equivalent of the central nervous system having a heart attack. The severely afflicted agoraphobic believes he or she will lose his mind or suffer a nuclear emotional meltdown equivalent to the China Syndrome if he or she is removed from his womb-like safe place.

This self-imposed imprisonment in the home makes for yet another bundle of results of sexual abuse such as unemployment, weight gain, chemical dependency, ill health and family and spousal relationship problems.

Not every victim of childhood sexual abuse suffers from all of these symptoms.

Most victims, however, suffer from some of them, and those who do continue to lead lives of desperation, usually quiet desperation.

The reason the desperation is quiet is that most victims do not have sufficient self confidence to stand up on their own feet and say: "Hi. My name is John Doe. I was sexually abused by my neighbor, Fred Fonebone when I was 7 and he was 45. He put his penis in my anus. It hurt. It continues to hurt today. It is part of my conscious being. He did it lots of times and as a result, I suffer from a number of things loosely described as Post Traumatic Stress Disorder. These things include depression, drug and alcohol abuse, panic attacks, anger, sexual dysfunction, flashbacks, fear and agoraphobia. I sleep with the lights on, am afraid of cops and judges, I don't take orders from anybody, I have to be heavily medicated or drunk just to leave my house and I like to kick the shit out of fags. Other than that, I'm just an average guy…"

It will be a while before any John Doe feels comfortable enough to give this speech, so I am giving it now for him and for all his brothers and sisters until they each find their own voice.

There are two final things to mention. Some women who were vaginally raped as little girls have difficulty becoming pregnant because of the damage done to their reproductive organs, and may have other, similar problems. This is a condition I have only recently become aware of because, like the men who go through life with anuses that leak, women are not keen on speculating how the pedophile's penis may have impacted her internally. Because they are ashamed, patients will not disclose this information voluntarily to doctors. Those people can now, if they want, take this book to their doctor and say "I think this may have happened to me."

I would like to say again for the kids who were raped and did not find their symptoms here that I could not write every symptom down. That does not mean that your particular symptoms are less valid or less worthy or less normal. They are normal because they are your symptoms. Write me. Honestly. I'll put your symptoms in the next book, if you want. Please contact me at:

www.unforgivablesins.com

This brings me to the next chapter on the pedophile's new tool…

Chapter 19

OMFG!! IT'S THE INTERNET!

Where dirty old men used to hang around schools and playgrounds in an attempt to lure children to their side for sexual purposes, they now employ the Internet. This is not to say that schoolyards and playgrounds are that much safer, but to emphasize how Internet technology has been transformed by pedophiles into a new means of sexually assaulting kids.

In the case of the Internet, the parents of the children who are targets of predators are often on the outside looking in. Any parent, if she thinks about it, knows that pedophiles congregate where children congregate. It's what pedophiles do. And a mother knows that a child in a playground, park or schoolyard is vulnerable to the dirty old man in the raincoat. Parents are familiar with this scenario and are accustomed to guarding their children against the man in the raincoat. They think they understand the playground problem.

Parents are generally not familiar enough with the Internet to guard their children from the pederasts who lurk there in their millions. These parents, in this generation, must become knowledgeable about what their kids are doing on the Internet. While the children, for the most part, are technologically superior to their parents, the parents are superior in their knowledge of the seamy ways of the world and that knowledge gives them the upper hand over their kids and the pedophiles.

Unlike the playground and the schoolyard, however, you cannot drive around the Internet to make sure the kids are alright. The kids will be able to look after their kids, but meanwhile what are you parents to do?

If the children have already been taught that bad people will try to touch them for sexual purposes and how to say no in the face of such a confrontation, they may still find themselves face-to-face with a pedophile they encounter in cyberspace unless special care is taken by their parents to learn what their children are doing on their computers for hours each day.

The Internet has become a place where children go to try their wings, to advance their social skills, to talk with kids of the opposite sex, to make the first halting steps toward boy-girl relationships, to make girl-girl friendships and boy-boy friendships. To become part of a larger society.

Fifty years ago these steps would have been taken at school dances or house parties chaperoned by adults who knew exactly what to watch for in the way of unacceptable behavior. The chaperones had been young once themselves…. Fifty years ago the kids would have gone to the movies together, or sporting events at school or otherwise.

Thirty years ago the site of these first steps toward interkid relationships became the malls, the convenience stores and the video game parlors. Parents were a bit buffaloed by how to crack this new social structure that their pre-teens and early teens had found, but if parents were buffaloed, so, too, were pedophiles.

Even the most engaging fifty year old pedophile would have difficulty blending in with a group of children hanging out at the mall.

The U.S. Department of Justice estimated in 2004 that one out of every 5 children on the Internet between the age of 10 and 17 is the target of an OPEN sexual advance at some point every year. The number of covert attempts to sexually ensnare children is unknown. However, we may take it as a given that any child on the Internet for an hour a day will be the target of a sexual predator at least once each year and probably a great deal more.

The question, of course, is how your child will respond to each sexual advance.

The Internet has given the children both a place to congregate and to speak with one another outside the hearing of parents and has given the pedophile a perfect way to disguise himself. On the Internet a pedophile can assume any identity. He can be a friendly father figure, an older teen, or a 13 year old girl worried about who likes her.

A skilled pedophile – and remember, they are very good at what they do – can adopt any persona that attracts the kind of children he is attracted to precisely because he knows these children so well. He spends time with them. He listens to their problems, shares their enthusiasms, sympathizes when they suffer setbacks and cheers them on when they have a victory. He learns how to talk like they talk. He is a perfect friend. Or would be if it were not for the fact that he needs these children for his sexual gratification. He will spend hundreds of hours talking to one child on the Internet knowing that at the end of the day that child will be in the same room as he is and he will rape that child.

This is part of the excitement for the pedophile, wooing the children into his presence.

The pedophile on the Internet is highly motivated by his sexual need. He is cunning. He is tireless. He feeds the small child everything that that child wants to hear about himself: that he is smart, good looking, well liked, cared for and loved – by the pedophile.

The pedophile becomes the most important person in the young child's life.

Because the child is getting from the pedophile precisely what she should be getting from her parents – love, respect, support and understanding, the child looks forward to her secret time with the pedophile more than she does to the 13 minutes the average child spends with her boringly clueless, out-of-touch parents each day.

When the girl's New Best Friend suggests that they meet – by coincidence he will be staying in a motel just two blocks from the young girl's house on Sunday afternoon when the girl's parents, as he has learned, are always out – the young girl can hardly wait to meet her new friend for the first time.

And he has a DVD with all her favorite videos that he's made especially for her – and they'll be eating pineapple pizza and banana ice cream – her two favorite foods. Why of course she'll go and meet her New Best Friend, and she'll only be gone an hour and he won't be back in her city for another six months and she won't have to tell anyone where she's going, not that there's anything to worry about or anyone to tell. They're going to play the new Xbox game she's been wanting to play!

She knows that her New Best Friend is a 14 year old girl, so nothing dangerous will happen, so she doesn't need to check with her mother, who'd just get all bent out of shape….and want to come along to meet her friend and that would be a drag.

Her New Best Friend is, in fact, a forty year old pedophile who has been convicted twice before of "sexual interference" (whatever that may be).

And her parents come home on Sunday evening to find their twelve year old daughter – the light of their lives – their only child - has gone missing and no one knows a thing about where she is and they call her friends – what are the names of her friends? – and then after another hour they call the police and the police know nothing until two hours later when they call back to tell the parents that their daughter has been brutally raped and strangled to death in a motel two blocks from their house and they hope to find the killer and they are deeply sorry for the parents' loss.

They have some of the killer's DNA to work with. There was some semen…

The Internet opens the door to propinquity.

Indeed, the Internet opens the doors to an infinite number of rooms where our children go for the sole purpose of testing their wings as social beings and making new friends.

If pedophiles had wanted to design a foolproof system of luring children to their sides, pedophiles would have invented the Internet.

Your job as a parent is to know as much as your child knows about chat rooms and to make every effort to spend time with your child so that he is comfortable telling you a bit about what he is talking about and about the various chat rooms and other sites he visits on the Internet.

Of course one of the reasons the chat rooms are so popular is precisely because there are no adults there – no one monitoring the kids' behavior and telling them what they can and cannot say. Like a tree fort in cyberspace, kids in a chat room expect to be able to behave like kids with no adults present.

All the more reason that parents should speak with their children, not at them, about who's saying what in the chat room. If this means becoming familiar with the comings and goings of Hannah Montana and who's a hunk at school and things that appear to you to be inconsequential, then get in there with both feet. It probably won't hurt you to know what Miley Cyrus' favorite shade of lipstick is on alternate Fridays, or that the rapper, Heavy Snoop Baby, has platinum grills.

Think of it as sharing in your child's interests.

You know.

Being a parent.

If you respect what your child has to say, your child will respect what you have to say. If a child respects you, the child will tell you that she has met a friend in a chat room who has a room in a motel this Sunday and she's been invited to go over for pizza and what do you think, should she go?

And that question makes all the knowledge you have gleaned about the names of Miley's seven shih-tzus worthwhile.

As I said before, Marisha Pessl has had one of her characters say, "life hinges on a couple of seconds you never see coming." When those seconds arrive you must be as sure as you can be that your child will act to protect himself from the disguised pedophile. The key is to ensure that when those seconds DO arrive, you have had the opportunity to put in place the wisdom you have which your child does not yet have.

An example of how the chat room works was reported by the FBI in 2006. A 13 year old girl logs on to an AOL chat room and, almost immediately, is besieged by men, the first of whom ask "r u a virgin?"

Well, the "girl" is not thirteen. She is an elderly male FBI agent. And unfortunately, the FBI agent says that finding people who want child pornography on the Internet is "like shooting fish in a barrel."

Well, we have to start somewhere.

Let's shoot those fish in that barrel and then let's clean out all the other barrels.

The phrase "r u a virgin" brings to mind yet another thing you will need to know – the latest short forms born of Instant Messaging. This is not rocket science, but it will require some research on your part. For example, if you do not know what the meaning of OMFG is, which I used to begin this chapter, look it up on the Internet.

And look up DILF.

And, yes, your little daughter talks like this.

Now, what do we do about a woman in Alberta who met a man from Toronto on the Internet. The man persuaded the woman to have sexual intercourse with her own son, vaginally and orally. He was six years old. She sent pictures of the sexual abuse to the man and he put the pictures on the Internet so that, for a price, any other pedophile wishing to do so could see the pictures. This woman was not emotionally well enough to have a child in her care. That has been remedied.

Her son has been taken from her. He is safe now. Except for the memories he will always have of his mother sucking his penis and being forced to stick his tongue in her vagina.

What is the appropriate punishment for such a mother? It is up to you, by your votes and your letters and your discussions, to tell the Judges what is appropriate for this mother. Judges don't know unless they hear from you.

Obscenity is defined as conduct which goes beyond the standards of the community. You are the community. Define things for your Judges. Otherwise, the Judges may think that what this mother did to her son is not as big a deal as you know it is. Judges sometimes need help, as we have seen.

Let me tell you for a minute about a young man in Kingston, Ontario. He's 21 years old and is very talented. His talent involves being on the Internet and talking to girls who are aged 9 to 15. Girls from all around the world. Hundreds of girls. He learned how to hack into the email accounts of these kids, and to read who their friends were that they chatted with, then he emailed those other girls pretending to be the girl whose account he had hacked into. Because he had read the girl's emails, because he was so good at being a pedophile, he could talk like her on the Internet.

When he emailed the girl's friends pretending to be the girl, he coaxed the friends into taking off their clothes in front of their video monitor. Then he had pictures of a naked teenage girl that she thought she was sending to her girlfriend for fun.

Once he had the girl's naked pictures, he sent the worst naked picture back to the girl and told her he was really a man and not her friend at all and said he would email the naked picture to her parents and all the girl's friends. With the benefit of the emails he had read, he would then name those friends.

So the girl masturbated in front of the camera when he told her to. The girl did anything he wanted after that, because the shame became worse and the threats became more violent. He threatened to kill the girl if she did not continue to commit debasing sexual acts on camera.

He stayed in touch with the girl for month after month.

Think of the terror, think of the shame that this young girl carried with her every day while this was going on. And for all the days after. Multiply that terror and shame by hundreds of girls. Because that's what this swine in Kingston did. To hundreds of girls. And if he can do it, anyone can.

The swine's name is Mark Bedford. He is unemployed. He lives at home with his parents. As I said, he's 21.

What should a Court do with Mark Bedford?

You decide.

Because the Court sentenced him in 2008 to three years in prison.

Out in two.

People like Mark Bedford would have no chance of hurting another child if the child came to her mother after the first contact and said "Mom, I just did something stupid on the computer. I made a mistake. Can you help me?"

That should be your son or daughter coming to you.

Only you can make that happen.

In a survey carried out by Kids Help Phone in Toronto in 2008, a group of teens responded to a questionnaire. More than half were under 14 and about 70% were girls.

About one-fourth of these kids said they had been "in love" with someone they had met only on the Internet. About half said they had a webcam and almost the same number had a computer in their bedroom.

And about half of these kids said they had given personal information to their online "friends" to prove their friendship.

This is how Mark Bedford was able to perform the evil that he did.

And this is precisely what your daughter and son need to know.

But even the best mother/daughter or father/son relationship can fail when the pressure is on for it to succeed – when the sexual and emotional wellbeing of your child is at stake.

To guard against this failure, or until you are certain that you have the lines of communication open with your son or daughter you may wish to consider monitoring your child's Internet activities. Yes, I know this is unseemly, an invasion of privacy, a breach of trust and a breach of the good faith you are trying to establish with your kids.

My suggestion is that you advise your child periodically, say once a month, "Be careful who you talk to and what you say on the Internet –you never know who's watching."

The kids will probably blow you off, but you've warned them, sort of.

And one of the people watching will be YOU.

There are a number of decent programs which allow you to spy on your children's Internet conversations. (You can, if you wish, use the word "monitor" instead of "spy." The correct word is "spy"). One you might wish to google is Spector Pro. For a few dollars and a few hours of your time a week, you can be relatively certain that your children are safe on the Internet.

You will learn things that make your head spin and you will hear things that make you wish you hadn't, but do not be drawn into correcting your daughter over some posting she made concerning what she imagines to be the sexual positions adopted by you and your husband. Stay away from that. You are there to keep her safe.

I am not comfortable with you spying on your son.

I am less comfortable with your son being raped.

The call is yours.

Or perhaps you have not made up your mind yet.

Alan Webster may help you to make up your mind. He's an Englishman who used to live in a little town called Hatfield.

Where he is now is in jail because, when he was 40 years old, he was babysitting a 12-*week*-old little girl for some neighbors.

And he raped that baby.

And he took pictures of himself raping that baby.

And he put the pictures on the Internet.

Because he put the pictures on the Internet, he was caught and sentenced to life in prison.

Had he not put the pictures up for the world to see, he would probably have gotten away with the rape.

Is life in prison – even if this guy stays in jail for life, which is highly unlikely – a sentence that you feel is appropriate for Mr. Webster?

In St. Thomas, Ontario, a man who raped his 4-year-old daughter live, on the Internet, so another pedophile could watch, was sentenced in 2007 to four years imprisonment. The Judge who sentenced him called the crime a "sickening" breach of the trust which should exist between a father and his daughter. Yes. It was a sickening breach of trust.

I wonder if the Court was concerned that this little girl would suffer because her father was in jail, and thus gave him less time in prison so he could spend more QUALITY time with his family upon his release.

The Internet, then, is a triple whammy for sexual abusers of children. It gives pedophiles access to like-minded pedophiles, who share tips on how to lure children; it provides a notice board for posting pictures of children being raped, and it provides a safe place for pedophiles to meet their intended victims.

Canada now has a law against luring children over the Internet for the purpose of sexually assaulting them. This law, like most new criminal laws, will need some shakedown time before Judges and lawyers know what the law is capable of doing and how best to use it.

In 2004 this law was the subject of what I would deem judicial negligence when a 35 year old man, who had posed as a 19 year old man on the Internet, lured an 11 year old girl to his apartment and kept her there for 15 harrowing hours while attempting to rape her. He managed to get his semen into the girl's vagina, but the Judge found that that did not constitute rape and the man was sentenced to 21 months in jail.

The public – that's you – should be outraged about such a sentence.

The maximum penalty in Canada for luring a child into a sexual encounter over the Internet is five years in prison, out in two-and-a-half to three years.

This is not enough.

The pedophiles who rape children have an extremely high rate of recidivism. That means they'll keep on doing it after they're caught and punished and released back into the world.

Raping children is what hardwired pedophiles do, what they want to do and what they will always want to do, no matter how many years they spend in prisons. If society is fortunate enough to catch them once doing what it is they do, these pederasts should never have an opportunity to rape children again.

Full stop.

People who vote can change the criminal law. Vote for someone who will increase sentences and consider the castration of pedophiles who offend more than once.

Castration is a drastic measure. But is it more drastic than the rape of a child? If you were forced to choose between your son or daughter being raped and removing the testicles from the rapist, which outcome would you choose?

And it is no help to your son or daughter to remove a man's testicles AFTER the rape. At best, this may help the son or daughter of an unknown couple, sometime in the future.

China has weighed in. In 2006 Chinese officials nabbed 28 year old Chen Hui, an entrepreneur who made his money by selling access to pornographic websites he had constructed. He was sentenced to life imprisonment. In China life imprisonment means life imprisonment. And, in case he missed the point, he also had to pay a fine of $12,500.

We have enough statistics now in order to say that after a pedophile gets out of jail – pays his debt to society - he will likely again do something sexually harmful to children.

Now, do we follow this guy around after he is freed? Do we put his picture up in Post Offices? On trees? Because if we did, the trees would be covered with pictures of men aged 20 to 90, most looking a bit scruffy, all wanting to sexually assault your children.

In the jurisdiction where I live, the government hires "handlers" to follow pedophiles released from jail wherever they go.

I kid you not.

Of course the pedophiles must first be categorized as "extremely dangerous predators" before they are entitled to this escort service.

The BC Corrections Service seems quite pleased with itself that it has managed to get Court orders to have handlers follow these swine. Brian Lang, Director of BC Corrections, said in 2006 that this method of safeguarding children is "setting precedents."

Well, there are good precedents and not-so-good precedents.

In late 2005 two of these Handlers were traipsing around in the wake of a swine called Shaun Deacon, a 40-year-old who had spent most of his adult life in prison. He was a repeat sexual offender.

Director Lang said that he was watching the Deacon case with a lot of interest because "however it turns out…" it will affect the government's ability to "manage people like him."

Whoa, Nelly.

"However it turns out"? Just what does that little phrase connote?

It might turn out well, do you think? And it might not. These appear to be the two options. I guess it could turn out sort of wishy-washy, too.

So three options, then.

And if it does not turn out so well? It turns out badly, is that right as well?

Badly for who? Badly for BC Corrections? Badly for the Court? Or badly for the child who may be raped by Shaun Deacon?

Is that what turning out badly might mean?

Deacon was such a likely prospect to sexually abuse more kids if he was let out that most of the halfway houses had rejected him as too risky a prospect to be in their care. One of the halfway house supervisors said "If you were to put Deacon in the community unsupervised for half an hour, he'd re-offend. I think his risk is extremely, extremely high."

Hmmmm.

Why is this man not in jail?

Oh, wait. His Court documents require him to take "libido-reducing" drugs every day. Well, that solves that. Just as long as he keeps swallowing those libido-reducing drugs and has a couple of Handlers on his tail... Handlers who are paid $20 an hour and work in two twelve hour shifts, seven days a week to ensure he does not sexually assault another child... we can all relax.

Yes, it must be tough on Shaun Deacon, having the Handlers around all the time. But apparently they do what they can to ease his burden. They dress appropriately, try to blend into the crowd, let him have a normal life. Try to be discreet. Eat an apple when he eats an apple. Like that.

And the Handlers only need about $180,000 a year to look after him

Sounds fair.

But wait!

Shaun Deacon is being oppressed! He says so! He's back in Court trying to get some of the more "onerous" terms of his supervision cancelled. Perhaps not appreciating the steps society and the Court have taken so he can be free, Shaun Deacon has also become "manipulative and spiteful," according to social workers.

And, for social workers, "manipulative and spiteful" are words equivalent to nuclear war because most social workers speak in a blathering fog of euphemisms or socialworkerspeak.

Apparently Shaun Deacon, no fool, began to take long, long walks for hours each day, looking back occasionally to see if his Handlers were keeping up.

For $20 an hour, damn straight they'd better be keeping up.

Deacon would go without food. So would his Handler. He would go for hours without bathroom breaks. So would his Handler. He would sit in a store for hours, doing nothing. So would his Handler.

Hey, no one said it was easy money, that $20 an hour.

But at least Shaun Deacon was not sexually harming kids.

On the other hand, anyone with a grain of sense would have to wonder why a Judge would make this kind of life for a man whose risk to re-offend was "extremely, extremely high."

I wonder if Director Lang has enough information now to conclude that perhaps it would be of benefit to society and the children to just lock Shaun Deacon up and throw away the key.

One of the problems we all face is that if and when the Shaun Deacons of the world are finally caught and convicted, we do not have a good idea what to do with them.

But time is our enemy here, and we cannot afford to dawdle.

If we put them in jail, we must ensure that no harm comes to them. As we know, pedophiles in prison are the slime on the bottom of the shoe on the lowest rung of the prison hierarchy. If other prisoners get near a pedophile, that pedophile will get a thorough drubbing, because prisoners have a code. I'm not certain what else is in the code, but I know this is. So, in jails pedophiles are kept in what is called "protective custody".

All the pedophiles are locked up together.

I recently went to a jail that has six living modules, or units, where prisoners are kept depending on the severity of their crimes, the likelihood they may attempt to escape, and so on. The module I went to was the one where the sexual abusers were confined. I spoke there with a man who had been convicted – unfairly, he said – of having sexually assaulted his stepdaughter. He told the Court that he had been drunk, and when he came home he went into the wrong bedroom, that of his 13 year old stepdaughter, and he was so unsteady on his feet that he fell over and when he fell over one of his fingers somehow ended up in the vagina of his stepdaughter and that's when she woke up and started screaming.

And that was the story he told the Judge.

He was in jail since the Judge, for some reason, did not believe the man's story.

Most jailed sexual abusers know that if they are released into the general population of prisoners, where bank robbers and murderers live, their lives are at risk.

I suppose we could do away with protective custody for pedophiles in jail.

Once the pedophile has served his time, out he goes again.

As I have said, some jurisdictions in the USA and Canada have set up registries for sex offenders when those people are released into society, having paid their debt to society for what it was they did to a little girl or boy.

In Ontario, Canada's most populous Province, there were about 7,000 convicted sex offenders on this registry in 2006. The purpose of registering sex offenders is to keep an eye one them, and they are required to tell police when they move into or out of an area in the Province. While this affords some protection for the kids, it is far from foolproof and approximately 5% of the sexual offenders in Ontario have gone underground, not registering with the police, lost to the system. The penalties for doing so are high – up to two years more in jail – but these pedophiles have decided to risk their liberty in order to avoid having to report.

What could they possibly be up to that they risk going to jail over?

Which brings us back to the Internet.

Every day comes some fresh horror thrown our way by sexual abuse brought about by the Internet.

In March 2006 a worldwide investigation beginning in Canada led to charges being laid against 27 people in the U.S., Australia and the United Kingdom on charges involving on-line video of the live rape of children. But these are just numbers.

One human face to put against the numbers is that of Masha Allen, a 13 year old American kid who defines bravery. In 2006 Masha told a U.S. House of Representatives committee about how she was used as a sex slave from the age of 5 on. She was born in Russia and ended up in an orphanage owing to her parents' treatment of her. In 1998 a man from Pittsburgh, Pennsylvania, showed up at the orphanage, adopted her and took her back to Pittsburgh. Things were looking up for Masha.

But when the man got Masha to his house in Pittsburgh, he began to rape her.

Then he took pictures of her being sexually degraded by him and put those pictures on the Internet where other pedophiles paid to see her, age six, having sexual acts done to her by the man who adopted her. But the money did not come in fast enough, so the man in Pittsburgh sold Masha to a friend of his in Detroit, who was also a pedophile and whom he had met through the Internet.

Matthew Mancuso was an engineer pedophile and he paid $15,000 for Masha.

Mancuso, her new owner, raped Masha. He tortured her. He fed her very poorly to keep her thin and looking young. He did not want her to look her real age – 10 – because that reduced her value on the Internet. Mancuso then took pictures of her having sex with him and sold them on the Internet to make back some of the money Masha had cost him.

Mancuso was known to the police for being involved in child pornography. He had once raped his own daughter. The police in Detroit found out that Mancuso had purchased Masha, they arrested him and put him in jail.

He is in jail now.

Masha has been adopted by another family.

The U.S. government is pondering whether to charge people convicted of downloading child pornography from the Internet up to $150,000.

And Masha may be able to sue people who looked at her pictures on the Internet when she reaches adulthood.

Not good enough.

In addition to being a magnet for pedophiles seeking meetings with children, the Internet has quickly become the most successful method in history of disseminating child pornography. A pedophile with a computer and a credit card can access any pornographic image he or she wishes to view as long as people are willing to debase children – including their own children – for sexual gratification and money.

Live acts of babies being raped by dogs, being urinated on, being defecated on, having penises put in their mouths and anuses and being burned by cigarettes, are common on sites that tens of thousands of perverts pay a lot of money to see EVERY DAY on the Internet.

Every day more and more people are using new technology to make and distribute pornography using children, resulting in more and more victims and every day the producers of this pornography destined for the Internet become smarter and more sophisticated – and more wealthy.

Every day the children who are violated become younger and younger. The universal truth about child-related pornography or any pornography is that the person who sees it has a stark need to see more and more graphic depictions of more and more degrading sexual abuse of younger and younger children to get the same thrill he once did.

It is this doubling and redoubling of graphic abuse which has led consumers of pornography to NEED to see depictions of women being killed in order to achieve sexual gratification through pornography. So-called "snuff" films have been available for years. The likelihood is that snuff films involving children – even babies – have already been made and that people are paying money to watch children being raped and then killed for their sexual gratification.

For all those who produce and profit from child pornography, the death penalty or life imprisonment with no possibility of parole is the only fitting punishment.

For those who consume this pornography and cause the children to be debased, the penalty should be castration and life imprisonment.

But that is just my opinion.

What do you think would be an appropriate sentence?

A collateral question is how do we catch these swine? Fortunately, this is an easy one. We instruct our legislators to put in place a massive police presence to monitor the Internet so that everyone who thinks about contacting someone else on the Internet for an illegal sexual purpose is never sure whether he is talking to the police.

In 2007, the entire number of police in British Columbia detailed to monitor the Internet for pornography was – wait for it – five. There are, conservatively estimated, 25 children in British Columbia defiled sexually every month to provide pornography for Internet pedophiles and there are five police officers scanning the Internet for pictures of these boys and girls.

If you want more police stopping children from being raped to make pictures and fewer police giving out traffic tickets or busting people for having drugs, call your local legislator.

While it is true that the anonymity of the Internet works both ways, we cannot turn that to our advantage without the numbers being higher on the good guy side. As it is now, the bad guys on the Internet outnumber the good guys by 1,000 to 1.

But if the swine who participate in the sexual abuse of our children on the Internet believe that there is a fifty-fifty chance that every time they arrange a sexual experience with a child they are dealing with a police officer who may throw them in jail and cut off their testicles, they may think twice and try to find a more acceptable outlet for their perversions, or just sit quietly in a corner.

They are not ungovernable people, slaves to their sickness, are they?

They have some self control, these perverts, do they not?

And there is yet another reason to track down these swine, as if another were required. The likelihood is that if a pervert possess child pornography he has already sexually assaulted a child. The National Center for Missing and Exploited Children in the U.S. has undertaken a study of 1700 people convicted of possessing child pornography. Forty per cent of those had already sexually assaulted a child. This is just one study and is probably a conservative one. Similar results have been recorded by the Center for Addiction and Mental Health in Toronto, where a clear link between possession of child pornography and pedophilia has been found.

In the spring of 2006, Carl Treleaven, the organizer of a child pornography ring with a worldwide reach over the Internet, where hundreds of pedophiles shared graphic pictures of child sexual abuse as well as information on how to avoid being caught and new and different ways to abuse children, was handed the longest jail term for such an offence ever given out in Canada to that point.

3 ½ years, out in 2.

The Judge who imposed the penalty was quoted at the time as saying "I am tempted to impose a higher sentence."

Hmmmmm. Well, Judge, we must all try to get a handle on these temptations. There's no telling what they might lead to.

In fact, Judges have not got a handle on sexual abuse yet. They have some abstract understanding of it, but are constrained, I believe, by their training in tort law which sees negligence and assaults in a different light. If a car smacks into your car, that's negligence. You sue the other driver because you were hurt in the accident and a Judge "weighs" your pain and your loss of income and awards you a sum of money. Is being anally raped by a penis analogous to being hit by a car? No, not even close. But it is the basis of what Judges have to go on. Judges do not often know what happens to a child who is anally raped. They have little to read on the subject and at a trial they may have one or two doctors to question about the effects on the child, and then the Judge makes a determination and that determination is then a precedent for other Judges. So if that Judge didn't understand the Doctors – or didn't believe the Doctors in his Court – or if the Doctors were not well informed about sexual abuse – or if he only halfway believed the victim, then the decision he arrives at is unhelpful for future plaintiffs.

An example: In March, 2005 a 32 year old man in Quebec was found guilty of sexual assault and using his assault on his daughter to make pornographic pictures, which he then$sold. His daughter was two years old when he raped her the first time and he kept raping her and taking pictures of her while he raped her for two more years, until she was 4.

He was put in jail for 15 years. The pedophile/father appealed, saying that was far too long a sentence.

The Quebec Court of Appeal agreed with the pedophile/father and said that he should only have been sentenced to nine years in jail because he was not violent during the rapes. For example, he did not gag his daughter or hit her. And he was a young man, only 32. And he had no previous convictions – other than for sexually assaulting some other, different child, but that had happened YEARS ago.

Plus, he had four children at home who needed a dad.

So now he will be out of jail, with time off for good behavior, when the daughter he raped is about 10 years old.

How will she feel when dad comes home, puts down his suitcase in the front hall and bends over to give her a kiss?

In my respectful opinion, this is a miscarriage of justice and it is only through education of our Judges that appropriate sentences will be handed down. This case has been appealed to the Supreme Court of Canada. I truly hope that the Court of Appeal of Quebec will be overturned.

Judges pretend not to listen to the chattering classes, pretend to chart their own way through thorny decisions, but they are always talking with other Judges, family members, and friends and reading newspapers to learn how they should make their decisions and how those decisions are viewed. Judges are not immune to being persuaded.

One Judge I know was sitting on a murder trial and after he had found the killer guilty and was about to sentence him, he was astonished to see his courtroom filled on that day with friends and family of the victim, all wearing tee shirts which had on them pictures of the victim's face. This Judge was moved by that show of caring and by the fact that the courtroom was filled with friends of the victim. Other Judges, too, can be brought around by the heartfelt positions of more vocal members of society.

A very good example of this suasion being brought to bear on a formal and organized basis is Mothers Against Drunk Driving, an organization which often has representatives in Court when a drunk driver is tried and sentenced. They are there ostensibly to record the sentence, but the Judge never fails to see them in her Court, and to be aware that there is the possibility that a low sentence will cause a commotion in the press. So the Judge is less likely to hand down a low sentence.

I say again: There is a great deal of work to be done in educating people about the damage done by the sexual abuse of children.

Fortunately, we are just the ones to do it.

Before we leave the ramifications of the Internet, I want to emphasize the fact that this technology has given pedophiles their own tree fort. Twenty years ago a pedophile would have to knock on every door in town to find out where the other pedophiles were. Now he just goes to a website and he can talk for hours with other pedophiles about whatever it is pedophiles talk about. Whatever it is, it can't be good for our kids, can it.

At the very least we need to have a cop at every pedophile website twenty-four hours of every day.

Chapter 20

GETTING A GOOD LAWYER

If you are a victim of sexual abuse or you are counseling a victim of sexual abuse who is determined to have her day in court, it is imperative that you get a good lawyer. Like doctors and therapists, lawyers are differently abled, to indulge for a moment in socialworkerspeak. For example, I couldn't do a real estate transaction if you held a stapler to my head. Likewise, lawyers who deal in real estate transactions or buy and sell businesses or work on issues involving intellectual property will be of marginal or no help to victims of sexual abuse or not particularly well versed in the dynamics of such a case, even if they had a desire to become involved.

In a civil case, therefore, the abuse victim wants a good personal injury lawyer who is practiced at helping people who have been injured by the acts of others. Very often we find that good sexual abuse lawyers come from the ranks of family lawyers or from those who have helped people who were in accidents which were someone else's fault.

Ask your local Bar Association for a list of lawyers who have a background in sexual abuse litigation or who have shown a willingness to become involved in it. Not every lawyer has the necessary level of understanding and ability to fight a sexual abuse claim for you. Work hard to find one with the right credentials, one whom you are comfortable with. Usually these lawyers will not charge money for their services until the case is over. If you get nothing, they get nothing. If you are awarded compensation, their fee will be a percentage of that compensation.

In Civil trials the pedophile is ordered to pay money damages if he is found to be guilty of harming you.

If you decide to lay criminal charges against the person who sexually assaulted you, the choice of which lawyer you have is not yours to make. The state provides a lawyer to prosecute the criminal case on your behalf. In Canada this lawyer is a Crown Counsel; in the States, she is called the Prosecuting Attorney.

In either civil or criminal cases there may or may not be a Jury.

It is possible to have either a civil trial or a criminal trial or both. If you decide on both, the abuser may be sent to jail and may also be required to pay money damages.

The amount of time your abuser will spend in jail is based on precedent, that is, what sentences have been given out in the past for similar conduct. The amount of money damages awarded is also based on precedent.

No two cases are ever the same, but Judges are required to make a rough approximation of the damage done to you and the damage done to people who have been in Court before and to try to make your case fit within a rough range of past decisions. Thus, there are some guidelines for Judges based on past experience, but it is possible that a Judge or a Jury will decide on a penalty far too great or far too lenient.

In that case, you and your lawyer will discuss whether or not to take the case to an Appeal Court to ask that a more appropriate penalty be put in place.

The lawyer for the pedophile has this option of appealing as well, if she thinks her client was treated unjustly by the trial court.

The length of criminal sentences and the amount of civil money damages are both based on a number of factors. What was the severity of the sexual abuse? Was it masturbation, oral/genital sex or rape? How many times did it happen? How old was the child? What was the relationship between the child and the abuser? Was the pedophile violent towards the child? What harm has the child suffered as a result of the abuse? Has the child abused alcohol or drugs as a result or a partial result of the abuse? Has the victim lost opportunities to work because of the sexual abuse?

In a case where a man has fondled the vagina of a ten year old girl on one occasion, a criminal court will impose a sentence of less gravity than if the pedophile had raped the girl on numerous occasions. Similarly, a civil court will award money damages that are in line with the nature and results of the abuse.

The maximum criminal sentence for raping a child in Canada is 25 years in jail. It should be more. The maximum in the United States differs from State to State. Some States impose life imprisonment. Some, like Louisiana, have opted for the death penalty, joining countries like Egypt, China and Saudi Arabia.

The highest award of money damages to a child whose life has been severely altered by the actions of a pedophile in Canada is approximately $1.7 million dollars in 2009. It should be more. In the United States, because of the infrequency of child rape cases coming before the Court, penalties tend to be much higher since they involve institutional defendants such as the Roman Catholic Church.

Generally speaking, the process of preparing a case for trial and giving evidence is difficult for a victim of sexual abuse. However, in many cases the victim benefits psychologically from confronting his abuser and from going over the nature of the abuse so many times that the fact of the abuse almost ceases to have an emotional hold on the victim. What was once a dirty little secret becomes a far less painful part of the victim's life story the more often she is required to revisit the abuse in her mind and to speak of it out loud. The first disclosure is difficult; the thirtieth disclosure, not so much.

Here the law of unintended consequences sometimes finds that a legal system which grinds down so many victims often lifts up those who have been sexually abused and can, in some situations, be therapeutic for the victim. The repetition of the story of the abuse preparatory to trial results in the victim becoming – not comfortable, that is the wrong word – but resigned to the fact of the abuse. Resignation is a far less harmful feeling than fear, shame and guilt.

Because the FACT of sexual abuse has a less deleterious effect on the victim as it is repeated over time, the repetition of the story of the abuse in preparation for trial may be just what the doctor ordered.

Or, in point of fact, what the doctor didn't order, but possibly should have ordered.

Doctors – therapists – who treat their patients in psychotherapy through "the talking cure" often allow their patients to dictate the subject matter of the discussions and, as I have said before, are loath to force their patients to return again and again and again to the incidents of childhood sexual abuse which so bedevil their patients and cause their patients so much pain.

The legal process, on the other hand, has absolutely no regard for the amount of pain caused to the litigant and will drag that litigant, against her will, back to the time of the abuse over and over again, before any trial begins. Doing what no doctor would ever think of doing – forcing the victim to re-experience the trauma again and again by reviewing it and talking about it again and again, under oath, in court-like surroundings, where the credibility of the victim is squarely placed in doubt by the lawyer for the pedophile, is always painful at the time, but often results in a purging of the power that held the victim in its thrall for so many years.

I often liken this process to digging a sliver out of the palm of your hand with a needle. Sliver's been there a while. Hurts like hell. Hurts worse to dig it out. Hurts most of all trying to dig that last bit out, the bit of the sliver that's gone in deepest. Feels good to get that last little bit. Feels good when it's over. Doesn't hurt so much after that...

Caution should be exercised, however. Not all victims of sexual abuse will derive a benefit from the litigation process and they and their lawyer must always be ready to weigh the possible psychological detriment of a trial against the benefit of a successful outcome. Success can be measured in many ways. My theory is that a successful court process is one where as many of the victim's demons as possible are banished forever. Sometimes that means the pedophile goes to jail; sometimes all that is required is that the pedophile admit his guilt and apologize; sometimes the reviewing of the evidence by the victim and finding that he is believed by his lawyer and his counselor is enough.

In very few cases is success measured in the amount of time that the pedophile must spend in jail or the amount of money damages that the pedophile has to pay. The victim seeks to have her pain acknowledged and diminished. Everything else is secondary.

If a way can be found inside or outside the legal system to treat cases of sexual abuse so as to focus on this result, those who fear coming forward to deal with their demons may be more encouraged to do so. The emphasis in sexual abuse cases in Court should not be on guilt and punishment. The emphasis should be on establishing the truth and healing.

The legal process is a clumsy one indeed when it comes to dealing with people's emotions. Law can put right a situation where someone has built a house on someone else's property or someone has sold a restaurant which had no oven, but law is an imprecise tool to use in trying to put right people's emotions.

Law tends to want to throw money at things. House on the wrong side of the property line? Here's $200,000. Move the house. No oven in the restaurant you just bought and they told you there WAS an oven? Here's $20,000. Buy a nice oven.

Can't have oral/genital sex with your wife because you were sexually abused?

Want the Court to return your carefree youth that was stolen by the abuser?

Here's......

a good time to adjourn the Court.....

Arbitration and mediation should replace the Court system in cases of sexual abuse and where plaintiffs have been emotionally damaged in other ways. However, for the time being we are stuck with the unwieldy process that has devolved from a case in England where a woman found a snail in a bottle of pop, got sick and sued.

Therefore, with emotions so much a part of each case, right from the outset of a sexual abuse case, it is best to have a therapist in place who sees the victim on a regular basis and who can stay in touch with the emotional consequences of the trial at each step. The lawyer should always be open to discussing the condition of his client with the therapist. The needs of the therapist's patient should always take pre-eminence over the needs of the lawyer's client.

There is no point in running a "successful" trial if the victim emerges more psychologically damaged than she was before the trial began.

Very often, in both civil and criminal cases, the evidence against the abuser is so strong that a trial need not be had. After a certain amount of evidence has been gathered and reviewed, the best result may be that a settlement is reached, the pedophile pays an agreed upon amount of damages or goes to jail for a time that both sides agree to, and the case is concluded. This is an important factor to consider.

In most jurisdictions, only about 5% of all legal actions that are begun ever get to court. In 95% of the cases, lawyers, working with their clients and the lawyers on the other side of the case, find a way to a mutually unsatisfactory conclusion.

In law, if both sides think a settlement is unfair, that is about as close to "justice" as any party is likely to get, even after all trials and appeals are finished.

Let me tell you how these settlements are often arrived at in a civil proceeding. At some point, at the very beginning of the process, in the middle, just before the trial, in the middle of the trial, in the bathroom on the last day of trial, the good guy's lawyer gets together with the bad guy's lawyer. It could be in an elevator, on the phone, in a little room in the court house or in the Court Room itself, just before the Judge comes back from lunch.

(Other lawyers are going to kill me for this bit, but it will save you three boring years of law school and about ten years of trial and error and possibly hundreds of thousands of dollars. Or you could just turn the page...)

Bad Guy's Lawyer ("BGL"): "So, some game last night. Damn Steelers never cover the spread. What does she want?"

Good Guy's Lawyer ("GGL"): (Feigning innocence) "What do you mean what does she want?"

BGL: "What does she want to make this disappear?"
GGL: "Oh, I don't know. We've never discussed it."
BGL: "You must have an idea..."
GGL: "Well, I was thinking around $850,000..."
BGL: "Dream on!"
GGL: (Ruefully) "Yeah. We'll see what the Judge says. Why?"

BGL: "Well, I think I could get my guy to go as high as $80,000, especially if he doesn't have to pay my fees for another ten days."

GGL: (Indignant) "Ha! 80 Grand? That would never work! Fucking Steelers. They need a new special teams coach."

BGL: "It's an offer...."

GGL: "What's an offer? You wanna coach the Steelers special teams?"

BGL: "No. I'm offering your client 80 Grand to go away."

GGL: "Ohh. Okay. I'll see...."

Now, any lawyer must take any formal offer to his client. So the GGL tells his client that the BGL has offered $80,000. Then the GGL says "I recommend you reject the offer. I recommend you make a counter-offer of $750,000." The plaintiff will usually agree. GGL makes the offer to BGL who goes to the defendant and says "I recommend you make a counter-offer of $125,000. The Judge may order you to pay $280,000." The defendant agrees and BGL makes the offer. This goes on for a while until both sides, reluctantly, agree. It may take two minutes. It may take two years. But this is how most cases settle.

And most cases DO settle, remember.

All of which is fine if your client is arguing that his tenant broke a lease in a shopping center because he had bats flying around in his pet shop.

Law is good at that stuff.

Not so good at broken hearts, broken dreams and broken spirits.

In years to come people will marvel that sexual abuse claims were once in the adversarial system in Courts.

People will also marvel that I had to write most of what is in this book because it was time to get the truth out.

For the time being, litigate we must.

However, in the United States there is a major impediment to successfully suing a pedophile in a civil action for damages. Most states have a limitation period that requires a victim of sexual abuse to be quick about suing the person who caused the damage.

As far as I can see, Alaska and Maine are the only states which have no time limits for launching an action for damages arising from felony sexual abuse.

Different states have different periods of limitation, and the limitations are changing. Indeed, they are growing longer, to the benefit of the person who was abused, with every year.

Most of the states have a time limitation which begins running upon the discovery by the person who was sexually abused that there exists a causal relationship between the psychological condition (say depression) from which the victim suffers and the fact that the psychological condition was caused by the sexual abuse complained of.

Other states take different approaches. In Connecticut, a person who sues for damages arising from sexual abuse must do so before he or she is 48 years of age. This is a number derived from the plaintiff reaching the age of majority (18 years old) plus 30 years.

I see what Connecticut is trying to do and it makes some sense, but it would have made a great deal more sense for Connecticut simply to have done what Alaska and Maine have done and removed all time limitations.

The states which have tougher time limitations, where a plaintiff has only two years or three years or four years from the age of majority to bring an action against his sexual abuser are those such as Arizona, Alabama, Hawaii, Indiana, Iowa, Kansas, Michigan, Mississippi, Montana, Nebraska, New Jersey, North Carolina, North Dakota, South Dakota, Tennessee, Utah, Virginia, West Virginia, and Wyoming.

Other states have longer periods of limitation. However, because this field is subject to change on an ongoing basis, if you are in the United States or seeking to commence an action in one of the United States, please consult a lawyer in the jurisdiction where you will bring the action.

If you were sexually abused as a child by your stepfather when your family was living in, say, Florida, then you will want to get a lawyer in Florida to explain the limitation period to you.

As we know, most kids don't figure out The Rules until they are in their mid twenties or early thirties, generally well past the time when they could successfully sue in the United States.

As you know, in British Columbia there is no time limitation for commencing an action for abuse that was done to a child in this Province.

Other provinces and territories in Canada that have no time limitations are Prince Edward Island, Yukon, the

Northwest Territories, Newfoundland (in certain relationships between the abuser and the abused) and Saskatchewan (in certain relationships between the abuser and the abused).

Alberta is somewhat antediluvian and requires that an action be commenced within two years, as do New Brunswick and Manitoba. The Supreme Court of Canada, however, overrides the provincial legislation with a version of the discoverability rule, and this, too, makes a great deal of common sense.

If a victim's doctor tells her after all these years that the reason she is depressed, for example, is because she was sexually abused, she has two years after finding that out to sue the pedophile. Even if the victim is 88 when the doctor tells her. She has "discovered" late in life the harm that the pedophile did to her, and now she can allege that he did that harm, and her doctor will help her tell the Judge that her doctor has discovered that her depression was caused, in part or in whole, by the pedophile.

Her doctor might also say that she has panic attacks, or an eating disorder, or nightmares, or is an alcoholic, or any one of a host of other symptoms in part because she was sexually abused by old Mr. Fonebone.

If she just now finds out that the sexual abuse had a part in causing any or all of these conditions, the victim can sue old Mr. Fonebone for raping her 80 years ago.

The law everywhere has to change to let these kids have their day in Court.

I am certain that sooner or later (probably sooner) the law will change to reflect the reality of the harm done when a child is sexually abused.

To my colleagues in the United States of America, I say that we have fought the war for you here in Canada; we have arrived at a workable manner of means of bringing actions in our Courts and recovering damages even in the face of inimical Limitations Acts. You are about to embark on a path we have already laid down for you.

Your adversaries in the US will not be the pedophiles so much as the institutions – the insurance companies, the Churches, the organizations where pedophiles thrive. These groups will retain lawyers who will argue and argue and argue that the child is depressed not because of the sexual abuse done to her, but for 10 or 20 other reasons of equal gravity and should therefore be awarded no damages or minimal damages by the Court.

Because your client will be so fragile and put under immense psychological pressure by the doctors and lawyers hired by the pedophile, the first cases will not likely go well.

My advice to you is to arm yourself with the best doctors whom you can find with expertise in this field and educate your Judiciary about the effects of sexual abuse on a child as he or she grows to maturity. Do this enough, and you will begin to succeed, and people will finally find justice. 10 years from now people will read this paragraph and wonder what all the fuss was about.

We just need enough lawyers using enough doctors to educate enough Judges to get their stuff together.

And we need this all over the World.

Let's get to work.

Chapter 21

BACK TO PROPINQUITY

The closer your child comes to being isolated with a potential sexual abuser, the more likely your child is to be sexually abused. This truism seems obvious but for centuries parents have not known it or acted upon it. In failing to guard against sexual propinquity, parents have been as neglectful of their children as if they had encouraged them to play blindfolded in traffic. Indeed, a broken arm or leg received by a child in a traffic accident heals faster and more completely and with fewer scars than a single incident of forced masturbation.

One of the most obvious places to begin to examine the Propinquity Paradigm is Pitcairn Island. Famous as the island in the South Pacific where HMS Bounty came to rest after Fletcher Christian and his mutineers took control of the vessel from the hated Captain Bligh, Pitcairn has been home to the original mutineers, the women they took from Tahiti and their descendants since 1789. The island is midway between Peru and New Zealand, as isolated as any inhabited spot on earth. In 2004, six men from Pitcairn were convicted of sexual offences against women and girls on Pitcairn dating back over 40 years.

On an Island 1 mile long by two miles wide with no permanent link to the outside world if the electricity is out, and where approximately 90 men and women live together under British rule, it is perhaps not surprising that the tradition of monogamy has fallen into disuse from time to time, even though that is the notional underpinning of the family unit on Pitcairn. More troubling by far is the fact that some of the six men have been convicted of having sexual relations – no more is known – with Island girls as young as five years old.

It may well be that the people of Pitcairn who began their families in the 1790s with women taken from Tahiti have often woken up in the wrong bed in the morning. Indeed, it is rumored that one such extra-marital affair led to the wound which ultimately took the life of Fletcher Christian. But no modern society, no matter how unusual its other mores, has ever condoned the sexual abuse of children.

On Pitcairn, in London, in Iran and in North Korea, the power of the state is always invoked to deal with those who sexually assault children.

It should be clear, however, that the likelihood of children being sexually assaulted increases when the size of the pool of available sexual partners decreases. A person who is not a pedophile, forced to choose between no sexual outlet and a sexual outlet using a child, may become a sexual abuser of children by default. This person, while not a true pedophile, commits acts as damaging to the child as if they were undertaken by a committed pedophile.

There are few places or communities in our society where children are the sexual outlet of last resort. However there are many communities of which we are aware where the size of the pool of children is large and where the pool of available adult sexual partners is concomitantly substantially reduced.

The British all-boy school is a good example of this. The male teachers often dwell in rooms alongside the dormitories of their young pupils, miles from the nearest town, with no available women on the school grounds. Those children, by definition, are at a high risk of being sexually assaulted by their teachers. Also by definition, any school teacher who sexually assaults one of his students in these circumstances should be imprisoned and the school officials who hired the teacher should be fined and fired as unfit.

Propinquity does not give license to the abuser. Propinquity, rather, is the klaxon that should warn every sentient mother that her child is in danger.

It does not matter that the teacher who anally rapes a young boy is a situational pedophile. The pain for the boy is equally as great as if the adult had been a hardwired pedophile.

And so it may be said for other institutions in society, with regard to male and female coaches, or in any other situation where young children come together under the tutelage of older people who have power over them and are physically near them, the danger signs should be manifest to all parents.

Chapter 22

THE CATHOLIC CHURCH: PART TWO

If anyone set out to build an organization where the sexual abuse of children would not only be likely, but more or less a certainty, the best blueprint they could use would be the Roman Catholic Church.

As I said earlier, the Catholics have survived for two thousand years in almost the same form. There is no other organization on earth which can even approximate the Catholic Church for the longevity, breadth and depth of its influence.

I'll just call it the Church here. We'll all know what it means.

The Vatican, in controlling the Church, has direct input into the lives of over a billion people around the world in countries as far flung as Nigeria, Australia, China, Chile and the Canadian Arctic. The mandate of the Catholic Church has always been one of reaching across the world to gain as many footholds in as many countries and cultures as possible. Every non-believer is a potential convert to the Catholic faith. For over two thousand years the Vatican has used the local churches in all the countries of the world as "talent spotters" to choose the best and the brightest Catholics from cities, towns and villages with the idea of moving them up the ladder within the Church from Priest to Bishop and eventually to Cardinal and to World Headquarters at Vatican City.

Because the Church has such a large talent pool upon which to draw and because the village Priests and Catholic teachers (who are often nuns in the early childhood years) are always on the lookout for the best and the brightest students, it is almost inevitable that if they have the requisite level of faith in the teachings of the Church, young people with potential will rise within the organization. Today it may be said that any young Catholic boy growing up anywhere in the world may aspire to be Pope. An office which was reserved for men of Italian birth until the 1970's appears to be open to any man to achieve.

With a hierarchy of men who guide the affairs of the Church and who report directly to the Vatican, there comes a sense of wellbeing and even arrogance that the matters which bedevil the rest of the world will have little effect on an institution which has floated over a sea of troubles like a golden vessel for two millennia.

From time to time there will be issues which affect the Church more than others. In recent centuries these issues, which have been bothersome to the Church – but far from fatal – have been the advent of Communism, which ideology preached in former Catholic enclaves that there was no God; the rise of Hitler, who struck a bargain with the Vatican that he would wage war on bits and pieces of the world, including Catholic countries, but not on the Catholic Church, provided that the Catholic Church did not attempt to turn its acolytes against Nazism; the social upheavals of the 1700s, which saw the creation of the United States of America; and revolutions in Europe in the 1800's, demanding liberty, equality and fraternity amongst the masses, which did away with a number of institutions and societal norms on which civilization had hitherto been established, but left the Church and its power largely unscathed.

Given that it was the most pervasively "established" entity in Europe, one wonders how the Church always dodged the antiestablishment bullet over these centuries of revolution.

Consider, too, the business in England with Henry VIII who ousted the Roman Catholic Church as the official religion of the British Isles so that he might get a divorce.

These potential crises for the Church, which appeared so dangerous at the time they were going on, when the rabble were literally loose in the streets and looking to kill authority figures, turned out to be nothing at all. The Roman Catholic Church survives today in the United Kingdom, the upheaval in Europe in the 1700's brought about little modification in the way the Catholic Church does business and arguably cemented the position of the Church as Napoleon – a product of those turbulent times – conquered a number of countries for France while at his side representatives of the Church were quick to plant their flags for Christ and the Vatican in formerly heathen lands.

Hitler's Germany, the Reich which was to have subsisted for a thousand years, barely managed ten years of existence and while homosexuals, Jews and mental defectives were eliminated in an attempt to create a Master Race, the Catholic Church again emerged largely unscathed from World War II. Although Mussolini ran Italy with as firm a grip as Hitler did Germany both before and during the war years, the Vatican and its business were left unmolested by Il Duce even though Vatican City is smack dab in the middle of Rome which was smack dab in the center of all that Mussolini, and therefore Hitler, controlled with iron might. Had adherents to the Catholic Church been urged by the Pope to rise up against the Fascists, or had the Fascists determined to wipe out the Catholic Church, the story of World War II would have been remarkably different. However, clearer heads prevailed and the Catholic Church lived cheek-by-jowl with Mussolini in

Italy and Hitler in Germany, France, Austria, Hungary, Poland, and Yugoslavia throughout World War II.

Communism, after getting off to a quick start in the 1920s and making inroads into such formerly Catholic countries as Mexico, Cuba, Hungary, Poland and East Germany, died on the vine and died in part because of the power of the Polish born Pope John Paul II.

Why the history lesson?

What has Henry VIII got to do with sexual abuse? (Quite a bit, probably, but that is not what this book is about....)

The reason for this historical overview of the remarkable ability of the Catholic Church to adapt and survive and even sometimes to go from apparent adversity to even greater strength, is to make it clear that a scandal involving the sexual abuse of children by members of the Catholic Clergy is not an issue of such magnitude as to cause the Church any lasting damage.

More like a pea, shot from a pea-shooter, bouncing off the hull of an oil tanker.

We probably all went to school with some smartass who sat in the back of the class and threw spitballs at other students, or at the teacher when her back was turned. This guy was rarely, if ever, caught, but other students were punished for his actions. In my more benign moments, this is how I think of the Roman Catholic Church. They cause a lot of trouble and then they sift out of the picture, relatively unscathed, leaving chaos and pain behind them. And just like the smartass in school, the Church can't help itself.

That's just the way they are. They do not expect to be caught firing spitballs. But if they are caught, they can weasel out of the punishment with a word here and a gesture there. For those of you of a certain age and provenance, the Roman Catholic Church reminds me a lot of Eddie Haskell. But that, as I say, is when I am feeling sort of benign toward the Church, which is not often.

When people read this book, they will say: "He has it in for the Catholic Church." I reply: guilty as charged.

If you are a Roman Catholic, what you read here will disturb you. You may have thought you were aware of the sexual abuse that has been done by Priests and nuns, but you are likely unaware of the scale of the abuse and the part that the Vatican has played in the aftermath of the sexual abuse. Perhaps only you can have a direct impact on Church policy, by taking up these issues with your Priest or your Cardinal, or by abstaining from making periodic donations to the Church but, instead, dropping notes in the collection plate and the mail asking that something be done to prove that the Church is finally on the right track.

You will need all the strength you can muster because the Catholic Church, as you will see, is pretty well entrenched in its position on the issue of childhood sexual abuse done by members of its Clergy.

So, then, back to first precepts.

If I wish to sexually abuse a child – boy or girl – what do I need? I need a child close by, a child who looks up to me or, even better, regards me with a mixture of fear and awe and friendship. That'll be Propinquity, for those of you following along.

I need to see the child over a period of time – a week here, a week there – to groom him. I need to make sure his parents are not around and, of course, I need to make sure the child's parents trust me absolutely with their son or daughter. I want 6 year old children. Five or six-year-olds. No older than eight. And I will need a certain amount of time each time I see the child to work on him. Say half an hour to an hour. I need the child to be alone with me. No family around and no other children, at least not for a while. I need to make sure that the child I have in mind will not tell anyone after I groom him and rape him.

If these are the things I, as a pedophile, want, I should become a Catholic Priest who teaches Sunday School.

All of these needs will be met without my having to lift a finger.

Or I could be a nun teaching Sunday School or a kindergarten class.

Or I could be a Priest who has the duty to choose altar boys and has absolute sway over them, sort of like a coach moves kids up in the organization. And their parents are so proud when their son becomes an altar boy...

Without knowing it, I suppose, the Catholic Church has institutionalized a set of circumstances for children around the world which any pedophile outside the Catholic Church would spend years trying to construct. Every possible requirement that a pedophile has to give him the best possible chance to rape a young boy has already been put in place by the Church.

If I were an aspiring pedophile, I'd march right down to the local Catholic Church, find the Priest in charge and ask: "Where do I sign up?"

Because as a young, aspiring pedophile who works as a counter boy at a Flickin' Chicken franchise, how am I going to get close to 5-year-old boys? Their parents are always with them, or their older siblings. How would I build a relationship with them? They're in and out. Would I take them into the bathroom? The broom closet? Wouldn't they tell on me as soon as I raped them?

Yes.

Far easier to be a Priest.

The parents encourage the children to come to see me every week and there is always a reason to keep a little one back after the bible studies are done to have a special, private word with him while I straighten his clothing and "accidentally" brush the back of my hand against his penis.

Put it another way around, though. Give the devil his due.

A young man who has always had a keen yearning to serve God throws down his apron at the Flickin' Chicken store, marches down to the Catholic Church and says to the Priest, "I heard the Lord speak to me last night. I've come to sign up."

This young former chicken flicker is sexually naïve. He has never had sexual contact with anyone. Woman, man, boy, girl, chicken. Now he is a Roman Catholic Priest, sworn to poverty and chastity, and living for Jesus, Mary and Joseph.

Every week, on Sunday, children come to learn bible stories from the former chicken flicker. Every week he teaches the children and enjoys his work and thinks the kids are wonderful.

Especially little Tim.

One day, because he just plain LIKES little Tim, he decides to ask him to stay after class because little Tim seems to be having trouble understanding the story of David and Goliath. And little Tim looks up at the freshly minted Priest with adoration in his eyes and then after a minute says "I have to go to the toilet." And the Priest takes his hand and watches him go to the bathroom and then, because little Tim doesn't seem to know what to do, the Priest helps little Tim shake the drops of urine off the end of his little penis. And the Priest, who has sworn to God that he will never have sexual relations with anyone, feels something stirring in his genitals.

The next week he asks little Tim to stay behind again and tells little Tim to go to the bathroom and the Priest will come and help like last week.

The Priest has taken a vow of chastity. He has never had sexual contact with anyone. The Catholic Church forbids him to have sexual relations with anyone. But he is sexually aroused by touching the penis of little Tim.

Is the Priest a pedophile?

He is now.

As for little Tim, he will be the first of many young boys abused by this Priest, who will work his way up from fondling boys to masturbating them, to sucking their penis to getting them to suck his penis to raping them.

Would this Priest have hurt so many little boys if he had stayed at the Flickin' Chicken store? No. Would he have sexually assaulted ANY little boys? I don't know, but I guess probably not.

Why did he end up sexually assaulting so many little boys like Tim?

Because the Church provided a ready-made situation in which Tim and the Priest became players in one initial act of sexual inevitability.

If the Priest had been able to have sexual relations with grown men or women within or outside the Church, would he have even started to sexually abuse little Tim? Don't know. Probably not. But it was almost a CERTAINTY he would sexually abuse little Tim if his religion forbade him any other sexual outlet with any other human being.

The Catholic Church has a great deal to atone for. A hundred years ago they didn't, because if this pattern of behavior was known in the Church then, it was known only to a few who kept it under their big, pointy hats.

Today, however, we know the whole story, and the time has come for the Catholic Church to do what must be done. Here I speak not of "spin" or "damage control" in the political sense of those phrases. This is not the time for an exercise in public relations to get the parishioners back onside and start looking like the guys in the WHITE pointy hats.

This is the time for fundamental change to be made to the Catholic Church and a time for those within the Church who say with impudence and arrogance and diffidence: "This, too, shall pass," to fade into the background while people truly and keenly interested in reform come to the fore.

Assuming, at all times, that there are people in the upper levels of the Roman Catholic Church who are truly and keenly interested in stopping the sexual abuse of children by its clergy.

I am not certain that these people exist in the Church, however, because it is my belief that, even in 2009, the culture of child rape pervades the Catholic Church from top to bottom.

Let's look at the record, and then you can judge for yourself.

As far as Canada is concerned, there was the investigation in 1939 into the sexual abuse of children who attended Kuper Island Indian Residential School. We know about that. The investigation was carried out by the British Columbia Police, who were responsible for policing the Province before the job was transferred to the Royal Canadian Mounted Police.

The investigation concluded that one employee of the Order of Les Peres Montfortains had been, at the very least, inappropriate with children for whose wellbeing he was responsible. The man was disciplined and sent away from that school. The results of the investigation were made known to the Bishop of Victoria, responsible for Vancouver Island who, in normal circumstances, would have passed these findings up to the Roman Catholic Archbishop of Vancouver, who would have passed the findings along to a Canadian Cardinal and from there the information should have gone to the Vatican.

We have no way of accessing Vatican records relating to this sexual abuse and its aftermath, but it is a fair conclusion to draw that the findings of the British Columbia Police Commission made their way to the Vatican. Whether they were drawn to the attention of Pope Pius XII or one of his functionaries is moot.

Those of you following along closely will know that in late 1939 Pope Pius XII was up to here with Mussolini and Hitler, neutrality for his parishioners in Spain and Portugal and the thorny issue of how the Germans were treating the Jews in Catholic Poland and elsewhere.

The Pope was also faced with a bit of a conundrum in that the Roman Catholics of France and Britain were waging war against the Roman Catholics of Germany and Italy, and all were praying in Roman Catholic Churches each Sunday to the same God to grant them, as good Roman Catholics, victory over, ummm, their filthy Roman Catholic enemies...

It was a dicey time to be Pope.

So, if a piece of paper landed on the desk of Pius XII to the effect that some underling in Canada had been found guilty of sexually assaulting a student, the Pope may have put the information to one side to be dealt with, oh, after the War sometime, maybe.

The alternative hypothesis is that the information respecting the sexual assault of a child at the residential school did not go past the Bishop of Victoria, or the Archbishop of Vancouver. If the information stayed in Canada, it may have been because this was not an event considered by Canadian Catholic officials to merit the attention of the Vatican.

Either way, so far as we are able to judge, life carried on not only at Kuper Island Indian Residential School but at all residential schools in Canada which were managed by Catholic clergy, as if nothing of significance had been unearthed by the British Columbia Police Commission.

So, too, it appears from reading the history and speaking with the former students, that the Government of Canada, which had forced the Aboriginal children to leave their families and go to the residential schools, did nothing to prevent the future sexual abuse of students after the 1939 Report.

Some fifteen years later, on the far eastern coast of Canada, another shoe dropped at an orphanage in Newfoundland known as Mt. Cashel. There, a member of the Royal Newfoundland Constabulary came upon a small boy who had escaped from the Orphanage which was located near St. John's, the capital of Newfoundland.

The boy told the policeman a tale of horror and sexual abuse at the hands of his keepers at the Orphanage, members of the Catholic order the Christian Brothers of Ireland in Canada.

The police officer returned the child to the Orphanage and made it his business to ask some pointed questions of the men in long, black robes who ran the Institution. How had the boy, aged about six, concocted such a graphic account of sexual assault? Where could he have learned of such behavior if he had not seen it or had it done to him? Where was his supervisor? Where was his teacher?

The Christian Brothers, to a man, denied any knowledge of what the little boy was talking about. The policeman was not convinced, but he had only a strong hunch and the evidence of a 6 year old to go on. He drove back downtown and went into the police station to discuss the matter with the Chief of Police, to see what could be done for the boys at the Orphanage.

The Chief of Police, whose surname was Penny, said he thought that there were some interesting bits of information here but they should wait on it a bit before running off madly in all directions with search warrants and questions for all the orphans. Later the Chief spoke with his brother and, in the result, nothing was done to follow up on the policeman's contact with the six year old boy.

The name of the brother of the Chief of Police was Penny, as might be expected. Like the Chief of Police, the brother, too, had a distinguished title: Roman Catholic Archbishop of Newfoundland.

Amongst other things, Archbishop Penny was responsible for the Christian Brothers of Ireland in Canada who ran Mt. Cashel Orphanage.

About ten years passed before the original policeman returned to the Orphanage loaded for bear and the result of his investigation was ultimately the bankruptcy of the Christian Brothers of Ireland in Canada and their being required to liquidate their assets to pay money damages to the boys they admitted to having raped.

We will never know when the first proven instance of sexual abuse of a child by a member of the Roman Catholic Clergy was made known to a Pope, or an Archbishop or Bishop. It may have happened two thousand years ago. It may not have happened until 1999.

My strong belief, however, is that certain members of certain Orders within the Roman Catholic Church regarded the sexual abuse of children as being as much a part of their ordinary lives as reading the Bible and praying.

I believe strongly, although we may never know, that certain Roman Catholic Priests, nuns and Brothers who were designated as caregivers for children at residential schools in Canada sexually abused these children with the knowledge and complicity and even the assistance of one another.

Of the thousand or so former inmates at residential schools whom I have interviewed, many have told me histories of their sexual abuse which leads me ineluctably to conclude that in some of these schools, at certain times, there was a network of pedophiles who found and groomed children and passed them amongst one another, even to the point of nuns acting as "talent scouts" and more, for the Priests.

Just recently, and not for the first time by any means, I reviewed with a woman her history of arriving at a residential school run by a Catholic Order and almost immediately being set upon by a nun. The nun took the girl, then five years old and frightened by being away from home, into her bed, under the guise of comforting the little girl, to stop her crying. The nun held the little Aboriginal girl to her, then showed the little girl that she wanted the child to move her hand back and forth on the nun's vagina. The little girl, new to white people, nuns, and being away from her family, rubbed the nun's vagina. That was what these strange women who spoke a foreign language did, apparently.

Meanwhile the nun put her finger into the anus of the little girl and moved it back and forth. This happened every night or every other night for about a month. The girl recalls the nun using larger and larger fingers, and then inserting objects into her anus.

Two months after the little girl had arrived at the school, the nun came to her and told her she had been a bad little girl and must go to the Principal, a Priest, for punishment. The frightened little girl walked into the office of the Principal – she had never seen the man before – and he offered her candy, picked her up, put her on his lap, took her panties down, took his penis out and inserted his penis into her anus, moving her up and down until he ejaculated. Because she was now bleeding from the anus and had semen oozing from her as well, the Priest told her to go back to see the nun and get cleaned up. The nun bathed the little girl and, while bathing her, put her finger in the little girl's vagina.

A week or so later, the little girl was told again by the nun that she had been bad and would have to be disciplined by the Principal. This time the Principal disciplined the little girl – who had done nothing wrong on either occasion – by raping her first in the vagina, then in the anus, and then sending her back to the nun again to be cleaned up.

This pattern went on for about one school year as the little girl was told by the nun time and again that she had been naughty and as the Principal continued to "discipline" her by anal and vaginal rape.

Other children who attended other residential schools have given similar accounts of how one religious Brother would break the child in for another Brother or Priest. On one occasion a little boy went to the Office of a Priest and the Priest told the little boy to suck the Priest's penis. The boy refused. "You did it for Brother Michael," the Priest said. "You will do it for me," and he struck the child hard on the side of the head and the little boy complied.

Some children who were approached by pedophiles at the schools fought back. Some screamed, kicked, cried and generally made the experience for the pedophile not as pleasurable as it could have been. Some went to the Principal or another Priest or their teacher and told them. This made no difference, and the children were often sexually attacked by the person they reported to, or otherwise disciplined by being strapped or hit for "lying" about a member of the staff.

Some children told their parents and when their parents confronted the teachers or the Principal, which occurrence was very rare, the Catholics responded "Do not interfere in how we discipline your child. Discipline is the business of the school, not the parent."

Other children were more cowed, more compliant, less argumentative. These were the children who were most likely to be used and used again first by a Brother, then a nun, then a Priest, then a Brother, and so on.

On some occasions a visiting Priest would have a child brought to him – boy or girl, his choice, apparently – and, as if he were being offered brandy or a cigar after dinner, he would be gifted with a sexually "broken in" Aboriginal child who was then raped by him and who stayed the night with him.

I have no idea how this worked, but far too many children have told me about it for it not to have happened.

I cannot begin to imagine what words might have passed between the local Church members and the visiting Priests to result in a child being passed around a school like a sexual toy. All I know is that I have heard enough stories of a similar nature to form the strong belief that this was an accepted practice at some residential schools in Canada as recently as the 1970s.

Nor was it always a Roman Catholic Institution where this went on. I have spoken with a boy who had similar treatment at the hands of members of the Anglican Church of Canada.

It is my strongly held belief that the Roman Catholic Church in North America has been rife with the sexual abuse of children during at least the years 1940-1970 and that any Roman Catholic Clergyman in North America during these years knew of the sexual abuse of children by Clergy, either directly or anecdotally.

Many Roman Catholics reading this book may take issue with these strongly-held beliefs. Some know the truth and are unlikely to break the silence.

One who has gone ahead to break the code, however, is Bishop Thomas Gumbleton of Detroit, Michigan. In January, 2006, Bishop Gumbleton, who was then aged 75, revealed that when he was 15 years old and a seminary student in Detroit, a Priest took him and some other boys to a cabin and "put his hand down the back of my pants." Gumbleton did not say what happened after the Priest put his hand down the back of his pants and out of deference to the privacy of Bishop Gumbleton, I will not speculate.

Suffice to say that the incident took place in 1946 and that the sexual assault had an effect on the Bishop. He said that there was "a strong likelihood" that there were other victims of sexual abuse at the hands of Catholic clergy who had not yet come forward and he argued in favor of doing away with putting time limitations on people who were sexually abused to come forward because he knew from his own experience how difficult it is to tell one's story of abuse.

This Bishop is not an insubstantial Catholic, having been a strong leader n the Catholic Peace Movement, Pax Christi.

Bishop Gumbleton also said that he had wanted many times to bring up the incident at his meetings with other Bishops, but the timing was never right. As with most children who have been sexually assaulted, Bishop Gumbleton found it very, very difficult to disclose the fact of his abuse.

In most states in the United States, as we have seen, you have two to five years to come forward before you lose your right to sue for having been sexually abused as a child. If you were raped when you were 6, you have from 2 to 5 years after you attain the age of majority to bring a lawsuit. This contemplates that by the age of, say 21, you know The Rules.

No one knows The Rules by age 21.

This is a stupid and uncaring law which has been done away with in British Columbia. If Bishop Gumbelton had his way, there would be no time restriction on being able to sue for sexual abuse. He knows firsthand how difficult it is to come forward, because even 60 years after what appears at first blush to have been a relatively minor assault, Bishop Gumbleton continued to have difficulty and to feel embarrassed while speaking about the sexual abuse he was put through by a Priest of his own Church.

If an educated Bishop of 75 has difficulty and suffers embarrassment speaking of a relatively minor abuse (we assume, for we know no more about his abuse than is written here), think how difficult it must be for an under-educated person of a similar age, not practiced at public speaking and never having had the benefit of speaking with the authority of a Bishop of the Roman Catholic Church, and being believed all his life in that capacity.

I suspect the Bishop got into hot water with the Catholic Church for coming forward. I suspect he came forward in part because, at 75, he was nearing the age of retirement. I further suspect Bishop Gumbleton was sent to Coventry for arguing against the 2-5 year limitation period, because that limitation period saves the Church a great deal of embarrassment and money.

How did the Catholic Church react to the announcement by Bishop Gumbleton?

Well, they could not very well disbelieve him. He was one of their leaders. Instead, the Church, in the persona of his fellow Bishops – the Catholic Conference of Ohio – said they were "saddened" to learn of Gumbleton's "alleged" abuse and emphasized counseling was available for victims of sexual abuse by the Catholic clergy, which, ummmm, "allegedly" included Bishop Gumbleton. So. Off you go for your counseling, then, Bishop! And that'll be that.

It does a heart good!

Of course, by 2006 the Roman Catholic Church was so lawyered-up over the issue of sexual abuse that any statement from on high would have been vetted by squadrons of litigators to ensure no admissions were made which could be used by other "alleged" victims to wrest more expressions of "sadness", back-handed apologies, counseling and lucre from the coffers of the Vatican.

And so it was that even the good Bishop Gumbleton was tossed in the heap of all those potentially money-grubbing troublemakers who "alleged" that Father So-And-So had touched their buttocks 120 years ago and now they wanted 10000000000000 dollars in damages to take away the pain.

And a declaration of the sadness of the Church over the alleged incident.

And counseling for the results of the alleged incident.

No wonder Bishop Gumbleton found "the timing was never right" when he thought of mentioning the sexual abuse at meetings with his fellow Bishops.

At a minimum he would have been given the old collective hairy bishoprical eyeball and made to eat lunch on his own, or with a nun, and at worst the other Bishops might have had old Bishop Gumbleton hustled off by Church ambulance to the local Church laughing academy, never to have been heard from again.

Any Church that can inspire The Inquisition and the circele (the little spiked belt that some members of the Catholic Order Opus Dei wear around their thigh, to make them more holy every time they go "ouch"), would think nothing of locking up some septuagenarian Bishop from Detroit who was going on and on about a dream he had of some Priest sticking his hand down his pants 60 years ago.

The Catholic Church – in the guise of the Catholic Conference of Ohio - summed up the case of Bishop Gumbleton and all others "allegedly" abused by Church members by saying:

"Healing is not achieved by lawsuits but by working with those who have suffered abuse, ministering to them pastorally and helping to meet their individual needs."

Oh me, oh my.

Well, this is just horseshit.

The Catholic Church comes at healing through a filter of religiosity so imbued with the Virgin Mary and Jesus that true healing cannot be done by a Priest counseling another Priest or a victim of a Priest.

Priests pray.

Prayer does not remove the pain of sexual abuse. (I should never say never. Somewhere, somehow, prayer may have removed the psychological effects of sexual abuse from a child.)

But if I posit a situation where an 8-year-old boy has had his nose inserted into the vagina of a Catholic nun and he has been forced to lick the vagina of that nun until she tells him he can stop, no other nun will likely be able to "minister" to this boy "pastorally" to take away his shame, his fear, his guilt and his revulsion.

Similarly, if a Priest has forced a boy to suck on that Priest's penis until the Priest ejaculates in that boy's mouth, another Priest, thirty years on, will not likely have much luck ministering pastorally to the boy to help him heal from the effects of the sexual abuse.

What the Catholic Church is doing in the case of Bishop Gumbleton, and every other child who alleges that a Catholic employee sexually abused him, is the same thing Dick Nixon did during Watergate.

First, get lawyered-up. The best: Sue the bastards back. Fight them at every hill, every valley, every bridge and every stream. We'll lawyer them to death, and if that doesn't work,

Bluff them. Tell them we're going to the mattresses and will never give up. Then, stonewall. Tell them nothing. But when a crack forms in the wall... Spin. Spin everything. It never happened. If it did, it wasn't our fault. Blame someone else. It was like that when we got here.

When the spin loses its effect, toss granny off the troika. Pitch Haldemann and Ehrlichmann under the bus. See if the wolves will stop.

And when the wolves keep coming, do a modified, limited hangout. A mea culpa, but not MEA, if you get my drift. Mistakes were made. See if that works. And when it doesn't, let them have what they want. Give them the tapes! Repay the money. Apologize if we have to. Conduct hearings. Take back the agenda! And when that is insufficient, resign.

Well, we aren't at the last two stages yet for the Catholic Church. We're static at the modified, limited hangout "mistakes were made" stage. The Pope has said so.

What the Catholics in Ohio and elsewhere have not yet learned is that the group who sexually abused the child cannot heal the child, that most children abused by Clergy have given up on the Church because its representatives did not act as Jesus would have acted but rather as Satan would have acted and, finally, that the process of suing the Church and the abuser in court really, truly CAN bring healing, where healing was least anticipated.

If, instead of adopting the modified, limited hangout plan, the Roman Catholic Church had laid its cards on the table and said: "We have all the money in the world. You can have that if it will help. We will spend that money getting the best possible counselors for all the children our people sexually abused and we will do it quickly and without fuss. Then we will get rid of the child molesters and pedophiles in our ranks. Then we will make sure nothing like this ever happens again by thoroughly screening new applicants for jobs with the Church. And, because some of these kids have had really rotten lives because of the sexual abuse, we'll give them a bit of money to help them out, to try to put them in the same position they would have been in if they had not been sexually abused by that nun when they were 6."

That would have been the enlightened thing to do. That would have saved money for the Church, made it look Big in the eyes of the world, instead of shifty, and would have helped rather than further hurt the children who, through no fault of their own, had had pretty rotten lives up until that point.

Ah, yes.

That would have been the humane and human thing to have done.

That might even be what Jesus would have done.

But it was not to be.

Instead, the Catholic Church followed the Watergate model, and they did it on a worldwide basis.

Have you ever heard of a little place called Apia, Samoa?

Nor had I. Nor, I bet, had Father Frank Klep, the Roman Catholic Principal of a boys' boarding school near Melbourne, Australia. In the 1970's and 1980's, Father Klep worked his way up from teacher to Principal. In 1986, former students at the school began to come forward to say that Father Klep had sexually assaulted them while they were at the school.

Father Klep, confronted by a mounting number of accusers, steeled himself, straightened his shoulders and took off for parts unknown, eventually heaving up on a beach in Samoa.

The boys in Australia whom he had sexually abused have tried without success to have Klep extradited to face criminal charges, or at the very least have him denied contact with other children while wearing the trappings and bearing the authority of a Priest. Of course, Father Klep could not BE Father Klep unless the Catholics said so. The Catholic Church, however, in particular the order Klep is a member of – the Salesians of Don Bosco – refuse to cooperate with law enforcement officials in Australia or anywhere else where their clergy are accused of sexually abusing children.

You may never have heard of it, but the Order the Salesians of Don Bosco is one of the largest Orders in the Roman Catholic Church. One of their major mandates is to educate children around the world, poor children, vulnerable children.

When one of their members – say Father Klep – is accused of sexually abusing the children his duty requires him to care for, the Salesians have a policy of moving that Priest to another jurisdiction, and doing so quickly.

Back in 2004, the head honcho of the Salesians was Cardinal Oscar Rodriguez of Honduras. No lightweight, Cardinal Rodriguez was one of those short-listed for the position of Pope after John Paul II died.

Cardinal Rodriguez was asked about his policy regarding investigating members of the Order he ran who had been accused of sexually assaulting children in their care. He replied (and any resemblance to Richard Nixon here is purely coincidental): "For me it would be a tragedy to reduce the role of a Pastor (namely him) to that of a police officer. I'd be prepared to go to jail rather than harm one of my priests. We must not forget that we are Pastors, not agents of the FBI or CIA."

In other words, there was no way, no how, that Cardinal Rodriguez was going to get involved in investigating allegations of wrongdoing by his staff. Sure, send HIM to jail, but let his staff go about their business unmolested.

So Father Klep lives among the children of Samoa and gives them candy and befriends them in the came of Jesus. One of his former victims of sexual assault is a former Salesian seminarian. He now has thorough contempt for the Salesians' policy of moving abuser Priests around and leaving them free to abuse again.

Meanwhile, Father Klep has said of his "exile" in the island paradise: "I have found a good measure of contentment. I'd be quite happy to stay here."

Yes.

Meanwhile, again, few of the local Samoan families are aware that Klep was convicted of sexually assaulting children in Australia, and has admitted to it, but refuses to face up to the consequences and in that stance he is supported by Cardinal Rodriguez and all the Salesian hierarchy.

A Judge in Chile has taken issue with yet another Salesian Bishop, saying there are grounds to charge the Bishop with obstruction of justice for having moved a Priest out of Chile to avoid his facing charges of sexually assaulting children in that country.

Similar charges have been brought against the Salesians in Costa Rica, Peru and Mexico.

What would Jesus do with the Salesians?

I don't know. I'm just a lawyer. But I know what I'd do. I'd be inclined to ask every child who had ever been sexually assaulted by a member of the Salesian Order to come forward in his or her country, and to tell the local police what that Salesian did to me.

Sooner or later even Salesians will run out of countries to hide their pedophile employees in.

But, you see, it's not just the Salesians.

For reasons having more to do with collegiality and a shared bond in a culture that tolerates child sexual abuse, Roman Catholics around the world have long played "move the pedophile."

The Catholic Church is a mighty big tent – larger by far than any system of justice in any country – and so when a Priest in Zambia is accused of sexually abusing children on a Monday, he can be in Boston by Thursday. And a Priest accused in Boston on a Monday can be in Zambia by Thursday. The police in Zambia and the police in Boston are left to scratch their heads and say, as did the Judge in Chile when speaking of the Salesian Bishop, there are grounds to charge the Bishop with obstruction of justice. But when the alleged perpetrator has disappeared and there is no criminal conviction and the children are ostensibly safe now, all any Judge can do is engage in some spirited finger wagging in the face of a Church official.

And, as it has done for Father Frank Klep of Melbourne, Australia and Apia, Samoa, life goes on.

Except for the children of the world who remain victims or potential victims of the moving pedophiles.

They and their parents should live in dread every time a new Priest gets off a plane to set up shop in their town.

Father Denis Vadeboncoeur was a Priest in a little place called Evreux, France. In the early 1990's he raped a boy many, many times and pleaded guilty to those assaults in Court. He was sent to jail. But he had been in jail before, in Canada, in 1988. He was in jail in Canada because he had raped four boys in this Country. The Catholic Church in Evreux knew that Vadeboncoeur was a convicted child rapist but it told no one and allowed him to minister to his new flock of children unmolested.

The Mayor of Evreux was quoted as saying "The Church knew, and that disgusts me."

It IS disgusting, isn't it?

And there's a lot of it going on.

In 2005, a Priest who had been living in a retirement home for clergy in Joliette, Quebec since 1984 returned to Massachusetts where he was convicted of sexually abusing

18 altar boys during the years 1978 to 1984. The boys in Massachusetts had known for some years that the Priest, Father Paul Desilets, was living in Quebec, but could not force him to return to face charges until his case was to be heard by the Supreme Court of Canada. Then, with the prospect of being forced to return to the United Sates staring him in the face, he admitted to 32 charges of sexual abuse and, because he was 81years old and in ill health, was sentenced to 18 months in prison in Massachusetts.

It is noteworthy that during the many years this case was before the Canadian Courts, Father Desilets was under the protection of the Roman Catholic Church in Joliette and, given that he had taken a vow of poverty, it is extremely likely that his fight to avoid returning to the United States to face charges was funded, in part or in the whole, by his employer.

In 2004, the Dallas Morning News ran a series of investigative reports concerning the Catholic clergy and sexual abuse. What they published was truly astonishing and received very little attention worldwide given the gravity of the newspaper's conclusions.

The Morning News, after following the stories of children in many areas of the world, came to the conclusion that Catholic Priests who had been accused of sexually assaulting children continued to work in the Church but were being hidden by the Church hierarchy.

This behavior on the part of the Catholic Church was found on almost every continent as Priests began new lives under the umbrella of the Church with no hint of their past sexual abuse history following them to their new posting.

All of this begs the question of how long the policy of catch and switch has been in place. I fear the answer is as old as the Church itself.

It seems that rather than deal with the miscreants, rather than take them to task, rather than attempt to learn what drives these men and women to sexually assault children, the Catholic Hierarchy has chosen to continue to move the problem to another neighborhood where the sexual abusers are free to rape and fondle other children half a world away.

In one particular case which I prosecuted, a teacher at a Roman Catholic school was masturbating and being masturbated by his 14-year-old male pupil. The teacher, who had a shred of decency and knew he was doing wrong, reported himself and his behavior in a letter to the School Board. The Catholic School Board acted on the information by taking the teacher out of the classroom for two weeks, and requiring him during those two weeks to speak with his local Priest. He did, confessing again what he had done to the boy. The Priest, having met with him once and having secured the teacher's promise that he would "try" not to sexually abuse the boy further, recommended that the teacher return to his class. He did.

Within weeks, he was again sexually assaulting the same boy.

This happened in 1979 in a major metropolitan area in North America. If this was the best the Catholic Church could do in 1979 in dealing with a self-confessed child abuser, it speaks of an organization that did not then and may not even today appreciate the gravity of the crimes being committed.

This case is almost unique in that I gained access to the teacher's file with the Catholic School Board and found there the letter in which he sought help and, effectively, turned himself in. As it was, he got no help, save from another Priest who suggested the benefits of prayer and knew nothing of psychotherapy.

My belief is that those sexual abusers who populate the Catholic Church even today are dealt with by fellow Catholic clergy rather than by psychiatric professionals who have no ties to the Church. The result, almost inevitably, will be a session or series of sessions more rooted in prayer and Catholicism than in attempts by a therapist to deal with the underlying cause of the problems of the pedophile.

I suspect that part of the reason for keeping the personal histories of the pedophile Priests "in house" is to ensure that the world at large does not gain access to the internal policies of the Church. Another reason to actively avoid having Priests and nuns attend the offices of non-religious psychoanalysts is to avoid the prospect of having the stories of sexual abuse falling into the hands of outsiders. As a lawyer prosecuting a pedophile, I am entitled to see the counseling records of anyone who has treated the pedophile. That would not sit well with the Church.

Yet another reason that trained professionals might be eschewed in favor of trusted Catholic Church therapists is that the Church probably has more faith in prayer and redemption and the concept of forgiveness than it does in some pseudo-science which purports to help pedophiles by urging them to tell their stories, not for the purposes of confession, but for the purposes of correction.

Thus, it is only when Catholic clergy are charged with a criminal offence and convicted that psychoanalysts in the penal system get a crack at them.

And there their stories are remarkably similar. Many have been sexually abused as children; most have agonized over their predeliction to sexually abuse young boys and girls; most have ended by convincing themselves that it is God's will that they continue to do so, and to disclose the conduct in the accepted form of confession, possibly confession to like-minded Priests.

This also explains how a boy who is being sexually assaulted by one Priest might soon be assaulted by two or three Priests. The confessional does more than establish sins and penance. It also transmits information to those on the other side of the confessional screen, who may have an interest in the subject matter being confessed.

Thus, when a Priest at a residential school says to a young boy from whom he is demanding oral sex, "You did it for Brother Michael," the function of the confessional may have gone far beyond that for which it was intended.

When people think of the sexual abuse scandals in the Roman Catholic Church, their mind often turns to Boston. It was there that the phenomenon of abuse on a massive scale first became apparent to many North Americans.

Father Paul Shanley was on point in this story, as was the Bishop.

Shanley was convicted in 2005 of having raped a boy at his Church in the 1980's when the boy was 6. He had raped the boy in the confessional and in the bathroom. Shanley's lawyers did as all lawyers for pedophiles do, saying that the boy made up the story for money or that he was "mistaken."

Shanley had done more than blot his copy book, however, when he had defended sexual relations between men and boys at a meeting of the North American Man-Boy Love Association in 1979. This should have alerted the Church to the man's sexual proclivities, but the Church allowed him to continue to have priestly contact with young boys until the 1990s.

In Shanley's case, the Judge believed the boy – who was 27 when he told his story – and sent Shanley to jail for 12 to 15 years. Because he was 74 at the time, Shanley may, in fact, have received what amounts to a life sentence.

Or he may have received what is indirectly the death penalty.

Father Shanley's lawyer was worried for the wellbeing of his client in jail, perhaps with some cause. Because in 2003, another Priest had been sent to jail – a Father John Geoghan – and he had died at the hands of a fellow inmate. The identity of the murderer of Father Geoghan has not been determined at the date of writing and I doubt that it will ever be determined.

While the stories of Father Shanley and Father Geoghan are tragic, there exist many, many more stories in the United States alone, stories where the numbers of children sexually abused begged thorough description.

In 2005 the Catholic Bishops of the US reported that 4,392 American Priests had been accused of "molesting" one or more children from 1950 to 2002. These are numbers generated by the Catholic Church, remember.

The numbers refer to accusations, not convictions. But the numbers do not – because they cannot – contemplate those children who have failed to make accusations when they might have. So, on balance, just looking at these numbers for a second, there are 80 Priests accused of sexually abusing kids every year for 50 years in the States, or about one every five days. The number, given the source, is possibly low. But even if it is low, it is very, very high. Children's lives were changed forever by pedophile Priests every week for fifty years.

This is a crime of major proportions with massive effects on humanity and on the children and on all of their families and loved ones. The reverberations of these sexual assaults will be felt in society for decades to come.

In cases like that of Father Shanley, it is clear that the Diocese in which he ministered knew or ought to have known of his sexual aberration from 1979 forward. Having spoken at a NAMBLA meeting, he was about as "out" as a pedophile can be. The fact that the Catholic Church did not immediately snap him up, isolate him from children and send him to a good psychiatrist, but instead allowed him to continue his priestly contact with children, is a direct connection between his sexual abuse of the children he hurt after 1979 and the responsibility the Church must bear for that sexual abuse.

In legal terms, the Church should be liable to those children Shanley abused after he disclosed his pedophilic propensity in 1979. The Church should be liable in that it must pay money damages to those children Shanley abused, to put them in the position they would have been in had they not been raped by Father Shanley.

Of course they can never be put in that position, but the job of a Judge is to decide issues like this. Father

Shanley, having taken a vow of poverty, had no money to give to the children he hurt, therefore the Church has all the greater cause to step into his shoes, open its wallet and pay for what it allowed Shanley to do to the kids.

But can the Catholic officials – the Bishops or Cardinals, say – who had knowledge of the sexual misconduct of its Priest be put in jail?

No.

A Grand Jury convened in Philadelphia determined that the Philadelphia Archdiocese of the Roman Catholic Church had covered up priestly sexual abuse of children for over 40 years, during which time 60 priests had sexually assaulted children in Philadelphia parishes.

The Grand Jury found in 2005 that the leaders of the Philadelphia Archdiocese had endangered and harmed children by keeping known pedophiles on the job or by transferring them to places where their pedophilia was unknown.

However, the officials of the Archdiocese could not be criminally convicted for putting the children at risk because of the manner in which the Church governed itself. The Archdiocese is unincorporated and, at law, its officers cannot be punished for the acts of its employees.

Well, then, if the people high up in the local Church cannot be sent to jail, surely the Catholic Church deals sternly with them when their negligence comes to light.

Wrong again.

Take the case of Cardinal Bernard Law of Massachusetts. Law resigned as Archbishop of Boston in

2002 after it was proven in Court that he had, for years, been in charge of a scheme in which Priests who were known to be sexually abusing children were moved from one parish to another to avoid detection. He was also Father Shanley's boss.

If this is all beginning to sound annoyingly familiar, that is only because it has happened time and time again in every part of the world that the Catholic Church touches with its organization.

The Attorney-General of Massachusetts concluded that Cardinal Law was legally responsible for the sexual abuse of over 500 children from the Boston area.

So, then Cardinal Law went to jail, right?

Cardinal Law did not go to jail.

Upon his resignation, Cardinal Law went to the tall cotton of the Vatican, where Pope John Paul II gave him a top position in the spiritual hierarchy of the Church. And in 2005, Law was one of only 9 Cardinals in the world who was permitted to deliver a homily on the life of the recently deceased Pope.

That'll show him.

That'll show him how seriously the Church treats people who help pedophiles hide from their victims.

That'll show all the others like him, too.

Get caught and we're just liable to promote your Holy ass to the Vatican

How do you like THEM apples?

Or how do you like the apples of Monsignor Bernard Prince? When he was a Priest in the Ottawa Valley, in Ontario, Father Prince allegedly sexually assaulted an altar boy. The former altar boy laid criminal charges. By then, however, Monsignor Prince was working at the Vatican and was very close to Pope John Paul II. The Ontario Provincial Police issued a warrant for his arrest; Monsignor Prince retained a lawyer in the Roman Catholic Diocese of Pembroke to represent him and, being "lawyered up," as they say, he declined to make any comment about the case when he was asked about it in early 2006.

Should the Monsignor choose to remain at the Vatican rather than return to Canada to face the charges, things look a bit grim for the alleged victim. A similar case arose in Arizona where a Prosecutor asked the Vatican to apply pressure to those dioceses where Priests facing charges of sexual abuse had been transferred to Mexico in one case, and to Ireland in another. The Arizona Prosecutor sent indictments against both Priests to the Vatican. The package containing the indictments was returned to the Prosecutor, unopened.

Canada may extradite people from Italy, but not from Vatican City. If Monsignor Prince chooses to remain in the Vatican, the prospects are slim that he will be extradited. If he steps over the line into the city of Rome, however, all bets are off.

The Vatican policy is the Roman Catholic Church policy.

Or how do you like the apples of Reverend Marcial Maciel, who founded the extremely conservative Catholic Order, the Legionnaires of Christ in Mexico?

Another favorite of Pope John Paul II, Maciel was given his orders by the Vatican in May, 2006, after Cardinal Ratzinger, now Pope Benedict, "invited (Maciel) to a reserved life of prayer and repentance, renouncing every public ministry."

In other words, no more sexual abuse for Reverend Maciel, who was accused by 9 former seminarians of having sexually abused them when they were young boys or teenagers during the 1940's, 1950's and 1960's.

Facing charges from officials within his own Church whom he had sexually abused, Father Maciel countered with this oath: "Before God, and with total clarity of conscience, I can categorically state that the accusations brought against me are false."

Well, that seems plain enough. The man swore he didn't do it. Swore to God. So any investigation, especially one by his own Church, will find him innocent…

Indeed, Maciel went on to say in 2002: "I never engaged in the sort of repulsive behavior these men accuse me of."

And he was tight with John Paul II, let us not forget.

But a year after the death of that Pope, with the advent of Pope Benedict, the Vatican lowered the boom, such as it is, on Maciel, described as the most powerful Catholic official to have Vatican sanctions imposed on him for sexually abusing children.

While it is my opinion that Maciel made the cardinal error of lying to God in front of Ratzinger, one result of the new Pope taking him out of the game will be to leave his Order, the Legionnaires, dispirited and rudderless. One of the fastest growing Catholic Orders in the world, with a leader who has been censured by the Vatican, the Legionnaires now face an uncertain future.

Reverend Jim Martin, a US Jesuit commentator, has said that the ethos of the Legionnaires comes from its Founder. Now that Maciel has been disciplined for committing sexual abuse, the wind will be knocked out of the sails of the Legionnaires. As Martin said in 2006 of the importance of Maciel to the Order, "his life is studied, his words are quoted, his pictures and statues are everywhere. Any critique of the Founder, especially one that's so serious, is a huge mark against the Order."

And what of Maciel, who swore to God that the accusations of sexually abusing boys were false? What does he say now that the Pope has forcibly required Maciel to retire?

Admitting no wrongdoing whatsoever, Maciel has accepted the Vatican's decision "with faith, complete serenity and tranquility of conscience."

But will God forgive his sins?

When Pope Benedict finally came to the United States of America in May, 2008, everyone expected great things from him in apologizing for his Church and railing against the sexual abuse perpetrated by his clergy in the United States and around the world.

What the Pope said on the subject was that the Church's response to the sexual abuse scandal had been "sometimes very badly handled."

Come again?

The RESPONSE of the Church to all the sexual assaults was "sometimes very badly handled"? That is tantamount to saying that the triggermen at the St. Valentine's Day Massacre in Chicago were looked at askance because "the garage was left in a bit of a mess."

To make sure that there was no real blame to be attached to the Catholic Church over all the ruined lives of trusting boys and girls, Benedict went on to say that there had been a moral breakdown in American society, that decent sexual mores in the United States were under attack on all sides and that pedophilia is found "in every sector of society."

Wagging a metaphorical Divine Finger of Chastisement at American society, The Holy Father concluded: "Children deserve to grow up with a healthy understanding of sexuality and its proper place in human relationships. They should be spared the degrading manifestations and the crude manipulation of sexuality so prevalent today."

The use of the passive voice here is most telling.

So the Pope, after ruminating about the misconduct of his clergy for over a decade, has gone from the Richard Nixon Defence to the Homer Simpson Defence, namely:

"It was like that when I got here."

In July, 2008, Pope Benedict made a further stab at sloughing off criticism of his Church while in Australia.

He condemned the misdeeds of his Clergy. And he said "Those responsible for these evils must be brought to justice."

He said the same in Ireland in March, 2010.

My advice to the victims is that they not hold their breath waiting for that Justice, since the Pope is the only one who can ensure that Justice – everywhere in the World – is done.

And so far, Pope Benedict has shown no sign that he wants that justice done.

Nor has he apologized to the victims on behalf of the Vatican for the lives ruined by his pedophile Clergy.

Pope Benedict, so long the one man in the Vatican who knew of all the worldwide sexual abuses by his clergy, is the embodiment of all that is wrong with the Roman Catholic Church and he will remain so as long as he refuses to speak the truth.

Chapter 28

CATHOLICS AND HOMOSEXUALITY

Earlier on, I danced around the issue of whether pedophiles were more likely to be homosexuals or homosexuals were more likely to be pedophiles. I said we do not have sufficient data to make a determination.

The Roman Catholic Church has probably always had a love-hate relationship with homosexuality.

As one of my clients succinctly put it in the midst of his tearful story of sexual abuse by a Priest, "Jesus, what do you expect when you tell men they can't have sex and then make them wear dresses?"

What indeed?

It has often been said that the Bible may be used to prove or disprove almost any religious or moral tenet. I have refrained from going to this source until now, but now I must, because the Bible provides me with the Highest Authority that something important has gone sideways in the Roman Catholic Church.

In the Book of Genesis, at 35:11, right at the beginning of the Bible, we find a direct heavenly requirement, spoken by God to Jacob. "Jacob!" God boomed, and in so booming, commanded all the people of Israel:

"I AM GOD ALMIGHTY! BE FRUITFUL AND MULTIPLY."

So God commanded his people to breed like bunnies. To spread His Word: To be fruitful and multiply.

You would think that the first people who would want to follow the Big Booming Voice would be the Roman Catholic Church.

The Catholic Clergy, then, the true believers, should be fruitful and multiply.

But instead, the Catholic Clergy is fruitless and subtracting.

The Da Vinci Code is a book and a movie which made a big to-do about the place of women in the Catholic Church. I will leave it to religious scholars to debate what the Sacred Feminine is all about and whether there should be a place in the Church hierarchy and its pantheon for women – perhaps women other than the Virgin Mary and Mary Magdalene.

My purpose here is to attempt to ascertain whether the absence of sexual gratification in the Catholic Clergy has led Priests and nuns to become pedophiles.

All men and women are imbued with biological sexual urges, save 2 or 3% of the populace who are truly asexual. If 3% of all human beings are asexual, then 97% can be one of three things only: heterosexual, homosexual or bisexual.

CELIBACY is not a state of sexuality. Celibacy is a denial or an abnegation of one's sexuality, a state in which a person's sexuality remains a part of his or her being but in which sexuality is not to be accessed for procreative or other purposes, such as pleasure.

But the Catholic hierarchy would have us believe that although Catholic Priests and nuns are celibate, they are celibate heterosexuals.

In 2005 the Roman Catholic Bishop of Calgary, Frederick Henry, wrote a letter to the parishioners of his Diocese in which he called upon the state to use its coercive powers to curtail homosexuality in the interests of a better society for all.

The Epistle of Fred to the Calgarians was part of an apparent Church-wide appearance of housecleaning in the wake of the pedophile scandal that had affected the Catholics for over ten years at that point.

Indeed, the Vatican put together a "flying squad" of investigators to go to over 220 seminaries in the United States expressly for the purpose of weeding out homosexual seminarians before they got to be Priests.

The Vatican had pronounced homosexual acts "intrinsically disordered" and seemed to be taking the position that even the homosexuals who had been celibate within its ranks would no longer be tolerated. Questions would be put in all the seminaries by these investigators, questions designed to smoke out any homosexuals studying to be Priests. The faculty would be asked if the seminarians had shown signs of "particular friendships" with one another.

The flying squad would be required to answer this question respecting every seminary it visited: "Is there evidence of homosexuality in the seminary?" (And are the altar boys eating the strawberries...)

There was a rumor circulating within the Church in 2005 to the effect that Pope Benedict would soon issue an edict that no homosexual could become a Priest. Presumably this edict would have grandfathered all the homosexuals in the Priesthood at the time it was issued.

But, sticking to its 2000 year old guns, there was no indication that the Vatican would amend the prohibition against women Priests or the requirement that all Catholic Clergy be celibate. At a time when the ranks of Catholic Clergy are shrinking around the world and parishioners, too, are dwindling, it seems odd to an observer that the Church would choose to unleash a campaign against American homosexual seminarians when there are so many other things it might do both to burnish its own image, work toward a better future for itself and safeguard children from pedophiles.

Question for the Pope: If your Clergy are celibate, why does their sexual orientation matter?

Only Possible Answer: Because they are not celibate.

Reverend Gerald Chojnacki, Head of the New York Province of Jesuits wrote to his Priests in light of the Vatican's anti-homosexual stance "I find it insulting to demean the memory (of gay priests who have passed away) and their years of service by even hinting that they were unfit for priesthood because of their sexual orientation."

Pardon me.

How, exactly, in a celibate clergy, does the Head of the Jesuits in New York know that there are dead gay priests whose funerals he has attended?

Well, of course, the fact is that homosexuals have always been attracted to the Catholic Church and every seminarian and Priest knows that fact. It has been suggested by Gilles Marchildon writing in the Toronto Globe & Mail (October 7, 2005) that the Catholic Church is "the world's largest employer of homosexuals."

If the true purpose of the homosexual hunt started by the Vatican is to stop the sexual abuse of children, then pedophiles should be the targets, not homosexuals.

Has the Vatican, then, concluded that homosexuals are more likely to be pedophiles than heterosexuals?

That certainly appears to be the motivation behind the flying squads rooting homosexuals out of seminaries in the United States.

And, to be fair, some vigilance after all these centuries is better than no vigilance at all.

But the likelihood remains that when this spate of sexual abuse news is at an end, things will return to normal and the Catholic Church will ride on unmolested for the next number of centuries. It may serve the Catholics well to carry out a supposed witch hunt for homosexuals, but at bottom this is merely a public relations ploy designed to patch up the holes in the image of the Church instead of striking at pedophile Priests and nuns – the root of the problem.

A second gambit employed by the Roman Catholic Church in the face of overwhelming numbers of sexually violated children accusing priests of raping them, is to cry poor. This one stretches the limits of disbelief and is proof positive of how ill-managed has been the sexual abuse response by the Vatican. Even with the vaunted Jesuits in the saddle – or perhaps because the Jesuits are in the saddle – the Catholic Church does damage control about as well as the Captain of the Titanic.

Time and again, around the world, in the face of admitted sexual abuse of children by its clergy, the Catholics have played the poverty card. Imagine Bill Gates in a Catholic Church when the collection plate is passed around, patting down his pockets, peering forlornly at his wallet and saying, as he passes the plate down the row, "I'm a little short of funds right now." The Catholics would not be impressed.

Nor should the world be impressed, in my opinion, when the Catholics, confronted with thousands of people whose lives have been forever altered by having been sexually abused by its Priests, say that they would very much like to redress the wrong done to these victims of sexual abuse, but they just don't have the money.

Well, okay.

As my grandfather used to say, "Thousands would believe you, but I don't."

In Newfoundland in 2005, the Roman Catholic Diocese of St. George's declared bankruptcy after 36 victims of sexual abuse at the hands of a Priest named Father Bennett sued the Church. The Bishop of St. George's said the Diocese was "determined to treat the victims fairly with the greatest possible value of our assets."

Now, as a lawyer who works with victims of sexual abuse, I can tell you that in 2005 in Newfoundland, the likely Court-awarded damages for these 36 victims would not exceed 15 million Canadian dollars. A settlement of these 36 actions would, absent extreme circumstances, be reached at perhaps $10 million in total. This estimate is based on a range of possible sexual abuses by Father

Bennett, Court decisions in Canada regarding pain and suffering and loss of wages that the abuse caused, as well as paying the greedy lawyers for their trouble.

It is difficult to believe that the Roman Catholic Church in Newfoundland, which probably has insurance to cover acts like the ones of Father Bennett, could not pony up twelve million dollars.

(Since writing this I have learned that six insurance companies in Newfoundland are being sued by the Catholic Church for the $13 million it paid to victims of clerical sexual abuse, arguing that the insurance companies were required to pay the damages under policies held by the Catholic Church. Stay tuned...)

Even absent insurance coverage, one would think that rather than prolong the suffering of the victims and the local church authorities, the Vatican would shoot over the twelve million dollars and sort out who owed what to who over the next two hundred years.

Not a chance.

The official policy of the Vatican is that each Catholic Church entity in Newfoundland, or Boston, or Vanuatu must financially swim on its own through these abuse-infested waters, or sink.

The policy of the Vatican has been to say to every Bishopric going through the financial/sexual abuse wringer, "Kids, you're on your own."

How much more enlightened would be a policy of the Vatican having a flying squad of lawyers and doctors who meet with the people making the allegations, verify the allegations, pay fair compensation for loss and for future counseling and get out of Dodge before the story even surfaces in the local news?

Any well-run modern corporation would give serious thought to proceeding in just such a fashion. The Vatican, in taking the position it has done, has effectively kept the sexual abuse stories around the world right in the face of its members, future members and clergy since the mid-1990s. There is no hint that it will change its policy. The Church only waits for the furor to die down.

This appears to me to be an inept way to run a Church, particularly one whose churches are closing down for want of adherents and whose ability to attract new Priests was far from stellar even before this public relations battering the Catholics have taken from the thousands of proven instances of sexual assault on children around the world.

To prove my point, let us look briefly in a couple of other corners of the Catholic Empire.

I have spoken of the Christian Brothers of Ireland in Canada and the boys warehoused in the 1950's and 1960's at Mount Cashel Orphanage in St. John's, Newfoundland.

When confronted by proven sexual abuse, the Christian Brothers went bankrupt and said to the victims, in effect: here, take us for all we are worth. That amounted to a few assets which I recall as being a bowling alley (2 lanes) a couple of buildings in Newfoundland of minimal value and some used bicycles. There were, at that time, about 100 orphans who had been sexually abused by some of the Christian Brothers. The total assets available, including the bowling alley and the bicycles, amounted to very little. But it was all the Christian Brothers had to their name.

The Vatican did not offer to help with cash for the victims, only strategy for the Christian Brothers.

Take it or leave it, said the Christian Brothers, turning out the pockets of their cassocks. That's all we have in the world...

"Not so fast!" said a lawyer in Toronto named David Wingfield. Wingfield was in charge of liquidating all the assets of the impecunious Brothers, and as he was poking around in their records he found a piece of paper that said one of the Christian Brothers in Canada had an interest in a school in Vancouver, BC. And there was another school in Vancouver that the Brothers seemed to have an interest in, albeit a tenuous one. Wingfield talked to me and a number of other lawyers and confronted the Christian Brothers with their apparent interest in the two schools.

"Oh, those!" the Christian Brothers said. "They don't belong to us. You can't have them."

"I think they may belong to you after all," said Wingfield.

Now these assets were valued at about $40 million in total, in other words a lot more than a bowling alley – even a two lane bowling alley – and some used bicycles.

Wingfield went after the BC schools with a view to having them declared assets of the Christian Brothers of Ireland in Canada.

The Catholic Church in BC got all lawyered up. The Archbishop of Vancouver got one, the first school got one, the second school got one and, of course, the Christian Brothers got one.

Wingfield had his teeth in their collective ankle and he was not about to let go. The Catholics circled the lawyer-driven wagons. The battle raged through the Courts. Time passed. About four years, in fact.

Finally, when the writing was all over the wall and the Catholics were running out of Courts to appeal to, they caved in and agreed to pay SOME money into the fund Wingfield was managing for the victims.

As a result, the victims were almost fairly compensated – I was the lawyer for two of them – and the Catholic Church got yet another black eye for failing to do unto others what they would want others to do unto them.

Lawyers will only grudgingly speak well of one another, especially trial lawyers who are ferociously combative when ferocious combat is required. I am pleased to be able to speak well of David Wingfield who is an almost unsung hero among the victims of the Christian Brothers, but who, through talent and tenacity, changed almost one hundred lives for the better.

He earned his money.

But the Catholic Church earned, and got, another black eye.

One would think that after the Catholics got down to used bicycles and bowling alleys – even the much sought-after two lane bowling alleys – they would have scraped the bottom of the barrel as far as pleading poverty goes.
Wrong again.

In addition to being insufferably arrogant and treating the world at large and their own adherents as if we were all a collection of village idiots, the Catholic hierarchy has overreached itself in playing the "poor me" card in Boston.

In May, 2005, the Catholic Archdiocese of Boston announced to an incredulous world that, owing to the vicious attacks of lawyers demanding millions of dollars for people who claimed they were sexually assaulted; Priests were going to have their pensions cut.

I'll wait for a second while you re-read that last sentence.

Yes. Priests in and around Boston were told by the Bishop that their monthly pensions of $1,889 would be frozen and that some Priests would have to pay more money for housing and medical benefits.

Pass the crying towel, Grace; pass the onion.

Which public relations firm is the Catholic Archdiocese of Boston employing these days?

Is there anyone left in the thinking world, who would fall for such blatant, maudlin, manipulative tripe as this?

Does the Roman Catholic Church truly think so little of the world at large that they believe that a story about impoverished Priests becoming marginally more impoverished will result in, dare I say it, sympathy for those Priests? Sympathy for the Church?

Sometimes I just marvel at the fact these guys have held sway for so long when they are so out of touch with those whom they purport to assist in speaking to God.

Catholic parishioners in Europe, though, seem to be prepared to give the Church a break. While sexual abuse has been rampant in, say, Poland, the Poles are not making a big stink about it because, well, simply put, they'd prefer to take their losses on this plane so long as they get to go to Heaven, and you'll never get to Heaven if you sue the Pope, as the old song doesn't go.

Ireland is a different story. The Catholic Church there has been dodging allegations of sexual abuse since the mid 1990's, and with some success.

In 2005, Archbishop Diarmuid Martin acknowledged that 102 Priests in Dublin were suspected of sexually abusing children. That's 102. Not one hundred and one, and not one hundred and three.

102.

The Church was quick to point out that this represents only 3.6% of the Priests in Dublin.

Meaning 96.4% of the Priests in Dublin are NOT pedophiles.

So there.

Ahhh, but all is not well in Dublin because, as the Archbishop sorrowfully relates, the Archdiocese will have to SELL some of its PROPERTY to pay for the abuse done to hundreds of sexual abuse victims by 3.6%, or 102 of the Priests.

Up until recently the Government of Ireland was paying for the sexual abuse committed by the Priests because, as in Newfoundland in the '50s and '60s, the Church and local governments were intertwined. The Irish taxpayer compensated the victims of priestly abuse at orphanages until the Irish taxpayer said: "No. Not any more from me, thank you," and, in 2001, changed both the government and its policy of stepping into the shoes of the Church with its wallet open.

It is estimated by those deeply involved in the Irish sexual abuse issue that one of every four people living in Ireland today has been sexually abused by a Catholic Church employee.

For the sake of those victims, let us hope that the property that Archbishop Martin proposes to sell consists of assets worth more than the Christian Brothers of Ireland in Canada found when they looked through their holdings the first time. Because the Vatican will do nothing to assist, as Pope Benedict made clear in 2010.

In the summer of 2006, the Christian Brothers of Ireland, who had educated Irish students for over two centuries, handed over 29 primary schools and 109 secondary schools to a charity that is to be run exclusively by lay people. The history of a violent, sexually abusive education endured by hundreds of thousands of Irish citizens has yet to be written and while the Christian Brothers have apologized for sexually abusing children, and while such acknowledgement and apologies are commendable, it boggles the mind that the Christian Brothers were able to hang on to their positions of power for so long. In fact, it appears not to be their brutal past so much as the decline in numbers of their Brotherhood which has forced the Christian Brothers to abandon the schools, leaving a sorrowful legacy for the Catholic Church and for Ireland.

And perhaps this is how it will end globally for the Roman Catholic Church.

The eradication of ignorance through education, the relatively higher level of sophistication in the Global Village, may lead to former preserves of the Catholics – like Ireland and Newfoundland where the Church was once above the law – becoming both more secular and less terrified of the ramifications of taking on the Church. It was always the intention of the Church, implied but not expressed, to bring its parishioners along to a certain level of sophistication and education but, past a certain point, the intelligentsia and the global and spiritual aspects of life were to be reserved for the Church hierarchy. This was all well and good when news traveled by foot, through the forests and the jungles and across the swamps and deserts, and where all education had as a centerpiece Jesus, his heart bleeding, fixed to a cross.

Now that formerly isolated people, such as those in Ireland and Newfoundland, are being exposed to a world view rather than one dictated by the Church, the absolute necessity of obedience to the Church is being watered down by minds free to think on their own.

When the Catholic Church held a virtual monopoly on both education and morality in this life and the one beyond – say from the year 0 to the year 1955 - it was a brave peasant indeed who doubted the word of the parish Priest.

Now, as power slips from the hands of the Christian Brothers of Ireland and other Catholic entities in a more and more educated and progressive world, it remains unlikely that children in the future will be subjugated by Priests and nuns who discipline at will and are predatory in their sexual abuse of students.

But beware.

The Catholic Church retains its power almost

undiminished in Third World countries whose level of exposure to the world is often akin to that of Ireland 150 years ago. When the parish Priest continues to be the most powerful man in the village, when the Archbishop continues to be among the most powerful men in the country, the likelihood of sexual abuse of children remains a clear potential danger. In April 2009, the Pope said, during a visit to Africa, that the Catholics were making great inroads on that Continent, but were meeting resistance from "local superstitions." Those "local superstitions" are otherwise known as African religions, which the Pope seeks now to brush away as his Church has done for millennia.

Pope Benedict made much of love and the family during his first months in office, weaving Church doctrine around a theme of love between a man and a woman, both the warm and comfortable love and the erotic love which leads "in ecstasy towards the Divine" which is, I believe, an allusion to the orgasm. It is true, in my experience, that upon attaining orgasm, many people, believers and non-believers alike, invoke the name of their favorite deity.

But it takes more nerve than a burglar for the Pope to try to ride over the crest of the sexual abuse scandal by employing sexual relations between a husband and wife in an attempt to regain the moral high ground, to say that the Church has had its hair mussed by the sexual abuse scandals but that the love between a man and a woman is what God and the Catholic Church are truly concerned with.

The Jesuit public relations spin control team lurches into action, and who knows but that they will hit a nerve.

Where a thoroughgoing housecleaning of the Catholic Church in order to remove pedophiles by inviting women into the clergy and by encouraging the clergy to marry is a practical beginning to thwart the sexual abuse of children, the Vatican has performed a lateral arabesque and danced over to another part of the world and otherworldly stage, calling for good, clean sex between married adults as one of the first statements of the newly elected Pope Benedict in the summer of 2006, followed by a series of non-apologies in 2008, 2009 and 2010.

This tactic of diversion, previously employed by such historical notables as the military tactician Sun Tzu (whose works were first translated in the West by a Jesuit, who took the liberty of adding a few of his own thoughts to those of the Master) and the magical guru Houdini, will not be sufficient to pull the Church out of the sexual abuse quagmire.

Nor will a search of Church ranks for homosexuals.

Since these scandals began to reach the media, the Catholic Church has done little to modify its views on the sexual abuse of children by its clergy. It has fought civil authorities vigorously on behalf of its Priests in every corner of the globe. It has hidden pedophiles. It has allowed pedophiles to flee to safer climes and employed them there. It has dissembled. It has not sought the root cause of pedophilia within its ranks and it is unlikely to do so because, despite all of the blows the Church has taken, the Vatican remains confident that this, too, shall pass.

By the Grace of God.

And with an arrogance born of two thousand years of wielding universal power, the Church adopts the attitude that the dogs may bark, but the caravan passes on.

Chapter 29

OTHER ABUSERS

The Roman Catholic Church has no monopoly on the sexual abuse of children by members of large organizations. The Roman Catholic Church has done many things on a broad scale, and pedophilia is but one of them.

As I indicated earlier, whenever children come into contact with a power figure, namely any elder who holds sway over them, those children are vulnerable.

When the actual, physical distance between the adult and the child is shortened to one where hand-to-body contact is to be expected, a teacher's pat on the arm or head, a doctors manual ministrations, a scout leader's checking the uniform, a stepfather's hug, then sexual abuse is more likely to occur than if the adult were a stranger or a non-arm's-length acquaintance.

When the relationship between the child and the authority figure is one which takes place over time, over months or years, as with a stepfather, teacher, doctor or scout leader, then the element of propinquity is introduced and the defenseless child is a sitting duck, relying only on the good sense of the adult not to rape him.

Of course, as parents, we cannot afford to rely on the good sense of any adult, male or female, so we must rely on the child to protect herself.

In 95 percent of cases of child sexual abuse, the child knows the pedophile perpetrator. There is already a bond between them, developed over time, before the first sexual assault takes place.

In the remaining 5 percent of the cases, the child is sexually assaulted by a stranger to her. Someone lures her into a car or befriends her on the Internet and the result can be both sexual assault and the subsequent death of the child.

Pedophiles who have developed a bond with a child seldom kill her after the sexual assault, hoping that their secret will be safe and hoping to be able to rape the child again. Strangers care only that the secret remains a secret. While kidnappers may keep the child alive and sexually assault her repeatedly while she is imprisoned by him, the ultimate death of the child has already been decided upon by the pedophile.

To protect your child from being taken against his will, raped and killed by a stranger is no easy task.

Essentially, the same rules apply as we have been reviewing. Knowledge of the dangers in the world should be passed to the children in age-appropriate language at age-appropriate times.

Children who already know that their bodies belong to them, who already know to say 'NO!" and to turn and run to an adult when they are asked by another adult to do something out of the ordinary, are protected to some extent from the stranger rapist.

A child who puts up a struggle will almost always be left alone by a rapist, who hopes that another more compliant child is just down the street.

The day will come, I hope, when there are no more compliant children for the rapist to find either just down the street or anywhere.

Some parents may be concerned that providing knowledge to their children about the dangers that await them may harm or even scar their children. This has not been my experience. Indeed, the opposite is more likely to be the case.

Children are very adaptable and not nearly so inclined to be traumatized by knowledge as they are by the act of abuse itself. I have never heard of a child requiring therapy because his mother told him how to protect his body, and his sexual integrity.

Properly couched, this is simply more language about growing up, more lessons from a mother to a child, like when to go to sleep, or like eating and going to the bathroom lessons. Children want to learn the rules. Children are sponges waiting to soak up information. Children know when information from Mom is important to listen to, important to remember.

When any stranger in a car, at the mall or, most especially now on the Internet talks to your child about his genitals or his bum, or her breasts, an alarm bell should sound in your child's head and he should immediately and reflexively seek escape from the situation he is in and get help fast, preferably from his mother.

Have the child phone 911 if there is no safe adult around.

In a day when most children have cell phones, those devices can finally be put to some good use. If your child has a cell phone, make sure she knows the most important number is 911. And make certain you use the G.P.S. function whenever you can, and that your child does so as well.

It is your job as his mother to make certain that your child knows these rules.

If all pedophiles knew that all mothers had taught these rules to their children, what a safe and wonderful world it would be for the children and the children's children to come.

Chapter 25

WE'RE ALL IN THIS TOGETHER

Children, parents, pedophiles, Judges, doctors, the Pope, you, me, we're all involved in the sexual abuse of children and how to stop it, some of us more than others.

I have tried to point out some of the ways sexual abuse can be stopped and I have made some suggestions about how to look at sexual abuse in what may be a new light for some people. The subject is as broad and as deep as humanity itself, and I know that I have barely scratched the surface of this massive problem we all have.

For those of you who were abused and who do not find your story here, please tell me about that story if you feel you want to. If you think it might help you to write down what happened to you so you can break the silence, find a computer and send me your story at www.unforgivablesins.com. I cannot promise to answer you, but the writing of the words may start you on your healing journey, or help you keep on going. I CAN promise not to tell your story to anyone without your permission.

For the doctors and the Judges and the politicians, I recognize I have been rough on you, perhaps unduly so. We all try to do our best in our own fields. I have attempted to broaden your field to include information you might not otherwise have had access to. If I have offended you, I did it for a greater cause than preserving your reputations as diligent, knowledgeable and caring professionals. You will get over it, as will the men in western society whom I have tarred with a broad brush as potential sexual abusers.

Well, guys, you personally may not be one, but that guy beside you at the bar, on the bus, in the locker room, at the stoplight... he looks a little squiffy, don't you think? Would you trust him alone with your daughter for a couple of days?

And that's my point.

I took a run at women, too, as sexual abusers. I know most women are not sexual predators and sexually abusing children is the last thing on the minds of almost all women. How, then, do we explain – how do we stop – the trend of teachers and other women to use young boys as sexual playthings?

The Roman Catholic Church did not come off too well, most deservedly so. I have no words here to ameliorate the damage that this book may have occasioned to the Pope and his Clergy. They have caused a lot of pain and have failed miserably in setting things right. I hold out little hope for this organization, and believe that even a multitude of defections by parishioners and a major drop in donations would have little impact on the Catholic Church.

They are just too big and too powerful for our own good.

To the pedophiles, many of whom struggle with their affliction but most of whom continue to seek new ways to have sexual contact with young boys and girls, I regret whatever it is that has made you into sexual abusers of children. After your second offence, I hold out no hope for you. You are a danger to children and children come first. Something more draconian will have to be done with hardwired pedophiles because the legal system in place in the western world today is failing our kids. I do not believe it is possible for a person who is hardwired as a pedophile to change into someone whose sexual preference is for adults. Because we cannot rely on pedophiles to be celibate, we as a society must stop them from doing damage to the children they stalk.

Finally, and always, to the kids and the adults who were kids when they were abused: this is a book about hope. You need not continue to be defined by what someone did to you ten or fifty years ago. You are free to become the person you were meant to be. Strive to find that person. There are tens of thousands of kids just like you who are fighting right this minute to reclaim the person they were meant to be. It will not be easy, but it is a battle you can win and a battle we all want you to win. As you heal yourself, you heal your family and as you heal your family, you heal us all.

You have all of my admiration for walking with courage and hope on your healing journey.

Good luck.

THE BIBLE SAYS THERE IS ONLY ONE UNFORGIVABLE SIN

Acknowledgements:

This book was written with much help.

For their strength and motivation I thank Darlene Hall, Joel Legate and Marissa Legate.

For sheer tenacity in putting up with me, I thank especially Erin White, Shirley White and Margaret Eaton.

For acting as sounding boards, my thanks go to Doug Lord, Michael Royce, Bob Raftis, Peter Freeman Q.C., Richard Legh, Sharon Smith, Tyler Luchies, Julia Nicol, Jennifer Nicol, Janis Libby, Julia Fountain and Arnold Gosewich.

For publishing, layout and cover design work I thank Michael Davie and Donovan Davie of Manor House Publishing.

For everything else, I thank Pat and Fergus Glencross Hall.

Scott Hall
Victoria, British Columbia
March 24, 2010

ABOUT THE AUTHOR:

Scott Hall, a lawyer based in Victoria, BC, was a prosecutor under contract with the British Columbia government in the 1980's when he first became aware of large numbers of sexual abuse complaints from youth. Hall came to devote much of his professional career representing abused children and bringing their abusers to justice and has worked with over 1,200 people who were sexually abused as children.

Manor House Publishing
www.manor-house.biz.
905-648-2193